PARENTS' MOST-ASKED QUESTIONS ABOUT KIDS AND SCHOOLS

In appreciation for your support of Focus on the Family, please accept this copy of *Parents' Most-Asked Questions about Kids and Schools* by Cliff Schimmels. Your contributions enable this organization to address the needs of families through radio, television, literature and counseling.

We believe this book contains helpful, informative answers to your questions about your child's education at home and in the classroom. We're confident this book, with its practical advice, will make a fine addition to your family's library.

Focus on the Family
Pomona, CA 91799

PARENTS' MOST-ASKED QUESTIONS ABOUT KIDS AND SCHOOLS

CLIFF SCHIMMELS, Ph.D.

VICTOR BOOKS®

A DIVISION OF SCRIPTURE PRESS PUBLICATIONS INC.
USA CANADA ENGLAND

Recommended Dewey Decimal Classification: 371.62
Suggested Subject Heading: EDUCATION

Library of Congress Catalog Card Number: 89-60159
ISBN: 0-89693-697-X

VICTOR BOOKS
A division of Scripture Press
Wheaton, Illinois 60187

TABLE OF CONTENTS

INTRODUCTION

Approximately 40 million Americans go to school every day. For some the experience is profitable; for others it is only bearable; for yet others, it is one of the most exquisite forms of punishment the world has yet invented. For some, the school experience is indeed, "the best years of your life," as we adults enjoy telling them; for others it is an ordeal that is only painfully endured as a thirteen-year-long preliminary test required to pass before one can enter "real life."

As parents, we sometimes feel we are caught in the middle of this whole process. We want more than anything in the world for our children not only to get something worthwhile from all that school endeavor, but we would also like to see them enjoy it. Yet, we often get the idea that we are somehow outside observers trying to catch a glimpse into that mysterious monastery set on a hill somewhere which swallows up our children, our most precious possessions, each morning and spits them back to us each afternoon.

We really want our children to get the most out of the experience and we are willing to do whatever we need to do to make that happen, but we don't know what to do. We cry for help, but we don't know to whom to cry and we never know if anyone is listening. And we are trapped with our questions. What can we do to make school bearable and maybe even profitable for our own children?

If this comes anywhere close to describing how you have felt at some time or perhaps how you feel all the time, this book should be of some help to you.

It was written for this very purpose: to help parents understand something about that institution called the school, how it works and how it affects our children during that time when they grow and change so rapidly.

Though the book isn't exhaustive, it does cover many of the areas where parents have expressed concern during the past several years, and it is rather long. For that reason, the book is organized with a question-answer format. You may not want to sit down and read the entire volume in one evening, but you can use the book as something of an encyclopedia, searching until you find the very question you want to ask. If you do find a question that sounds rather familiar, that may be because all the questions have actually come from parents during the last few years. In other words, these are the questions that real people are asking about schools.

As much as possible, I tried to keep the answers objective by consulting with several people before developing a response. However, most of the answers do carry at least a hint of my own personal opinion. I do think, though, that my opinion is worth something. I visit schools every day. In the course of a year, I visit more than 200 classrooms in more than seventy-five schools. During the past five years, I have worked as a teacher in twenty schools and I even spent some time as a high school student. Thus, my opinions are based on personal observation.

My greatest frustration with this project is that it is incomplete, and always will be. The questions we have about schools are endless. Every day when I wander out to shop or to eat out or to go to church, I meet somebody who has another question or another observation. From start to finish, this book has been much like a fungus, just growing out everywhere from a central root.

Since I have not and cannot answer all the questions, perhaps I can leave you with some general themes.

1. If we are going to be able to achieve the best possible education for our children, parents and teachers must cooperate in the effort.

2. The classroom teacher is the center of education.

3. Schools are the results of the opinions of common people working together positively.

CHAPTER ONE
Motivation and Self-Concept

It is altogether fitting and proper that this book about schools and parents should begin with the topic of motivation and self-concept. There may be more controversial subjects to concern ourselves with, but there is none more important. There is no single factor which has more influence on how successful any student is or how successful the schooling process is than what that individual student thinks of himself.

This whole process of schooling would be a lot easier for everyone concerned—parents, teachers, and students—if this business of motivation and self-concept were a simple, one-dimensional aspect of one's personality. But it isn't. It is very complex. For one thing, it is not a one-time once-and-for-all-times affair. How nice it would be if motivated people became that way sometime during the third grade and stayed that way the rest of their lives. How nice it would be if the high school girl with a fairly good sense of self-assurance was self-assured every day and in all activities. But it doesn't work that way. Growing up and probably living in general is a constant process of trying to get motivated or trying to stay motivated once you get there.

This chapter includes both motivation and self-concept in its title. It would probably be easier to discuss these if we could separate them into two distinct entities, but after spending thirty years as an adult trying to figure out that strange animal called the adolescent, I'm convinced that we can't do that. Motivation and self-concept may not be synonymous terms, but the two aspects are so interrelated that we can't just look at one or the other. We have to look at them both at the same time.

Permit me one more word of warning. This topic is too important and too vital to a student's success to be taken lightly. It is not the domain of responsibility for the teacher or for the parent. A healthy attitude toward learning and toward oneself requires all forces in the student's life to work together.

My son is a normal teenager, but in the last year, his grades have slipped to Cs and Ds. What are we to do with him?

Our daughter's teacher tells me that she is very bright but she is not working up to her potential. What is the problem?

The questions about the motivated student are endless and almost universal. Every teacher would rather teach motivated students than unmotivated ones. Every parent would much prefer that their children be motivated. Not only do motivated children cause fewer problems, but they also make us look better as parents.

Yet, despite all our talk and all our concern, we are not quite sure we know what it is we are talking about when we talk about this strange animal called motivation. Oh, we know the difference between a motivated person and an unmotivated person when we see one, but we have never been sure how anybody got to be that way, and we don't really know how to prevent someone from getting that way.

Just to check, have you ever heard of a good, succinct definition of motivation? See what I mean?

Well, I probably don't have any better insight than anyone else, but someone has to start the ball rolling so let me begin with an operational definition.

MOTIVATION IS THE ABILITY OF THE LEARNER
TO SEE THE APPLIED VALUE
OF THE LESSON TO BE LEARNED.

How's that for starters! But I am serious. Every student comes to class every day with one burning question on his mind. The teacher's ability to teach and the student's ability to learn depends on how satisfactorily that question is answered. Without a good answer, there isn't much learning; with a good answer, there is much learning.

What is that burning question which every student brings to class every day? Well, it shouldn't be a surprise because it is the same question we asked when we were in school. Don't you remember? "Why are we doing this?"

Again, let me repeat the importance of the question. Every student comes to class every day with the question on the back of his mind. Most ask it silently, but once in a while, some of the bolder ones will just blurt it out, "Why are we doing this?"

When we were in school, the question was easier to answer than it is now. In those days we still believed that the mind was something of a muscle that needed to be exercised, so when we held up our hands and asked, "Why are we doing this?" the teacher would scowl at the impudence and exclaim in a tone of finality, "Shut up and diagram those sentences. It will make your brain grow."

Well, we can't really tell students that we are doing it just to make their brain grow anymore. Somehow we have to come up with a better answer.

That is the first problem of motivation. The student who sees the applied value of the lesson or who sees the reason for doing it is simply going to be more highly motivated than if he sees no worth in the activity at all.

For whatever reason, some students are still willing to work just for the grade. For them, the answer to, "Why are we doing this?" is, "Because it will be on the test tomorrow." Again, this will work for those students who value grades, but it won't work for all students. They need to see a more realistic reason for this expenditure of energy.

The easy response to the problems of the two students mentioned in the questions above would be to offer them some kind of reward for better grades. That would be the simplest solution if it would work. Just tell the students that they get five dollars for an improved grade, or they get a car if the grades stay up where they belong, or put some such material value on the grade itself.

But as parents everywhere are finding out, this reward system isn't as successful as it sounds like it ought to be. Again, it works with a few students but it doesn't work with all of them. What this kind of reward system does is cause the young person to unconsciously establish a priority of his own personal values, and to make a choice on those values. Now, on the surface, the student may think that he would value a car, but in reality, he values his goofing off in class more. So he chooses not to keep his part of the bargain.

The other problem with this reward system is that it only rewards the grade and not the learning itself. Most students know the difference between those two, so unless we find some way to reward the learning as well as the grade, we might make the students feel that they are hypocrites, and most high school students will rebel against that possibility.

So this is the trick of motivation—to find some way to help the student see the applied value of what the teachers are asking him to learn.

Let's explore some possibilities.

1. Show your son or daughter how you use aspects of your schoolwork on a day-to-day basis. I once heard of a middle school writing teacher who assigned her students to survey people in the community to determine what adults wrote on a day-to-day basis. After the students compiled the list and found out what was required, they became more highly motivated to learn to write.

2. Model your use of what you have learned for your children. Let them catch you reading and writing and working math.

3. Let your adolescent get a part-time job. Frequently these jobs will demand skills which the student is working on in school.

4. Help your children think about the future and help them see themselves as adults.

With the season rapidly approaching and the excitement building higher each day, the kindergarten teacher decided to use the natural motivation. "Today," she announced to the class, "I would like for each one of you to draw something which reminds you most of Christmas."

Since the students were already excited and since they liked the assignment, they all went to work on their creations. Some drew pictures of trees; some drew presents; some drew Santa Claus. But one little girl, with more of an understanding of the true meaning of the time, went to work on an elaborate drawing of the Nativity scene. Throughout the process, she was careful and thorough. She drew Mary and Joseph and the Baby Jesus in the manger. But she also drew shepherds and angels and even wise men. Over in the bottom right hand corner, she drew a little fat figure, half standing and half lying down.

The teacher was properly impressed with the little girl's work and told her so. But she did have to ask, "What is this little fat figure over here in the corner?"

"That," announced the little girl in all seriousness, "is Round John Virgin."

I hope you found that story funny because I meant for it to be. But at the same time, I hope you saw the larger point. That little girl was almost clear on a concept, off by just a bit, but off far enough to have the completely wrong idea. I wonder how often this happens. I wonder how many students are sitting in classrooms with a piece of the concept but with a completely distorted idea and don't even know they are in error. When we talk of lack of motivation, when we talk of poor scores, when we talk of poor study skills, we need to remember that little girl.

Our daughter makes good grades in every course except math. She seems to be intelligent, but she can't get simple arithmetic through her mind. What is the problem?

Well, of course, this could be a complex problem of some kind, but it could also be a simple case of math block.

Actually, this is rather common. Some students simply can't get some subject because they are scared to death of the material. This irrational fear, or perhaps we should say phobia, doesn't make any sense. We don't know where it comes from. We don't know why some people are frightened of one thing and not of another. We don't understand why an intelligent student would have a debilitating fear of any material. But some do.

Math seems to be the most common source of fear. Most teachers will tell you that they have at least one student with an unhealthy fear of numbers and math problems. Many adults will confess to a fear of math, particularly when they were in school.

But this phobia can occur in other areas as well. I have seen several students through the years who had a writing block. They were just afraid to put words on paper. Sometimes they would even go so far as to write the assignment, but then they would tear it up and throw it away before the teacher could see it.

I also suspect that there is something we can call reading block as well. I firmly believe that there are some students who develop such a fear of the printed word that they can't read well and they hate reading.

The unfortunate problem with this fear is that the people who don't have the fear don't understand. Thus, the poor student is usually dismissed as being unmotivated. I hear the talk in the teacher's lounge. "Bobby does all his work in my class. But when I give a writing assignment, he just sits and stares out the window, completely unmotivated." "Sally may make good grades in your class, but she is certainly unmotivated in math." I hear the talk, and all the while, I suspect that we have a case of fear.

Frankly, I know something about the nature of phobias myself. If I were a student in a physical education class and the teacher asked me to tuck my shoulder down and roll forward into a somersault, he would just have to flunk me. I am not going to tuck my shoulder down and roll forward. Threaten me with an F if I don't. Promise me M & M's if I do—I am still not going to do it. "That's dumb," you say, "Just a stupid fear." Well, of course it is. That is what a phobia is, an irrational fear. But how many students are sitting in classrooms with an irrational fear of the material and can't convince the adults in charge of their lives and destinies that they have the fear? Thus, we label them unmotivated and make little effort to correct it.

Now, the next question is a tough one. How do we work with a student who suffers from math block or writing block or reading block? To answer this, I am going to offer a neat list of suggestions, a rather logical list, if I may say so, but the problem is that the fear isn't logical; probably the reason the student has the fear in the first place isn't logical; and the cure for the fear isn't logical either. But now that I have explained why my suggestions may not work, let me offer them anyway. At least, we can try something rather than just accusing the student.

1. Break the task down into manageable chunks. The student may have a mental block against mastering the whole endeavor, but he may be able to conquer one portion of it. As he gains confidence with that one task, perhaps he can begin to work on the next step. When I have worked with students with word block, I would begin by having them put words on paper. The words did not have to make sentences or be in any sequence. I simply asked the students to put the words on the paper as they came to mind. After some time of doing this, the student was then ready to move to sentences. Eventually, he moved into paragraphs and even essays. But the beginning was to start with building confidence with words on paper.

2. In a personal conversation with the student, ask a series of questions to determine if he fully understands the principle and the concepts involved. I suspect that the block often develops because the student misses some simple concept early in the instruction process. If you can identify that missing concept, perhaps you could work on that

and help the student gain his confidence.

3. Don't force the student too soon. The block is there because the student doesn't have any confidence in himself. Putting too much pressure on the student will only make matters worse.

4. Help the student understand himself. If you know of someone else who has a block, have your son talk to that person. Perhaps he can get an understanding of himself and not have to live with so much guilt.

The young art teacher came into the classroom bubbling with excitement. "Today," she said, "we are going to draw a lion," and she held up a pencil drawing of a lion lying among some grass and reeds.

Since I am an upside-down left-hander whose entire art ability consists of trying to find two socks that match every morning, I hid my anxieties and fears behind a big sigh and decided that I wouldn't even try. Nope, not me. They may draw that picture that she was holding in front of us, but I wasn't going to draw. I could assure you of that.

But then, the young teacher, still bubbling, held up another sheet of paper with four circles drawn on it. "Can you draw these four circles?" she asked as if she were sure we could do it. So I did. I can draw circles all right, but I can't draw a lion lying in grass.

Next, she held up another sheet of paper with some lines drawn among the circles. Of course I did that; then I did the next step and the next one, and by the end of the period, I had drawn a lion lying in grass. Mine wasn't as good as hers, but it is good enough to hang in my office to remind me that I can draw, and to remind me of something even more important. Good teaching requires that we break the task down into manageable chunks that the students can accomplish.

We could probably all do more than we think we can if we could just divide the task into the right components and the right sequence.

Roslyn prepared herself to be an English teacher, and she was quite good at it. She had more than an understanding of great literature. She had an appreciation for it, and she personally used literature to enrich her own life. Often she would quote a line from a poem or some other work of literature just as a means of enriching the moment at hand.

During her student teaching experience, she used that appreciation

15

in such a way that the students soon caught the habit themselves. Often in her classroom some student would quote something from yesterday's lesson just to enrich the moment at hand.

Needless to say, I was thrilled about what Roslyn was going to be able to accomplish when she graduated and became a high school English teacher. She would surely be a bright, refreshing experience for her students.

But Roslyn never made it to the English classroom. Actually, she never graduated from college. The college requires all students to complete one college math class, regardless of the major. It sounds like a good requirement to me. But Roslyn who had such a personal mastery of literature could not pass that math class. She tried five times and never passed. She worked hard; she studied thoroughly, but she just couldn't pass a simple college math class.

This is the most dramatic case of math block I have ever seen. But as I worked with Roslyn during her five unsuccessful attempts to pass that class, I came to realize that this irrational fear was not just something she had created for herself. It was real and debilitating. Roslyn has suffered a good deal because of it.

How many other young people are suffering from some kind of mental block, against math or writing or even reading?

Our sophomore daughter is taking geometry this year. She started the year working hard but doing well. She worked on homework almost every night. She studied hard for the tests, and she had a strong B average. But just after Christmas, she missed three days of school with chicken pox. Since then she hasn't even tried and she is now failing the class. What happened? Could missing three days of class make all that difference?

What an excellent question! Students and teachers everywhere will thank you for asking it. The answer is an emphatic yes. Yes, missing three days of a class like geometry could have made all the difference in the world. The reason is actually rather simple when you think about it. Geometry and other classes build concept on concept. Every day the teacher sets out to present a new concept to the class. In fact, the good teacher will write that one new concept on the board so the whole class will understand the objective for the day. This is wonderful. But what the teacher doesn't understand is that he covers three other concepts before he gets to the main one. If a student misses any one of those preliminary concepts, he won't be able to get the main one. When a student is absent, the good teacher will be very deliberate in showing the student the main concept, but even the best of teachers forget about all those other concepts en route. Then when the student struggles and doesn't understand, he begins to blame himself for being stupid, and he very soon loses all motivation for doing the work.

Let me see if I can describe how your daughter must be feeling just now. Don't you have a specific multiplication fact that you hate to see in a problem? You are balancing your checkbook multiplying by twos and fives and doing quite nicely. Then all of a sudden, you hit seven times nine and you say, "Oh, well, I will do it tomorrow when I have a calculator." Admit it. Aren't you afraid of something like that? So is your daughter. She is short a concept. She is blaming herself. And she has lost all interest.

For the adults in her life—you and her teacher—she is just another unmotivated student who has quit trying and now quit caring. But I'm afraid she represents thousands and thousands of students across the nation. Somewhere they have missed a concept, and now they can't go on, so they just lose interest. The seventh-grader who hasn't learned to read; the ninth-grader who doesn't care about grades anymore; the geometry student who lost motivation right in the middle of the year— it may all be as simple as one missing concept.

But the question now is how do we know which concept is missing so we can know how to correct the damage. We don't get far asking a general question such as, "What don't you understand?" If your daughter knew what she didn't understand, she could probably find it somewhere and learn it on her own. At this point, she doesn't understand any of it, so she needs to go through a series of specific questions until she and her teacher can identify the missing concept. I know this sounds like tedious work, but I don't know of a shortcut.

DATELINE: SEVENTH GRADE

The seventh-grade reading teacher was quite thorough. She wrote the concept for the day on the board in big letters—METAPHOR = AN IMPLIED COMPARISON. Then she went through an animated and lively presentation of the meaning of the word "comparison." She gave appropriate illustrations and used metaphors as examples.

Now, let me ask you. Why did 70 percent of those seventh-graders not hear a word of what she said and still don't know what a metaphor is after all that fine lesson? Maybe they just aren't very highly motivated. Maybe they have already decided that they don't care about school anymore. Maybe they don't get any support from their parents.

Those are all good reasons and probably the ones the teacher presented when she discussed this whole ordeal with her colleagues in the lounge after class. But maybe the answer is simpler than that. Maybe those seventh-grade students didn't know what the word *implied* meant and without that concept they couldn't master the rest of the lesson.

The teacher was thorough and quite good. She made just one mistake. She assumed that all students knew a basic concept when they didn't.

DATELINE: SECOND GRADE

The teacher was good but the concept was hard—borrowing in subtraction. The teacher explained, used matchsticks to demonstrate, had the students use the matchsticks to demonstrate, explained some more, and had each student explain the concept to a partner. When it was all over, every student present that day could not only work the problem which required borrowing in subtraction but could explain the concept to someone else. I was quite impressed.

Afterward I commended the teacher and asked about anyone who might be absent. "Yes," she told me, "one little girl is absent, but I will explain it to her tomorrow."

Yes, I know the teacher will explain it tomorrow, but I don't think she will be as good or as thorough as she was today. If that little girl is not very bright, she is going to struggle some to know the concept as well as her second-grade colleagues know it, and she could begin to look like an unmotivated student after a few years.

DATELINE: HIGH SCHOOL CHEMISTRY

Because I can get lost in high school chemistry class in a hurry, I was working particularly hard to listen this day. The young teacher was thorough and sensitive to my learning problems, so I was staying with her on this lesson about balanced equations.

Then she wrote some number on the board that looked something like this: $2OH_2Ph3$. At that point, the young teacher made her mistake. She assumed I knew how to read that number—what the two and the subset and all that means.

Well, that was the wrong assumption. I don't know what those numbers mean, so I quit listening and wrote her a critical evaluation of her teaching style.

DATELINE: COLLEGE SENIOR SEMINAR

After hearing of the death of Glenn Cunningham a couple of weeks ago, I went to class prepared to have some kind of meaningful discussion about the life and ministry of a truly great man.

I opened the discussion with a simple statement. "As you all know Glenn Cunningham died last week." That piece of vital information was greeted with twenty-seven blank stares. Now, this is ridiculous. I know that he might have been someone out of their generation, but his death had been in all the papers. How could intelligent college seniors miss such an important piece of news?

I decided to try another route. "How many read the CHICAGO TRIBUNE?" I asked. About twenty hands shot up. "How many read SPORTS ILLUSTRATED?" About fifteen hands shot up. "How many read TIME?" About twelve hands shot up.

Now here's the mystery. Those students and I had read the very same pieces of material. From each one I had learned of the death of a man I admire and respect, but those students had not only not read but they had not even seen the account. What could be the difference?

Here's the lesson to be learned. To receive a piece of new information or a new concept, we need something already inside us to attach that new piece of information on. Since those students had no reason to recognize the name of Glenn Cunningham, they had not even seen the information. It just flew over them. Yet, in reading those very same pages, I with my background saw the story and received it into my knowledge bank.

How often we ask students to listen to new information or to read new information and we just assume that they have the background to handle it. When they don't get as much from it as we want them to have, we say they are not motivated.

My friend Tal Bonham tells a wonderful story in one of his joke books. The Sunday School teacher had told her class of kindergartners about God's decision to destroy Sodom and Gomorrah. As the teacher explained it, "God wanted to spare Lot, so He told him to take his wife and flee." With that, the teacher sat back and watched the silence of comprehension take over the faces of each class member.

Finally, one little guy ventured a question. "What happened to the flea?"

That is probably funny to us, but to the one who holds the missed concept, just that much of an error could become at least an embarrassment and maybe even more.

My son wants to drop out of school when he reaches sixteen. What can we do to change his mind?

It is much easier for me to answer this question than for you to ask it because we are dealing with your son instead of mine. If this were my own son who felt this way about school and himself, I would probably cry myself to sleep every night. I can tell you that it doesn't matter all that much that a student completes high school, that he can still get a good job and lead a full life—I can tell you that and philosophically I believe, in fact, know it for sure, but on a personal basis, such a problem as this would crush me.

Given my reservations about offering you sound advice which is going to seem so empty, let's see if I can offer any help at all.

The first thing you need to do is to decide why your son feels this way, and that may be more difficult than it sounds. Sometimes adolescents know their own minds, but often they don't. They just know that they are unhappy or tired or seeking a change. They really don't know the reason but they just feel that they don't fit. If this is where your son is, then you need to help him explore the possible reasons for his unhappiness in school. Let's list some of those, because by your having the list, you will be in a better position to help your son explore and make some meaning of his own feelings. Keep in mind as we go through this list that school dropout is a very complex problem with no simple explanations or answers.

1. He is struggling in his classes. This would seem like the most common reason for students to drop out; but about the time I get comfortable with this as an explanation, I run into a dropout who was on the honor roll, and I realize the complexity of the problem again. Nevertheless, if this is your son's problem, we need to look at it. To simplify the problem of struggling, we can say that he has trouble reading, writing, and perhaps doing math computations. Of course, the problems inside this could be quite involved, but on the surface, these are the skills needed to succeed in high school classes. If your son is

behind in developing some of these skills, he has to work harder than the other students and he has less to show for his efforts. I don't blame him for feeling as he does. That combination would make me angry too.

If this seems to be his problem, you may want to convince him of the need to go see a counselor or a testing specialist (most school districts have such people on their staff, but if not, there are always very capable private testers who can do this work for a fee). You will want to find out just exactly where your son's difficulty is. Perhaps he can pronounce all the words in a reading assignment but he can't comprehend. Perhaps he has some fear of writing or just doesn't know how to organize his thoughts. Perhaps somewhere in the past he missed some fundamental concepts and now he is lost in class without those concepts. A good, professional testing session may be able to reveal that to you and your son, and could even tell you how you could get special help. For many students, just knowing the source of the problem really gives them a boost and a fresh attitude about themselves and life in general. They know they have been struggling but since they don't know the reason, they blame themselves and begin to think that they are just lazy or indifferent. To have an expert tell them that it really isn't their fault is one of the best pieces of news they will ever have.

2. He doesn't have any friends in school. I suspect that this is a common problem for school dropouts, and it may be one of the most difficult to deal with. This is particularly a problem for a student who has made older friends through the years. When the older friends leave school, the place becomes rather lonely for the one left behind. If this sounds like something your son is dealing with, get those older friends to help you talk to your son. Unless they are really selfish people, they are probably on your side.

3. Your son doesn't see the need for a high school education. The most common reason for this is that your son has skills which are not always taught in high school—he wants to build houses and they want him to learn the causes and results of the French Revolution. If this is the problem, investigate the vocational programs available in your area. There could be a program suited to his interest.

4. Your son has difficulty accepting the regimen or tough time schedule of the high school day. He just can't accept the kind of life where every moment is controlled by someone else or he can't learn in a typical classroom filled with people all lined up in rows. This too is a legitimate concern. Some people just have trouble with that kind of

existence. If this seems to be the problem, contact the local school officials (such as the county superintendent if you live in a state with such an office) and ask about alternative high schools in your area. There are special schools designed for this kind of person. Thus, the student can feel some sense of freedom and still complete his high school education.

5. Your son is just in a hurry to grow up and take on an adult existence. This is another common reason for high school dropout. These young people just get in a rush for their own independence— jobs, cars, their own apartments, their own schedules. Again, this is a particularly tough problem to deal with because the solution may be to offer your son some independence while he is still in high school. Just getting an after-school job may be sufficient for him, but probably not. He will probably also need his own car and maybe even his own schedule.

6. Your son feels that he is in danger at school. In spite of all my optimism about schools, there are some places in this country where some students are in danger at school. In other words, for some, per- haps very few, this is a reality. If this seems to be your son's problem, and you feel strongly about his need to be in school, you may want to take radical steps—move if you can, and if you can't, see if he can move in with a friend or a relative so he can attend a safer school. I realize that this is a cop-out—that I ought to be telling you what you can do to make the present high school safe, but frankly, I don't know how to do that. So I am just recommending this to help the present situation with your son.

Obviously, this list is not complete. Because the problem of dropout is never simple, this list could go on and on. But perhaps the process can help you begin talking with your son to see if perhaps you can identify some reasons for his feelings and perhaps come to some solu- tion for how he should deal with those.

Ray was already two years older than the other sophomores, and it looked liked he might have to be a sophomore again. Though Ray was not the most brilliant student I have ever had, he had more talent than he was using. Besides that, he was a pest. He chose not to do any work, and he hated to be alone in that decision so he encouraged the other students to join him in his indifference.

After all my noble efforts to motivate him had failed dismally, I gave Ray up as a lost cause and spent my energies trying to rescue those he would drag into nothingness with him. Sometime after the second semester had begun, during that time of the year when it looks like it's going to be winter forever and you can't see a break in sight and one day of class runs into the next one, I introduced those sophomore English students to a unit on careers. My educational objective was to use the unit as an introduction to research. The students would need to select a career which might interest them, read five sources of information about that career, interview someone in the career, and write it all up nicely as a research paper. As an assignment, it had some merit.

On the day I made the assignment, Ray announced to me, the rest of the class, and all the other humans within a five-mile radius that his ambition was to become a cop. Everyone snickered appropriately, but Ray assured us that he was sincere. He wanted to research being a cop.

I agreed and gave him the name of a local state patrolman who lived on my street. I assumed that we were all safe because, based on his past record, Ray wouldn't call. But to my surprise, he did call the patrolman. That patrolman spent hours with Ray, and even took him on part of his rounds.

The next few class periods were given over to listening to Ray recount the excitement of being a cop. But after that, something strange occurred. Ray went to work. The patrolman had told him that he would have to take a spelling test to become a policeman, so Ray began to study spelling. The patrolman told him that he would have to read, so Ray began to read, particularly in the area of current events and government. The patrolman told him that he would have to write, so Ray started working on the research paper.

In a matter of weeks, Ray's work and his grades had improved significantly in all his classes. Again, Ray never was the best student in school, but by the time he graduated he was working near the top of his ability.

I ran into Ray a few months ago, quite by accident. He now patrols part of the stretch of turnpike which I have to travel regularly.

Our son makes Ds, but he is much brighter than that. What can we do to help him?

Rather than repeating what I have already said about motivation, let me add just one more piece of advice. If your son is making Ds for no particular reason, make sure he knows that you love him. Let's be

23

honest. A few Ds in high school aren't going to ruin his life. Now, don't tell him that, and don't tell his high school teachers I said that. But if he has the ability—if he can read, write, compute, organize, use the language—he can do about anything in life he wants to do when he finally decides he wants to do it. The problem is hanging around long enough to let him decide he wants to do it.

Whatever you do, don't panic over those few Ds. Don't let those grades drive a wedge into your friendship (I assume that you and your son are friends). Let him know that you are unhappy. Remind him that those grades are his choice. But don't nag. Get on with life. This may be funny in ten years when he takes time out from a busy professional life to spend Christmas with you.

Our high school son goofed off and just barely passed in every class. Should we make him take summer school to catch up?

Perhaps I answer in the interest of your son, and perhaps I answer in the interest of whomever might be teaching summer school, but I would say no. More schooling just doesn't seem to be a very fitting punishment for someone who didn't like it in the first place.

If your son goofed off during the school year, he will in all probability goof off in the summer, and you are right back where you started.

Until he decides to make the most of his God-given abilities, your forcing him probably won't have that much positive outcome. Your task, which is a difficult one, is to try to find out why he goofed off in the first place. Is he tired of school? Is he going through a stage where he is insecure socially? Has he lost track of the value of what he is doing?

Sometimes we dismiss all these possibilities by saying something like, "Aw, he's just lazy." But I don't believe I have ever seen a high school student who is lazy. They are all quite willing to spend a ton of energy on what interests them. The mystery is how to get them interested in the things we think they ought to be interested in.

But as you are searching for this, let me make a couple of other observations. Your son's low grades are not necessarily an indication of what he got out of the past year. He might not be as far behind as you may think. Sometimes students listen enough and do enough work to master the material, but they don't complete the assignments or function well on tests. The grades go to the cellar, but actually, the students

24

are learning about as much as some of the others who are making better grades. If this is the case, your son could catch up in a matter of days, maybe even hours, when he decides he wants to.

It is also obvious that you are more concerned about your son's grades than he is. I do hope that you are careful not to let this become a barrier in your relationship. So your son goofed off a year in school. We wish people wouldn't do this, but it is not the end of the world, for him or you. He can bounce back. After being in this business for almost thirty years and seeing lots of people like your son, I have to realize that there isn't as much connection between a high school junior's grades and the kind of person he is at forty as I once thought. In other words, if I could be permitted to preach here, I would say, "Don't let your son's grades destroy your relationship."

I would recommend that you counsel him into finding a good job for the summer. Let him relax from school pressures, and build some self-confidence. This should do him more good than summer school would, unless summer school becomes his first choice.

Our son is not doing well in school. His counselor says it's because his self-image is low. What is he talking about?

Self-image, self-esteem, self-concept are words we use to identify how we think about ourselves. In its simplest terms, a healthy self-image is simply feeling confident that we can do the job. We are assured; we are positive; we are confident. On the other hand, a person who has low self-image doubts himself, worries about himself, feels that he is inadequate, and doesn't think that he can get the job done.

I have come to the conclusion that the student's self-image is one of the most vital tools in his learning. In fact, I am convinced that the two major factors which affect what your child learns in my classroom is what I think of myself and what your son thinks of himself. If your son thinks he can learn and thinks he can master the material, then he probably will. But if he thinks he can't learn, he probably won't. Since my ability to teach and the student's ability to learn depends so much on what he thinks about himself, then it would seem that we have the simple task of helping the student, your son, feel better about himself. But that task isn't as simple as it sounds. Let me suggest some reasons why self-image is such a complex area in the lives of children and adolescents.

1. Children and adolescents are in a constant battle to maintain and keep self-image. It would be much simpler if we could just build up a young person's self-esteem and he would stay that way the rest of his life. But it doesn't work that way. When you are young, self-image is a day-by-day and even moment-by-moment affair. (Actually, it may not be all that different when you are older.)

2. In young people, insecurity rarely looks like insecurity. Again, it would be convenient if the person with low self-image would just give us some definite, conspicuous hints that that is his problem. Then we could at least know what we are dealing with. But insecurity rarely looks like insecurity. Frequently, particularly among the males of the species, insecurity looks like arrogance—bragging, bravado, even bullying. Don't be deceived by this arrogant swagger. It just might be a way for the young man to tell you, "I don't like myself very much and I am not very confident."

Sometimes insecurity looks like apathy. The other day, I stood on the sidelines of a game at a picnic and heard parents try to encourage their young daughter to enter into the fun and frolic. She thwarted all their best logical persuasion with the age-old, "That's a dumb game." Translated, she was probably saying, "I don't think I can do it, and I am not going out there to make a fool of myself."

With the convenience of television, sometimes insecurity looks like listlessness or even laziness. The young person who is spending his time lying in front of the TV while his colleagues are out involved in some activity may just be feeling insecure.

3. Young people don't have as many ways to build a healthy self-image as adults do. To analyze that, let's look at some of the avenues any of us has to build a healthy self-image.

A. We compete and win. How's that for beginning with the controversial spot. But I do think it is true. Most of us rely at least some of the time on the feeling that we know that we are better than someone else. We bid for a job against our competitors and win. We win a prize. We play a game and win. We beat the other driver to the parking spot. We do something that no one else is doing.

Now be honest. Don't those kinds of accomplishments make you feel good about yourself, give you a sense of confidence and security?

Now I have a confession to make. As a teacher, I need for your son to feel good about himself or I won't be as effective in my attempts to teach. If your son is suffering through a period of low self-image, I will try to build him up. But what I will probably wind up doing is creating some kind of competitive situation where he can win. I will give a spelling quiz, a math drill, a butterfly assignment, or something that your son is better at than the other people in the class. If I am creative as a teacher, and if I know my students, surely, I can find something at which your son is good enough to beat his colleagues. Then hopefully, this will suffice for the time and I can teach and your son can learn.

If you are yelling foul, I can understand why. This is a cheap approach. You don't want me to use those techniques by themselves to build that healthy self-image. I don't blame you. I see the inadequacies too. Building self-image on competition can be dangerous. Not everyone can win. Besides, when the circumstances for the winning disappears, the feeling of security and assurance may disappear as well.

Yes, I know the dangers, but as a teacher, I will still employ this method to build self-image. That is why I recommend that parents make sure they work hard at helping the child have a healthy attitude toward himself before he even comes to school.

B. We achieve; we accomplish; we finish the task. I do a job, and when I have finished the job, I feel good about myself. For most of us adults, we have those kinds of positive guideposts worked into our lives day by day. We clean the room, make the sale, teach the class, finish the report, and then we feel confident and positive. Unless young people are very committed to making good grades, they don't have as many opportunities in their lives as adults do.

C. We know where we stand in our relationships. I am assured of my wife's love. Regardless of where I go or what I do or how badly I fail at something, I am still assured that Mary loves me. This assurance is vital to my self-image, to my confidence, to my feelings of security. I am not sure I could survive without it.

Young people need the same assurance from their relationships. But the problem is that they are not always convinced. There is so much change in their lives that they are never really sure where they fit into any relationship at any moment.

That is one reason why they do so many compulsive and irrational things in the name of friendship. If they need to go to the mall to see a friend, they must go to the mall to see a friend. It is almost a life-or-death matter. They must have the assurance of that friendship. They wear strange clothes or earrings or fingernails, not so much for the aesthetics of the look as for the social identification. They must know where they fit in the relationship.

D. We are confident in our relationship with God. We have the assurance that we were created by God with special talents and abilities, and we are excited about those talents.

Now that we have looked at the means we have available for us to develop our feelings of security or assurance or, in other words, a healthy self-image, let's consider some things you might try in attempting to help your son gain confidence in himself and consequently do better work, both as a student and as a person as well.

1. As much as possible, provide him with a consistent, dependable, predictable environment. Let him know what is expected of him.

2. Assure him of your love for him. But remember that this is not a one-time affair. He will need for you to assure him and reassure him every day. If you can catch him, run him down and hug him. When he is not expecting it, tell him how much you enjoy having him for a son. A good time to do this would be after he has goofed up in some small way. Catch him off guard and don't punish. Just tell him that you are pleased with the privilege of having him for a son.

3. Help him find some area where he can succeed. Direct him to a hobby or extracurricular activity where he can find some success. He may not be the best at the activity, but he does need to succeed.

4. Give him some responsibility around the house and expect him to fulfill his end of the agreement. In other words, treat him as if you respect him as a person.

5. Try not to be negative about his grades. He is probably feeling bad enough. If you just don't mention his school work and direct your relationship somewhere else during this time of his low self-image, he may even regain some confidence sometime soon.

Let me tell you about the day I taught composition to my high school students. I was actually employed to teach composition to high school students for fifteen years, but I did teach one day.

One Tuesday morning during the late '60s, the first order of business for the school was an announcement about a new school policy. At their regular meeting the night before, the school board had established a new hair and dress code for our school. The boys' hair was to be above the collar and above the ears. The girls' skirts were to come within four inches of their knees. (Do you remember those times?)

As soon as the principal had pronounced the new edict via the intercom, the uproar began. According to the students, this new policy was unfair, un-American, and Communistic. They may as well be living in Russia, they all agreed. But when the name-calling ended, they asked me what could be done. I suggested that they express their feelings to the school board.

That day those students learned to write. Students who had never cared before about such things as subject-verb agreement or commas or capital letters learned the rules and wrote flawlessly. Some of the letters deserve the title of masterpieces. Those students learned to write because for the first time in their lives they saw the real purpose for learning to write.

Of course, I called the president of the school board and told him what they had done. He commended me for the way I had handled the situation, and agreed to read the letters. Later, some of the students were even called in to meet with the board and to work through some of the protests and the problems. Not only did those students learn to write, but those students even learned the value of dignified protest.

Let's suppose a military drill for a moment. (Since I have never been in the military, I am only guessing here; but I hope my example seems realistic enough.) Suppose there is a building filled with poisonous gas. In a few minutes the whole outfit will have to put on gas masks and go stand inside that building.

Now, think about the teacher who is telling the troops how to put on the gas mask. That teacher does not necessarily have to have a sense of humor. He does not have to speak correctly. He does not even have to be particularly well-organized. Those students are going to learn how to put on a gas mask no matter what the teacher does or says.

That's called motivation—the ability of the learner to see the applied value of the lesson to be learned.

Maybe that is what we need in schools—a gas chamber.

I was explaining concept mastery to a group of college seniors when one of the brighter students held up her hand and offered a word of personal confession. When the other students and I eagerly agreed to hear her confession, she made us swear to secrecy. "My fiancé doesn't know this and my parents don't know," she warned us. So we moved to the edge of our seats and pledged absolute secrecy. Then she told us. "I can't divide." Now remember that this is a bright college senior making this statement.

"Why not?" we all asked in amazement.

"Because we moved four times when I was in the fourth grade," she told us, "and I never learned to put it all together."

Of course, this does make sense. Dividing requires not only mastering a sophisticated set of propositions but it also requires putting them together in the right order. If a person misses any part of it, he will never be able to divide, or at least he will never have any confidence at it.

After she had told us her fascinating story of how she had learned to compensate through the years and had learned to hide her weakness and had even learned to cheat, she then concluded with one final threat. "Don't try to teach me," she warned us. "It's hard and I can't learn it."

This young lady is a high school social studies teacher getting excellent reports from her supervisors, who probably don't even know that she doesn't know how to divide.

I must believe that this story is not unlike thousands of others. Somewhere sits a student in a classroom who missed one simple concept and he can't go on with the task at hand.

If I tell you something, will you promise not to laugh? All my life, when I heard about the Philippines, my mind went to the Caribbean. I realize now that this isn't any big deal, but I have been wrong all my life.

I almost did get caught in an embarrassing situation a couple of years ago. I was at a committee meeting with a group of world travelers when someone suggested that I should go to the Philippines and take a look at a program at Faith Academy, a very fine school for missionary children there. I quickly agreed. After all, a week in the Caribbean in the middle of January sounded all right to me. But in a few moments I realized that I didn't know where the Philippines are. With some maneuvering, I managed to cover my ignorance until I could run out from the meeting to find out for sure where the Philippines are.

At that point, I learned that I had been wrong all these years, but I still didn't know why. About a month later, I was visiting a high school history class. The young teacher was doing a rather nice job of explaining the Spanish-American War. Here we were down in Cuba with Theodore Roosevelt charging up San Juan Hill and being wonderful and victorious. In the process, we liberated Cuba and the Philippines. And then I understood why I have been wrong all these years.

My error was a simple one which didn't really cause all that much damage. But for all these years, I had had a wrong concept just because of the context of the presentation. How many thousands of students are in the same place?

CHAPTER TWO
Schools and Values

When I taught high school English, I made a rather big deal of the American poet, John Greenleaf Whittier. I have heard comments that he wasn't much of a poet, but I liked him; and when you are the teacher, you get to teach what you like. Besides, he was a Christian and he was an honorable man, standing firmly on the principle of abolition.

In 1962, I taught literature and John Greenleaf Whittier to a class of high school sophomores in a small school in rural Oklahoma. I remember the class, mostly guys, mostly football players, meeting first hour in the morning. As usual, I taught Whittier, doubting all the time that any actually learned anything. Nevertheless, I taught.

At the end of the year, I left that little town with little cause to remember much about it later. But in 1982 one of those students from that first hour English class called me. He is now a medical doctor. Looking me up is not in itself an easy task, because we have moved several times since 1962, but I did enjoy hearing from a former student.

In the course of a very informative conversation, he told me the good news that in recent years he had developed an appreciation of poetry and had begun to read poetry in his spare time. I was thrilled to hear the good news. You teach 1,000 and one gets the message.

Then my former student said, "In fact, I've just discovered a poet that I think you might like."

Now I am really encouraged. Not only has he begun to read poetry but he is going to recommend someone to me. "Whom have you discovered?" I asked with eagerness.

"John Greenleaf Whittier," he answered with much enthusiasm.

After twenty years, I had lost my right to yell at him. This was not the place for me to chastise him for not remembering Whittier from class discussions twenty years ago, so I bit my tongue and pride a bit and asked, "What have you discovered about this wonderful poet, Whittier?"

Do you know what he had discovered out of his own mind and imagination? He had discovered my lecture, point for point and word for word.

If I know the way former students talk, this young doctor probably went to the hospital the next day and said something like, "I remember old Schimmels. He was a good old boy but he didn't teach us much."

But I will take that. Without his knowing it, I am already in his mind, and he will never get over me, regardless of how much he tries.

It is because of this that we put this chapter on schools and value formation second in this book. We must understand that education, the product and process of schools, is the process of acquiring skills and facts. But it is more than that. It is the process of acquiring some insights, a vision, through which we look at ourselves and our world. Those insights or that vision can be joined together and called our value structure.

We just have to believe that every day in a young person's life something is happening that will have a major impact on that person's life ten, or fifteen, or twenty years later. Some way that lesson will come back to present itself—in how he relates to his spouse, in how he relates to his children, in how he relates to his Lord, in his integrity at work, or in what poetry he reads. Someday in some way the lesson will be there.

Knowing this is both reassuring and frightening. What we teach and how we teach does make a difference. It is important for us as parents to know clearly what is happening to our children, so that we can coordinate, supplement, and direct their moral and value growth.

It is important for us to know what the schools are doing in the overt moral areas such as drug education and sex education. But it is also important for us to understand what is happening to our children in the day-by-day activities of classes and extracurricular activities.

Value education is broader than whether or not a young person uses drugs or alcohol or engages in sex. It includes the love of learning, the definition of success, the respect for others, and yes, even the kind of poetry one reads.

Is it possible for my child to get a value-free education in the public schools?

No. How is that for a short but frightening answer? Let's face it. There is no such thing as a value-free education. There never was and never can be. Education is by its very definition an enterprise in preparing people for a future. To do this, someone has to guess about what that future is to be and how is the best way to prepare for it. Those guesses constitute values. We just can't escape it.

Let's look at some of the ways human values are consciously or unconsciously incorporated into the school process. For one thing, just the structure of the school day teaches certain values such as the importance of being on time, the importance of following instructions, the importance of the mind. Students really don't have any options. If they go to school, they are going to learn that we Americans believe in being on time. That is part of the way the program operates.

Determining what is and what is not in the curriculum is another way we teach values. For example, in any school in this country, a student will quite soon get the idea that things like math and English are essentials while music and art are luxuries. You can protest that categorization all you want, but the tone is already written into the requirements. You must have math, but you don't have to have music.

Teachers make hundreds of value decisions every day. They decide which piece of material will get three days of emphasis and which piece will get only one day. They decide what they will explain and what they won't explain. They decide what is a good piece of work and deserves an A or what isn't a good piece of work and gets a C.

I don't want to frighten anybody, but a lot of what we adults value is what we learned from some teacher whose name we probably don't even remember. No, there simply is not something called a value-free education.

We have heard so much about the humanistic values taught in the schools. What can we as parents to do counter those?

That is a very thoughtful and difficult question. It is particularly difficult for two reasons.

1. We are not always sure we know what we are talking about when we talk of humanistic values. The most dangerous definition of humanism is that man has been left in this world to take charge of his own

destiny without any help, support, or interference from a divine Being.

Another definition of humanism frequently used in school circles is that one human being ought to treat any other human with respect and dignity.

Yet another definition that sounds more classical is that humanism is the study of the thoughts, the art, literature, philosophy, and history of the human race.

Obviously, if two people are trying to communicate with each other, they need to be using the same definition of the word lest they develop a chasm of misunderstanding. Unfortunately, this is what has happened in some places in recent years. We have this document, The Humanist Manifesto, which gives some uniformity to the definition; still, not all people have read that document so they are using the word in a different slant.

2. If we are not careful, we can become alarmed about some educational and noneducational practices in the schools and in society in general, and we can miss some of the more dangerous things which happen to our children. Deception is still one of Satan's most powerful tools. Let me see if I can illustrate. Many teachers rely very heavily on the use of competition as a factor in motivating students. Sometimes these competitive battles are obvious. The teacher divides the classroom into groups and conducts a contest. The teacher gives prizes to the students who do the job better than the others. Now, at this point, you may be protesting, "Come on, Cliff, a little competition never hurt anyone. This is what makes this country strong." OK, I don't really agree but now let's talk about how the teacher uses a rather vicious form of competition without even knowing it. The teacher gives a test, has the students exchange papers, then the teacher calls each student by name and has the student tell his grade as the teacher records the grade in the grade book. In my opinion, that practice which is far too common teaches one of the most vicious kinds of competition there is, and I don't want my child learning that. Teachers who do this probably don't mean to be teaching any significant lesson. They are just trying to save some valuable time and effort. But the practice still teaches an unhealthy lesson. These are the humanistic practices which concern me.

But now that we have looked at the problem, let's see if we can answer your question. We as parents must assume that we have the full responsibility for teaching values to our children. They are going to meet values head on in every place in their environment—from the TV, down the street with friends, at Grandma's house, in the classroom, and they must have some vehicle, some measuring stick for recognizing those values as values, for evaluating, and for making a decision about them. That is an enormous task for parents. Let's break it down into workable steps.

1. Let your children see your value structure in practice. In this modern age of rush, we sometimes forget to share all of our lives with our children. We keep our professional life and our family life separate. This may be convenient, but it doesn't do much to help our own children see how a value system works in practice. As a boy, I knew that my father was a man of his word. At times, I saw him go out of his way to keep his side of an agreement. This boyhood impression of my father has made a significant impact on the kind of man I have become. I am not always sure I can live up to the value he taught me, but I know that I want to try. I at least have the goal.

Teach your children. Let them watch you live. That in itself should be more powerful than anything they get from a book or a teacher.

2. Teach your child the Bible. As we all know, the best defense against Satan's deception is a good understanding of Scripture. The best defense any of us has against falling into the trap of living values which are contradictory to what we know we should do is again a good understanding of Scripture. Since knowledge of Scripture is so important in your child's growth and education, assume the role of teacher yourself. I'm afraid that one hour of Sunday School per week just won't get the job done. Your child needs to get into the Word every day. Does this sound like I am advocating family devotions as a method for countering the humanistic values your children are going to meet in schools? Probably so.

3. Maintain the kind of relationship with your child which will permit him to share with you honestly and openly what is happening to him day by day. I think what frightens most people about schools is that it is such a giant unknown. We pack those kids on the yellow vehicle at 8 A.M. and they disappear into existential nothingness until about 3 P.M. During that time, we don't even know whether they exist or not, much less what is happening to them and what they are learning. Your task in trying to get some handle on that vacuum time is to maintain the kind of relationship where your children will talk to you. If you hear something you don't accept, decide whether it is insignificant

or a major issue. If it is insignificant, you can probably correct a wrong idea with a simple statement to your child. Frequently as a teacher, I have had students come back to me and say, "My mother disagreed with a point you made yesterday." Frankly, I am encouraged by that statement. It means that the child and mother are talking, and it means that the mother cares enough for her child to take some responsibility in the education process. It is also apparent to me that the mother has more impact on the child than I do. That's wholesome too.

4. Develop and maintain a working relationship with your child's teacher. I believe so strongly in this suggestion that I have devoted one whole section of the book to it. But if you have any concerns about the kind of education your child is going to receive, make sure you know the teacher and the teacher knows you.

The other day a college student was telling me how much things had changed since his high school days. To illustrate, he picked a story from his own family. The student reported that while he was in high school, he sat with his father one day to watch a football game on TV. After one particular play, the student blurted out his commentary, "That sucks!" And for that comment the student's father slapped him.

Four years later the two sat again watching a ball game, and after one particular play, the father blurted out his commentary, "That sucks!"

Yes, things are changing.

What can be done about all the profanity in school?

I wish I knew the answer to this question. If there is one thing that appalls me about schools, it is the profanity. I think we probably knew all those words when we were in school, but I do think we had some sense of appropriateness, some sense of when to use them and when not to use them. Maybe I am just getting older, but it seems to me that in recent years, the use of profanity has grown rampant and indiscriminate.

As adults, the one thing we can do is to maintain our own standards and require young people to respect our standards when they are in our presence. Maybe we can't stop them from using profanity, but we can prevent ourselves from hearing it.

As parents, the one thing we can do is to realize that our children are exposed to that kind of talk. Knowing this, we can then assume the responsibility ourselves of teaching our own children how to communicate without engaging in words that offend God and other people. As parents, we must assume this task ourselves because their environment is not going to teach them.

Not long ago I overheard a conversation at a conference for school superintendents. They sat around in an informal meeting sharing ideas and proposals, and someone introduced the possibility of having a Bible study group form under the Equal Access Law. Some of the superintendents were quite nervous about the possibility and could only see such negative results as community reaction and lawsuits. Others seemed to think that the idea wouldn't be so bad.

In the midst of the discussion, with the group about equally divided for and against, an old veteran superintendent with more than thirty years of experience walked in. Since he is highly respected, not only for his experience but also for his wisdom, one of the group suggested they ask him his opinion of these Bible study groups in the schools.

He was not only quick with his answer but he was firm. "Permit them," he said. "In fact, if you get a chance, encourage them."

"Why?" the group wanted to know.

"Cheapest way I know to cut down on building vandalism," the old veteran answered and walked on with his thoughts and wisdom.

When Carl was a college student studying to become a math teacher, he would frequently come into my office and we would have long, meaningful conversations about ideas and principles.

When Carl graduated and went to work as a high school teacher, he was immediately popular with everyone—students, fellow teachers, and administrators. At that time, his career choice seemed to be a perfect match. He was happy in the profession and the profession was happy with him.

After three years, Carl quit teaching and took a high-paying job in the financial district of our city. Since this is not really that unusual, I wasn't all that surprised or even disturbed. Good math teachers can almost always find better-paying jobs in the business world, and too often someone makes that choice.

I hadn't seen Carl since he had made the move, but I bumped into him the other day on the train on the way into work. Again we had a good conversation, but unlike the conversations of the other years, this time we talked about things rather than ideas. He told me about his new home, new car, new VCR, and new big-screen television set.

As we were getting off the train, I sensed the need to say one more thing just for closure to our conversation, so I asked, "Do you ever miss teaching?"

Since he was ahead of me on our way out, he had to turn slightly to establish eye contact, but I could still detect a look of sadness in his eyes. "Every day and every way," he answered. "I miss the kids, the classes, the excitement, the sounds, and even the smells of school. But I don't miss having to grovel for my pay." And with that he turned and went off to his high-paying job that he didn't enjoy as much as teaching.

Here is the American tragedy. Here is the value structure we need to be concerned about. I don't hold anything against people who have high-paying jobs or who delight in owning things. But when our definition of success is so narrow that we can't be happy in our pursuit of it, we have somewhere learned the wrong lessons.

Next year our daughter is to enter high school. We have heard reports that there are drugs in the public school she is scheduled to attend. Do you think we should make the financial sacrifices to move her to another school?

This is a difficult situation for you and your daughter. We are all frightened to hear that horrible word "drugs," and rightfully so. Not only are we as parents concerned about the availability of drugs to our children, but drug activity in a school could mar the quality of the education and affect even the spirit and climate of the entire school.

Let's face it. A student who smoked marijuana during noon hour isn't going to be too sharp a student the hour after lunch. He isn't going to make much of a contribution to the class, and that will affect the education for all students. You have a right to be concerned. Any wise parent would be concerned about sending a child to a school with extensive drug activity.

But now let me frighten you even more. To be on the safe side, we parents need to realize that drugs are a part of our culture. They are everywhere. I seriously doubt that there are very many schools in this country where there is not some drug activity.

I say this to remind us all that we simply cannot protect our children from drugs. We cannot build a shield around them. Let me state this in emphatic terms. Every young person growing up in the United States must make his own decision about drug use. Our task as parents is to teach our children how to make that decision. We must give them the equipment they need to protect themselves with their own decision-making process.

"What is that equipment?" you ask. Well, we need to provide them with some tools for building their own self-confidence. We need to provide them with a sense that someone loves them and appreciates them. And we need to provide them with opportunities for success in their lives.

Whether you move your daughter to the private school is a family matter, but regardless of the decision, you still have your work cut out for you.

My son is in the eighth grade. His school has just begun a semester-long course in drug education. What can we expect from the course?

Of course, the answer to that question will vary from program to program and teacher to teacher, but by and large those courses in drug education or substance abuse consist of two general components—information and decision-making skills.

Perhaps the strongest feature of such a course is the providing of information. This may be the strongest feature simply because teachers are most skillful at providing information to students. But also there is much information to be taught. We now have some good evidence of the dangers of drug use, of the deception of addiction, of the costs of drugs both in money and brainpower. Frankly, I am pleased that we have some method for providing that information to young people. I am pleased that your son is going to know this.

But as we have learned through the years, information alone is not enough to help a young person make the right decision about substance abuse. There must be another dimension. That is why the school programs often contain a decision-making component. In these sessions, the students are given some principles and some practice on how to make a decision in the face of such obstacles as peer pressure and the desire to belong.

Your attitude should be that the course has been implemented to assist you as a parent. The course itself won't do your work for you. The course itself, regardless of how good it is, is not enough. The course is just a beginning, a stepping-stone to assist you in your work as a parent. Let me make some suggestions.

1. Since your son is already in the course, this should be a good time for the two of you to have some excellent discussions. I would recommend that you talk to him a bit every day about what is happening in the course and what he is learning. Make the conversation as light and open as possible so that your son will feel that he can be open with you during this time.

2. Model for your child the kind of behavior you want him to have. It is rather tough to give your child a persuasive lecture on substance abuse while you have a beer in your hand. Regardless of what you say to your child, he will probably be more influenced by what you do.

3. Don't give your child cause to doubt the consistency of your love.

4. Keep an open relationship with your child so that you can tell if he has sudden mood changes or attitude changes.

The sixteen-year-old daughter wanted to go see a movie rated PG-13, but the mother was hesitant. In fact, the mother was holding her own in the discussion and even looked to be slightly ahead until the daughter pulled out her best shot.

You can always tell when they are on their best shot. They pull up their shoulders a bit to show defiance but pucker their lips at the same time to show a bit of pouting.

The girl went through all the visible signs and said, in a plea, "But, Mother, the world is R-rated."

Unfortunately, she is accurate. It is an R-rated world that they live in—the one at school, the one on TV, the one on the streets. It is an R-rated world which they didn't create, but now they must learn to live in.

Don't you really admire and respect them, those who pass through it all and maintain a sense of dignity and self-control?

I first met Helen when she and I were on a panel at a conference for high school English teachers. Immediately, I could discern that she was a Christian. I could tell from her responses to the questions, from the way she looked at her students with respect and treated them as intelligent human beings with worth and dignity, from the way she dealt with administrators and fellow teachers. Her Christianity was obvious in her attitudes and approaches, but it was also obvious in her face. She was happy and she loved life in such a way that she urged others to love life too. I thought she looked like the Samaritan woman must have after she met Jesus and went back into town to convince those people to come see the Saviour.

But I must admit that Helen was something of a puzzle. She had the maturity of a person who has been a Christian for a long time; yet she had the freshness of one who has only recently discovered the wonder and majesty of a personal God.

My curiosity got the best of me, so during one of the breaks in the panel action, I leaned over and asked, "How long have you been a Christian?" Now, that could be a dangerous question to ask of someone you have only met an hour ago and have only interacted with on a professional basis. But somehow, I just knew that Helen would respond to the question.

And I wasn't disappointed. A big grin came to her mouth and eyes, and she looked even happier than she had before. "About three years," she answered, and then as if she wanted me to know and she wanted everyone else sitting by us to know, she added, "One of my students led me to the Lord."

I nodded as if I understood and she told the rest of the story. "One of my brightest students, cheerful and happy and a school leader, kept writing such beautiful essays about the role Jesus played in her life. And I just said to myself, I need to be like this girl. So I called her in and asked her how I could have Jesus play a role in my life. She told me, and I became a Christian right in my own classroom."

With that, we went back to the panel business of telling other English teachers how we teach such important things as commas and semicolons to high school students.

What is values clarification and how is it used in our schools?

Values clarification is a highly organized theory of how we develop values plus a rather thorough set of curriculum strategies for helping students clarify and identify their values.

Though many names have been associated with the concept since its beginning in the late 1960s, the two principals include advocates Louis Raths and Sydney Simon.

In short, the theory states that in order to have a definite value or value structure, a person needs to choose a value from several options; he needs to affirm that value by expressing it; he needs to identify it clearly; and he needs to apply it in a practical situation.

Values clarification is not so interested in labeling any value as right or wrong, but rather the idea is concerned with helping the individual identify and clarify the value he has chosen.

After the initial concept was developed, the proponents worked out elaborate and thorough strategies for helping students clarify their values. Some of these classroom strategies included such things as:

1. The magic circle where the students sat around in a circle and explained how they felt at the moment without any fear of rebuke or correction. The idea is that we need to be honest with our feelings.

2. The mask of the inner you—In this activity, the students would take a paper sack, some string, construction paper, and crayons and make a mask of their inner self.

3. The affirming sheet—in this activity, the teacher would write a student's name on a sheet of paper and have several students say what they like about that student.

4. List of likes—The teacher would have the students write down a list of ten things they like or that give them pleasure. To make the activity even more precise, the teacher might then have the students put those ten things in some order of preference.

Values clarification activities seemed to be far more prevalent in classrooms in the mid to late 1970s than they are now. I am not sure I know all the reasons for the popularity during that time, but one of the reasons is rather simple and obvious. The curriculum materials and activities were so clearly written step by step that teachers could use the activity without much creative thought or preparation on their part.

I have heard that in some schools there is an organization of Christian students who meet regularly for prayer and Bible study. Is that legal?

Yes. In all probability, what you are referring to is an organization which comes under the Equal Access Law which is a federal law passed and implemented in 1984.

What the new law provides is for a group of students to get together on their own initiative to have a student-initiated and student-led meeting for Bible study and prayer at the school at a time during the school day which is not instructional time. In other words, the organization cannot meet during classes.

Teachers can be present if they wish, but the school officials cannot require that any teacher attend. At the same time, according to the law, the organization must be led by students rather than by teachers.

This organization is to be treated like any other noncurricular organization. In other words, it is to be treated like a chess club or a travel club or some organization that is not an extension of the curriculum.

Though the Equal Access Law is not widely known and though there have been some initial fears on the part of school officials about the possibilities of such organizations forming, several schools throughout various areas of the country are taking full advantage of the law. A couple of months ago, I spoke with young people in the Dallas area who had actually first heard the Gospel in the Bible study at their school.

Willie was an excellent football player and a dedicated Christian. He had looked forward to becoming a junior in high school and moving up to varsity competition. The coaches had looked forward to that moment too because Willie had the potential of being one of the best.

But when the time came, Willie wasn't as excited as he should have been. He did enjoy the competition and he was distinguishing himself as he used his God-given talent to his best ability. But the head coach used profanity, and frequently the players would too.

Willie was not used to that profanity and he found it repulsive. So after a few days, he went to see the rough-spoken and outspoken coach and told him his plight. Rather than being upset, the coach was embarrassed. He thanked Willie for his conviction, and that afternoon before practice the coach ordered the profanity to stop.

Incidentally, Willie went on to become all-state and eventually played on a team that played in the Rose Bowl.

As every junior high and high school English teacher will tell you, we always have those students who want to shock us when they write their papers, so they write about the most shocking subject they can think about at the time. Sometimes there may even be a hint of truth or reality in the vivid accounts of rampant sin, but most of the time the real purpose of the papers is to get our attention and shock us a bit.

When I first started teaching in 1959, those students wrote me vivid details of their smoking habits. I was appropriately shocked, and I went to see the counselor. Together, we decided to take action, and started a program in our school for those students experimenting with tobacco. Actually, the title and theme of that program seemed rather original at the time, "SAY NO TO TOBACCO!"

In 1969 those students who wanted to shock us were still around, but by then they had progressed to writing about drugs and drug usage. Like the tobacco issue of a decade ago, that got our attention.

Twenty years later, those students are now writing about suicide.

Do you see the plight of the poor adolescent, especially the one with a hint of rebellion in his soul? In this age of worldly sophistication and callousness and acceptance, it just takes a whole lot more to get our attention than it used to take.

Do Christian students really have much of a testimony in the public schools?

Yes, yes, and a thousand times, yes. Christian students have a testimony to other students; they have a testimony with teachers; and they can even have a testimony with the community at large.

There may be a few laws restricting what Christians can say in a public place such as the school, but there is no law keeping a Christian from being a Christian; from thinking as a Christian; from looking at other people through the eyes of a Lord of love; and from keeping a lifestyle which is not conformed to this world, but is transformed by a spiritual commitment to a righteous God.

I have heard students witness to their Lord openly and directly in classes or in private conversations with fellow students. They quote the Bible at appropriate times and they are frequently called on by the teacher to comment on any biblical passage which might come up in the school material.

I have seen other Christian students witness just by being Christian. Last spring I overheard a conversation in a freshman physical education class. One rather boisterous young man said to another, "I've never heard you cuss."

"I don't cuss," the other said. "I am a Christian."

"Wow, I admire you," the boisterous young leader said, with complete sincerity.

Some Christian students witness by doing quality work. Frequently, teachers will comment that students from "church" families are easier to teach. What they are probably saying is that the solid family unit which has God at the center makes a difference in the lives of young people.

Yes, Christian students do have a witness in the schools.

Why do schools use the Planned Parenthood materials in sex education?

I suppose there could be a couple of reasons why schools use the materials prepared by the Planned Parenthood organization. Perhaps some educators are fully convinced that these materials are the very best available, so they use their own judgments in selecting what materials will be used. On the other hand, I find that, too often, schools use those materials simply because they don't know what else is available.

In either case, parents who do not endorse the thrust and intent of the Planned Parenthood materials can become actively involved in the process of selecting and adopting the materials used in the sex education courses in school.

The first thing you need to do is to make sure you know what is available yourself. Do your own research and do it well. But let me give you a head start on that project. Dr. Dinah Richard of San Antonio, Texas has conducted and published a tremendous piece of research in a little manual called, "Teen-age Pregnancy and Sex Education in the Schools: What Works and What Does Not Work." Any parent trying to rear children in the last quarter of the twentieth century ought to own and read fully that piece of material. You can order it from the Research and Education Division of San Antonio Pregnancy Center, P.O. Box 792011, San Antonio, Texas, 78279-2011.

Order your copy today. I don't know what it costs, but the material is worth the price. Find out for yourself what the research says. Then show the publication to your local school people. Let them know that there are materials other than Planned Parenthood.

We have received a note from the school telling us that our sixth-grade daughter is to be in a sex-education class next semester. How should we respond?

You should first respond by accepting the fact that the school really wants you to respond. The school didn't send that note through simple courtesy. The school is really seeking parental input, advice, and endorsement. I really recommend that you respond.

The first and least that you can do is to go to any public meetings to discuss the program. Just recently, a father told me that he had received a note just like yours. He went to the public meeting to discuss the new program and met with four other parents who were interested enough to come. Too often we complain and worry and fret about what is being taught our children, yet we don't go to the schools when they are making a genuine effort to find out what we think.

The next thing you can do is to ask to review the materials. Since the school sent you the note, I am sure the principal or teacher would really cooperate if you ask to see the material. Take whatever time is needed and consider the material carefully.

You will want to spend some time thinking about what you like and don't like; but more than that, you will need to spend some time thinking about how you are going to supplement the material when it is presented to your child at school.

By sending the note out, the school has actually said to parents, "Look, we can't do this job by ourselves. All we can do is help you in this very important part of your child's education. Now, come and find out what we are doing so we can do a better job of helping you."

Our son is in a Quest program. What is that?

Quest is an international curriculum organization with offices somewhere near Columbus, Ohio. (They move so often I can't keep up with them.) About ten years ago, the founder and president, Rick Little, supervised the development of curriculum for high school students called Skills for Adolescents. The curriculum basically consisted of a series of lessons designed to help high school students develop skills of making decisions, considering alternatives and, in general, living with the pressure of being an adolescent.

The curriculum can be implemented into the school program in a variety of ways. Some schools offer one semester. Other schools put the curriculum into another course and use it as a supplementary lesson. Still other schools offer the curriculum as something of an option to another class.

One of the unusual aspects of the Quest curriculum is that the organization requires the teachers to take special training. Thus, the people in charge of writing the curriculum have a bit more control about how it is used and about how the objectives of the program are to be accomplished.

In recent years, Quest has expanded to include a curriculum for junior high schools which in addition to the lessons on making choices and living with stress include some highly endorsed material on substance abuse and the decision-making process.

The junior high curriculum also includes a manual for parents, and part of the program includes some regularly scheduled seminars for parents.

Why do schools even consider sex education in the curriculum?

In a recent survey, seven out of ten high school seniors reported that they had participated in sex at least once.

Pregnancy is one of the major causes of high school dropouts.

Sexually transmitted diseases compose one of the major health threats to this nation and to the entire world.

We all agree that there is a problem.

The next question is, "Who's going to provide the instruction that young people need to deal with this problem?"

The most acceptable answer would be, "Parents!" But the recent survey also told us that two out of every ten high school seniors said that they had had some kind of discussion about sex with their parents. Now think of that. If these people are representative, and it seems that they are, eight out of every ten high school seniors are left on their own to find out about their sexuality and how to use it. Or, in other words, they are going to learn about sexuality from the street or from the television, and neither seems to be a really reliable source.

In the face of the problem, someone must (let me emphasize *must*) assume some responsibility for the education. By default, if nothing else, the school seems to have inherited the job. And that is why sex education is in the curriculum.

Many have protested that it isn't a very suitable study for schools. And there are some valid reasons for that argument. Schools and teachers are primarily concerned with providing information for students. Thus, when they inherit a class such as sex education, which is more about forming an attitude than learning facts, they struggle with the assignment. It is much easier to teach the facts of American history than to teach the proper attitude about how to use the beautiful God-given gift of sex.

Of course, there is some valuable information which needs to be taught. These young people need to learn how the body works, how diseases are transmitted, and the facts of the responsibility of your own actions. They also need to learn how to make decisions so that reason rules over passion. They do need to learn this, and these are lessons teachers are comfortable with. So by and large, this is the material of the sex education curriculum.

I agree with the protesters that this is not enough. We should teach these young people the sheer joy and beauty of saying no until marriage. We should teach them that their bodies are sacred temples and not their own to mar and blemish. I agree with this. But these are hard lessons because they are lessons about attitudes and lifestyles. These are lessons that young people need to learn or at least have reinforced in places other than classrooms. But in the meantime, someone has to assume the responsibility for laying out the facts. So that is why sex is in the curriculum.

Our school has sex education beginning at sixth grade. What is left for us parents to do?

Thanks for asking that question. Probably every person at school connected with that sex education program would hope that every parent would ask the question. Any educator who is worth his salt knows that this important lesson must be a cooperative effort if there is going to be any success at all. The parents must get involved. I am sure your school people would be happy to offer even more suggestions than I have to offer here.

First, you should find out what is happening in the school sex education program. Go up to the school and explain to them what you want to know. I am sure they will cooperate. If the program uses handouts or textbooks or films, ask to see them. This may take a bit of time on your part, but the time will be well spent. You do need to know how the school is approaching the issue and what materials they are using. If you react to any of the material, speak to the teacher in charge. You may not convince the teacher, but you do deserve an explanation. If you find something offensive for your child, ask that your child be dismissed for this portion of the program. This should all be fairly easy.

But you aren't finished here. Now that you know what your children are studying, be prepared to help them with the information and even ideas that they will get in school. I find that children will want to talk about this material with some adult they respect. Since you know what they are experiencing, you are in a position to offer some prompting to get the discussion started. It is perfect for a dishwashing activity or riding in the car or just a casual conversation. The school curriculum will go fairly fast for them. They will need some time to reflect on what they are learning with you.

But you still aren't finished regardless of what your school is or is not doing, regardless of how effective your church youth group is, regardless of how much you are embarrassed by the topic, you are still the one responsible for helping your own children learn the proper attitude toward their sexuality and feelings. The school program may provide some good information, but that program can't prescribe a lifestyle. It is your task to help your children learn that lesson. For this, the New Testament provides excellent material. Paul tells the Corinthians that their bodies are the temples of the Holy Spirit. You need to tell your children that too. It is too important a lesson to be trusted to someone else. You need to do that yourself.

The other good source of material is yourself and your own lifestyle. I don't want to put pressure on you, but there is a good chance that your children will grow up with your attitudes toward sexuality. Don't be afraid to tell your children about how you dealt with those feelings and questions when you were their age. They will respect you for it.

Sometimes we forget that young people ask us questions because they want answers. One of the best responses to the questions they are asking or even to questions they are thinking is a simple, "Well, I don't know about you, but this is the way I dealt with it."

Roger and Sue were a perfect match in high school. Sue was a cheerleader, a straight-A student, and the homecoming queen. Roger was president of a couple of school organizations and captain of the football team. It seemed obvious to everyone that the two should be dating.

But there was one small glitch. Sue was a Christian and Roger wasn't. Finally, when Roger got up the nerve and got around to asking Sue out for dates, she agreed only on the condition that Roger would attend church with her each Sunday night. Since Sue was one of the prettier girls in school, Roger decided the price was not too high so he agreed. Shortly after they had begun to date, Roger responded to the message of the Gospel and became a believer himself.

The two dated through high school but when they went away to different colleges, the romance faded into just other high school memories.

Roger is now a quite successful and well-known minister, pastoring a large church in the Midwest—an effective servant of God who was first introduced to the Gospel because a high school girl was not afraid to stand on her convictions.

Our freshman daughter has asked our permission to date a senior boy who has asked her out. Should we give in?

I wish you hadn't asked that question. But since it has come up, let's talk about this problem. In developing any kind of response, there are several questions which you have to ask yourselves first.

1. How old should a girl (or a boy for that matter) be before she begins dating. I suppose there are many factors to that question—the maturity of the person, the attitude of the parents, the kind of dating. But it is a question which must be faced by every family, and it is a family question. I would never presume to be smart enough to answer that kind of question for any family. But it is a question which the family needs to address before the fact. If you have not already, the mother, the father, and the girl should sit down together and establish a consensus of dating boundaries. When does dating begin? What kind of dates? How often? With whom? All three parties need to be reasonable, and the discussion may even call for diplomacy and perhaps even some compromise. But the ground rules need to be established and agreed on.

2. Why does this boy want to date your daughter? Where did they get acquainted? How long have they known each other? What does she think of him? Though I am not sure what is right in this case, I would be much more sympathetic if this were a neighborhood friend, or a friend from the church youth group or a son of family friends rather than someone she met at a rock concert. If your daughter is the only girl this guy knows, perhaps I can understand his request, but you must realize that he is still about twenty percent older than she is. That is a lot of life's experience.

3. Why is your daughter interested in this guy? Is she not comfortable around boys her own age? Of course, that is a good possibility. Ninth-grade boys can be about the most immature three-year-olds on earth, given the right set of circumstances; and quite frequently ninth-grade girls grow bored with that kind of behavior in a hurry. On the other hand, is your daughter attracted to this guy because he has a car and independence?

Now that you have begun to ask yourself the questions, you still have to make a decision about whether you let her go. First, aren't you glad she asked? Whatever you do, you must regard that respect she has shown for you, and you must do whatever you can to keep it.

However, as a general principle, I am not very optimistic about this kind of relationship. I base my pessimism through having watched these kinds of relationships through the years. Almost always, the girl winds up getting hurt in some way. Most often, the guy dumps her after a couple of dates, and she suffers through the first broken heart earlier than you would have wanted her to. If he doesn't dump her, and the relationship continues, the guy, simply because he is older and has to make some more permanent commitments, pushes the thing faster than the girl can handle. At that time, somebody, usually the girl, has to call a halt; and then she suffers the broken heart, combined with guilt.

Of course, my little scenarios do not cover all situations, and perhaps this is the one that is different. You and your daughter are in the best position to decide that. I don't envy you the decision you have to make because whatever it is, you still have to respond to the cry: "You don't trust me." And when a daughter of that age seasons the cry with the salt of many tears, then I suffer a broken heart.

Why are sex education courses necessary now when we didn't have such courses when we were in school?

We could say that these kids just aren't as smart as we were when we were that age, and there might even be some truth in that. Most generations prior to this one did get some training about sexuality and birth processes from a closer association with animals than most suburban or urban students now have. If we could just remember, we might realize that we had the same questions; but somehow as we watched the process with a cow or a horse, we put some things together and came out with a rather accurate idea of what was going on. Most young people now don't have the ready access to a cow.

But there are a couple of other reasons, and perhaps more reasonable ones, about why the young people of today need more instruction than we had.

First, the world has changed some since we were that age. For whatever reason, young people are exposed to more temptations to lust in a week than we were exposed to in our whole adolescence. If you want to see this in vivid detail, compare an old "Leave It to Beaver" television program with any prime-time show made in the last three years. If you listen carefully, you will be shocked with the tone, the suggestions, and the graphic portrayal.

When I was in elementary school, we all went to see a movie called *Gone with the Wind.* It was a great movie and a great memory, but the most powerful memory of all, and the one we giggled about for weeks, was when old Clark Gable in his finest Rhett Butler voice as he was walking out the door, uttered that shocking piece of profanity, "Frankly, my dear, I don't. . . ." Well, you know the rest of it. But do you remember how shocked we were to hear such a statement in a movie? That was "behind the barn" talk, and not suitable for a movie—at least not then. But now, our young people live in an R-rated world. They didn't create that world. They didn't make it R-rated, but it is the world they inherited. It is the world that my generation has let develop during our lifetime. Despite all our protests about the reality of this trend, it doesn't really seem that we are having much success in reversing it, so we must do something to help our young people survive and develop normally in a much tougher setting than we had.

Another reason for the added pressure on these young people is the elongation of the adolescent age. When I was an adolescent, most of my friends were considering marriage right after high school. Their commitment to remain pure until marriage was a commitment to make it through high school. Now, most young people aren't considering marriage that early, so they have to make a much firmer commitment and one that is grounded in both factual information and moral fiber.

When I was in high school, a dirty movie came to our town. Though we didn't have the sophisticated rating system which now tells us beforehand where we will be comfortable and where we won't, we nonetheless knew this was a dirty movie. In small towns the grapevine communication system is both faster and more reliable than any form of rating labels could ever be. This was indeed a dirty movie. I will never forget the title: *The Moon Is Blue.*

One night I mustered my courage and went. It was time for me to see what everyone else had been gossiping in the halls about all week long. Though I was not a Christian at the time and did not even know that I had a sense of right and wrong, within fifteen minutes, I became embarrassed and ashamed and guilty and I got up and left.

About two years ago that same movie, *The Moon Is Blue*, came on late-night television in its original uncut version. Now that I have gone to a couple of county fairs and have grown a bit more sophisticated about the rawer side of life, I decided to watch that movie that I couldn't handle as a high school student.

I put the family to bed (after all, it is my role to protect them), got out the sodas and popcorn, and settled in for a long evening of shocking reality. This time I watched about fifteen minutes, turned it off, and went to bed. That movie is not shocking; it's boring. The 10 o'clock news has more sex and violence than that movie.

Suddenly that night I became painfully aware of how complacent we have all become in letting all sorts of trash into our lives. Our children have more temptations and more enticements to lust than we ever had. They indeed live in an R-rated world, and an R-rated world that they didn't create but they have to learn to live with somehow.

I frequently speak to high school church groups about the subject of values and value formation. After some discussion about what a value is and how one works in our lives to dictate the decisions we make on a day-by-day and moment-by-moment basis, I ask these adolescents to identify in their minds a couple of values they hold and operate from.

"Now," I ask with my friendliest face, "where do you get those values?"

"From our friends!" The shout rings out from around the group, and those who did not shout at least nod in agreement.

"But where else?" I ask, as if I am hoping this is not the only answer.

"From our parents!" This time the shout is not quite as enthusiastic and not quite as universal, but it is still convincing.

"But where else?" I ask with a hint of pleading in my voice, and then I wait and wait and wait and repeat. "But where else might you learn a value?"

One young man with glasses holds up his hand and says, "I think I learn some values from what I read—you know, newspapers and books and such."

I nod my approval in such a way as to make him feel good about himself, then I ask again. "And where else might you learn a value?"

The room grows silent, and as any teacher can tell you a room full of silent teenagers is a scary thing because you can never tell whether it is permanent or only temporary. But I am a good teacher. I can wait through that silence so I wait and wait, and plead (now I am pleading), "Where else might you learn a value?"

"That's about it," they say, assuring me that we have about reached closure on this topic.

"No," I am still pleading; "where else might you learn a value?"

Again they grow silent and ponder either the content of the question or my determination in continuing it. But I repeat the question and wait and stare as if my feelings will be hurt if someone doesn't give me the right answer, which, as any student will tell you, is the answer I want them to give.

Yet no one comes up with anything, so I decide to prime the pump. "What about teachers?" I ask, trying to hold back the tears in my eyes.

"Yes," some pleasant young person responds; "we did have a teacher who taught us something valuable once."

I don't want to scare anybody with this little account but since it does happen to me at least once a month as I speak to these people, I think there may be a message here. We need to pay attention to all our children's teachers—and that includes ourselves.

Why does our daughter insist on doing her homework in the noisy family room instead of the quiet of her own room?

If you ask her, she would probably give you a variety of reasons, but I am going to propose one that may generalize them all. Perhaps she studies in the family room because that is where the family is. Isn't that wonderful? You have such a nice family that the family gives your daughter a sense of security and a feeling of warmth. And if there is any time that we need security and warmth, it is when we are doing our homework.

I know you are not pleased with that answer, but cherish your daughter's choice. She obviously wants to feel like part of the family. She wants to be part of the family. Sure, her room with all that quiet is the logical choice, but the spirit of family is more important than logic ever was or could be.

Someday you will enjoy the memories.

CHAPTER THREE
Parent-Teacher Relationships

For most of us, there are five teaching agencies—the home or family, the school, the church, the TV set, and the peer group.

Statistics which tell us the relative impact are staggering. According to some recent research, the average American child between the ages of six and eighteen will spend about twice as many hours in front of the TV set as he will spend in classrooms. Obviously, television is a powerful teacher in any person's life; as a parent, I feel almost helpless in setting any guidelines about how that teacher is supposed to operate. The best I can do is to restrict my child's watching habits.

In a similar manner, I am rather afraid of that nebulous monster called the peer group. Since I am not sure what the peer group is and I don't understand how it works, I find the whole process a rather frightening mystery.

Fortunately, I can depend on the church; but my child is in church so little of his life that I realize that influence cannot be all that strong.

That leaves two teaching agencies over which I feel I must have some control if I am going to achieve any kind of peace while watching my children grow. I must assume that the lessons he learns at home are accurate and significant, and I must assume that something positive is happening in school.

Thus, the thesis of this chapter and, in fact, the thesis of this whole book is that those two teaching agencies, the home and the school, must talk to each other, must work together, and must coordinate efforts. As you can readily see, that thesis is based on several assumptions. Let's look at these.

1. Parents and schools can cooperate. I have already pointed out why they must cooperate but, to assure ourselves that this is not an

impossibility, I want to affirm the idea that they can cooperate.

2. Teachers represent the schools. In fact, as far as the student is concerned, the teacher is the school. The principal and the superintendent and the school board as well as other school officials may be quite important to the life of the school. But the truth is that most students don't even know those people. Thus, if a parent wishes to talk with and work with the school, he must direct most of his efforts toward establishing a working relationship with the classroom teacher.

3. Most teachers and most parents want the same thing. I do hear teachers say that parents don't care and I hear parents say that teachers don't care. And I suspect that some parents and some teachers really don't care. Mostly, I think those people are in the minority. I still must maintain that most teachers and most parents are really working for the same end—to help in some way to get this child through childhood and adolescence into some kind of thinking, mature, conscientious, and moral adult. If we begin with that assumption, it is much easier to unite our efforts and work together.

So there it is—the thesis and underlying assumptions of this chapter. Now let's look at some of the questions which parents just like you have asked.

Those teacher conferences are always scheduled right in the middle of my workday. How important is it that I go?

Isn't it the truth? You look forward to going to those things like you look forward to having a toothache; yet you have characters like me yelling, "The teacher conference is one of the most important activities of parenthood," until you are up to your elbows in guilt. Then they schedule the conference at a time when it is almost impossible for you to get there. At best, the world is unfair. At worst, there is a giant conspiracy among educators to make you look bad as a parent.

But I still stick to my guns. To me, the teacher conference is one of the most important activities of parenthood. I know at times those conferences seem like just so much routine. You really get the idea that the teacher is bored with it all. Or what is worse, the teacher uses the conference to vent hostility, either at you for having children in the first place or at least at the school and the teaching profession for causing her all her trouble and anxiety.

But in spite of it all, that conference is still important. If nothing more, it shows your child a bit of unity between you and the teacher, and that ought to worry him some—when he considers that the adult authorities in his life scheduled a regular time to plot against him. Your attending the conference also reminds the teacher that you do care; it shows her that your child has parents (and that often comes as something of a surprise, particularly to the younger, less experienced set). And who knows? You may even learn something that will be valuable to both you and the teacher in dealing with your child in the future.

No. I know your excuse is a good one, but I recommend that you go. Now, what I do suggest is that you call the school and tell them your problem. If the school administrators are on their toes, they have realized the inconvenience to you and other parents like you, so they have already built alternative times into their schedules to accommodate people like you. If the administration has not already considered the need for alternative times, tell them they should; then communicate directly with the teacher. Express your desire to meet; then ask for an alternative time. You may have to be creative—breakfast on a Saturday morning—Sunday evening after church at the teacher's house—but show a strong desire to meet the teacher. This is the most positive thing you can do to help your child have a successful school experience.

What can I expect to accomplish at a teacher conference?

That is a great question so you will have to pardon me if I get long and involved here. Too often, too many people look at those conferences as the "teacher's" conference, so both parents and teacher alike let the teacher organize the time, set the objectives to be accomplished, and control the conversation. In other words, parents learn what the teachers want them to learn. So after so much of this, parents begin to look at those conferences as a time to come in and listen to the teachers complain about how badly our children are performing. And this isn't very helpful to anybody.

Consequently, I am going to suggest something radical. Why don't you set some objectives you want to accomplish, go to the conferences with those objectives in mind, and assume enough control of the time to make sure you achieve your objectives. Let me begin by listing some things a good teacher should know which would help you better understand your own child.

1. General characteristics of the age-group—Since you have only

seen about three or four children the age of your child, and the average teacher has seen scores, hundreds, and maybe even thousands, the teacher ought to understand some general characteristics. In other words, the teacher ought to understand some general characteristics and be able to tell you something about the feelings, the emotions, the social patterns, the adjustments which your child is going through at this particular age.

2. How your child relates to peers—You may not agree with me at first, but hear me out. As a parent, I can never know for sure how my own child relates to his peers. I may even work at trying to know this. I may invite other children over just to observe my child work with friends; I may observe my child in church activities; I may stand at the window and watch him run through the neighborhood; but still I can never know for sure because those situations are more often artificial than real. When my child is in our yard playing with the neighborhood children, he is on his turf, so he will naturally be in charge, or at least an equal. This may not be true in other social settings, so you may need to rely on the observations of a good teacher.

3. How your child relates to other adults—Again, most situations for me to observe my child with other adults are artificial ones. To get a better understanding of how he relates to other adults, I need an outside opinion. A good teacher can be invaluable.

4. How your child compares to other children his age in academic skills—Since this is usually the obvious purpose of these meetings in the first place, this discussion should be a given.

Of course, this list is not complete, but it should be sufficient to stimulate your thinking. A good teacher should be able to give you some invaluable insights into your own child, but you may have to be bold enough to ask some questions on your own. In addition to learning some things yourself, here are a couple of goals for a teacher conference.

1. You can provide the teacher with information which may help the teacher better understand your child and be able to create a better learning climate. Don't exaggerate, don't brag, don't make excuses, and don't sound like a doting parent. But if you have observed something about your child through the years that the teacher may not be able to spot in a classroom of thirty other children, do your child a favor and share that information with the teacher.

2. You can develop a positive, encouraging relationship between you

and the teacher so that both of you can understand and appreciate that you are working on a cooperative project here—getting your child through childhood and adolescence and into adulthood as a thinking, responsible, moral human being.

QUESTIONS YOU CAN ASK AT A TEACHER
CONFERENCE
1. Who are my child's friends, and is she a leader or a follower with those friends?
2. Does my child do better work before lunch or after lunch? (This knowledge will help you plan meals and bedtimes.)
3. How do my child's skills compare to those of children her own age?
4. How does my child respond to authority?
5. What seems to be my child's strongest learning skill?
6. Have you seen a pattern of good days and bad days? (You may want to consider the family schedule.)
7. What is normal behavior for a child this age?
8. How can I help my child improve academically?
9. What adjustments can we expect next year?

I am a teacher. All my friends are teachers. I visit schools and talk to teachers every day. I think that I think like a teacher. One day a few years ago, my business took me to the school where my son was a high school senior. I walked into the building, happy, cheerful, and very much like a teacher. But my son's English teacher was standing at the door, almost as if she had been waiting for me. She pointed a straight finger, eyed me, with no indication of mercy, and said in an icy voice, "I need to see you before you leave this building." Then she turned and walked away.

I immediately ceased being a teacher and became a parent. For the next hour as I conducted my business, I went through all the emotions of a parent. In case you have never been through those, let me name them.

First, there was fear. "Oh, no! What has he done now? I will never be able to hold my head up in this building again. What has he done? I know it has to be terrible to get her so upset."

After a while, fear gave way to anger. "I'll kill him,'' I decided. "Grounding is not enough. Only death is suitable for this crime, whatever it may be."

Then somewhere in the midst of this emotional struggle, anger gave way to defensiveness. "Who does she think she is?" I asked myself. "She isn't perfect. After all, he is out for football. He has a part-time job. And she isn't perfect."

It was in this stage of defensiveness that I made my way back to her classroom, prepared to counter all of her accusations with some of my own. But to further add to my humiliation, she made me sit in a student seat.

But there I sat, contrite and humbled and a bit tired after spending one of the worst hours of my life. She hovered over me, and at that point, I remembered getting in trouble in the sixth grade for throwing rocks on the playground. Then she gave it to me with both barrels. "Cliff," she said, "my parents are sick. Could you pray for us?" I had just spent an hour of sheer agony for this. "I'll have to get back to you," I told her.

The next day I called and asked for Miss Brown. "She's in class," the secretary said. "Can I take a message?"

"Yes," I answered. "Tell her Larry Schimmels' father called." Now let her go through an hour of agony.

I have always made a point to know my child's teacher, but now that she is in high school and has six different teachers, what do I do?

You probably have two problems here. First, you may be getting all kinds of protests from your own daughter. At that age, they become rather convincing at saying something like, "I would just die if you go to school to meet my teachers," and you're obviously not the kind of parent to inflict mortal wounds, at least not premeditated ones.

Of course, the other problem is the one you address—breaking into that seemingly austere beehive of activity of high school instruction. At this point, even the scheduled conferences lose their appeal and charm, because too often those are with a guidance counselor who has been assigned by some random system to take a deep and abiding personal interest in all of your daughter's problems and plans though he has probably never even met your daughter personally. And conferences with those people are always fun. Since the counselor has been to some seminar on office etiquette, he comes out from behind the desk, takes a seat next to you, says something cheerful like, "Let's talk about Alyssa's life," then he proceeds to read about Alyssa from a file folder and recite the same list of instructions and proposals that he has already recited to the 300 sets of parents who preceded you.

I realize that I am coming down hard on these people when I really don't blame them, but frankly, that kind of conference simply can't provide the kind of help and insight into your daughter's school life that you need. And by the same logic, you can't really start any kind of a helpful relationship with a teacher.

So, yes, you will want to go to those conferences, but now you must go even further if you want to make a significant contribution to your daughter's education. And that next step may require some effort and creativity. Let me make some suggestions.

1. At this stage, the notes to the teacher are especially important. As quickly as you catch any teacher doing something right, send a note. For high school people, I recommend mailing it, because your daughter surely doesn't want to carry it herself. The note is not the same as a face-to-face friendly meeting, but it is at least identity. The teacher now knows that your daughter comes from a home and lives a life outside the classroom. This alone could give him some encouragement.

2. If you want to go a step further with showing appreciation, make a little gift—cookies, a cake, something from the garden (except zucchini). Call the school, find out when the teacher's free period is, make an appointment, go, deliver your gift, and leave. If you handle this right, you could look every one of those six teachers in the face within a thirty-minute period.

3. Invite the teachers, one at a time, out for breakfast or lunch. In a couple of weeks, you could have a solid conversation with all six.

4. Go to the school functions, such as ball games and open houses. You may be able to meet several at such places.

5. Now, I don't want to change my advice. Meet all six of the teachers every semester. You need to know what they look like when your daughter talks about them. They need to know what you look like when they call the roll every day and look in your daughter's face, and they need to know they have your support. But for the depth of relationship, you may find it easier to concentrate your major efforts with one teacher. Listen to your daughter. See who her favorite, or most important, teacher is, and work especially hard at establishing a hearty, cooperative relationship with that teacher. You may need someone with whom you can be honest before the year is out.

I witnessed a tragedy today. I saw two women meet. I know both of these people. I have been in church with them. I have prayed with them. I have listened to their stories about the children in their lives, listened as their eyes glistened and the excitement rose in their voices as they described some small incident in the annals of childhood, but to one involved, a significant moment worthy to become a memory.

But today there was no glistening, no excitement because they did not meet as two women only interested in children or even two women in prayer. They met as teacher and parent.

The air in the room was heavy, reeking of professionalism. The one woman, the one who today was the teacher, spoke of the third-grade boy's problems as if she were describing the behavior of a germ in a sterile laboratory seen through the distant haze of a microscope. She spoke of such things as time on task and word attack skills and comprehension and falling behind, but there was no excitement in her voice. She described her new program, something with an official government name, Chapter One or something like that, and she told how often the boy would be pulled out of his class, away from his lessons and friends, to get the individual attention which could help him. She talked, but her eyes didn't glisten.

The other woman, the mother, listened hard, but she didn't hear it all because the tears in the backs of her eyes flowed backward into her auditory canals, plugging up her ears.

There was talk, but no communication. There was talk, but no honesty. But how could there be? How could that teacher tell that mother how she had stayed awake the night before, and several nights before, worrying about this little boy, so charming, so helpful, and so behind in his reading? How could that teacher tell that mother how she had prayed for the boy that he wouldn't have to be pulled out of her class for the Chapter One program, but how, despite the risk, it still seemed like the best thing for him?

How could that mother tell that teacher how she had cried and prayed the night before? She didn't want her child to be different. She had never heard of the special program. She had no idea the advantages or disadvantages involved. She couldn't even think of the risk, much less weigh it. All she could hear through the teardrops in her ears were words like, "Trouble," "Behind," "Special program," "Different."

We can pass all the laws we want to and we can spend the big dollars on buildings and programs and textbooks but we really haven't done much for that third-grade boy until we find some way for those two dear women to talk to each other—honestly.

How can we tell our child's teacher that we appreciate what he is doing?

Don't worry about the method. Just tell him, quickly and often. Every teacher needs all the positive feedback he can get. Don't worry about embarrassing your child or the possibility that someone will think that you are trying to butter up the teacher. You have a right and maybe a duty to express your honest opinions.

Write a note. Send a gift. Call the teacher. Call the principal. Invite the teacher home for dinner. Do any or all of the above.

Of course, it never hurts to be specific either. If there is something you particularly like, mention that in your communication. This kind of feedback helps the teacher make decisions about which methods are working and which aren't.

My son's teacher said something on the spur of the moment which hurt his feelings. Now he doesn't want to work for her, and I'm afraid he is going to lose the whole year. What can be done?

These things do happen. It is unfortunate when they do, but with the right kind of effort and cooperation, you may be able to turn this into a learning situation instead of a loss.

First, you can begin with your own son. I don't blame him for feeling as he does. Learning is such a private and personal affair that the student is always vulnerable in the relationship with the teacher. In fact, for the student, that relationship with the teacher is one of the most vulnerable he will ever have. Any little thing the teacher says could be taken completely out of context, misinterpreted, or taken too seriously, and the student would be hurt for a long time, maybe even the rest of his life. Teachers need to understand this, but some don't.

Yet, though I understand how your son feels, he needs to deal with the idea of forgiveness. Maybe you could explain to him how often people say unfortunate things on the spur of the moment, things they wish they could reach out and grab back, but life doesn't work that way. The injured just has to grow up, forgive, and get on with the relationship. If you want, you can even borrow a definition I like:

"Forgiveness is starting the relationship anew as if there is no past." Perhaps your son can learn something about forgiveness from all this, and if he learns something about forgiveness now, he will be a happier person the rest of his life.

You may also want to try to help your son realize that his method of protest is hurting him more than it is the teacher. Frequently in our lives we choose a course of action which simply isn't wise. Your son's course isn't wise. (Now you want me to propose an alternative for him, and I can't think of anything except putting tacks in her chair. But I guess that is out of the question.)

Your next step is to go see the teacher. In this case, I would recommend that you not tell your son that you are going. You want to speak to the teacher by herself first. Go assuming that the teacher is an honorable person. If so, she will know that she made a mistake. Unfortunately, the finest and most caring teachers sometimes make cutting remarks in the heat of the day. The honorable ones know at that moment that they have made a mistake and they regret it. I know teachers who cry themselves to sleep over slips of the tongue. They would do anything to be able to undo what they have done.

If your son's teacher is this kind, just remind her of what she said and how it has affected your son. She might not have realized that her statement caused so much damage. In this case, give her an opportunity to apologize to your son, and pledge your support to help her help your son understand. (TO CORRECT A MYTH—Wise adults are not ashamed to apologize to children when they have been wrong.)

On the other hand, if she is the kind of teacher who meant to hurt your son and has no remorse for what she said, go see the principal with your concern. Maybe your son can get reassigned.

Can parents ever do anything to help teachers improve?

Of course they can—in fact, during this time when there is so much talk about moving education from mediocre to excellent, during this time when teachers are being blamed for almost every national problem from the success of Japanese-made automobiles to indiscretion among the Marines, during this time when teachers are subjected to all kinds of evaluations and tests, parents could be quite instrumental in helping specific teachers improve.

"How?" you ask. Simple! Take every opportunity you can to do what you can to build a teacher's confidence. Good teachers have a variety of characteristics which distinguish them from their colleagues who are not quite so good, but one of those characteristics is confidence. Good teachers have some kind of assurance that they know what they are doing and they can get the job done. A third-grade teacher going through a period of personal confidence is simply a better teacher than that same person going through a period of personal doubt and insecurity.

I have said it before, but I will say it again. If you want your child's teacher to improve as the year progresses, seize every opportunity to make that teacher confident. Send notes, make phone calls, brag to the principal, invite the teacher for lunch. Regardless of how you do it, seize every opportunity to make that teacher more confident.

My son's teacher doesn't seem to like him. What can I do?

This is a rather tough problem, actually. Most teachers will try to deny that we have favorites and not-so-favorites, but after all, we are human. There are just some students that teachers like better than others. Most teachers will also try to claim that though we may not like someone, we can at least be totally objective, but that's not true either. Objectivity is a rather rare condition in a classroom. If one student says something, the teacher laughs. If another student were to say the same thing, the teacher would punish him. When a teacher reads the paper of a student she likes, she tends to ignore little errors or glitches; but when that same teacher reads the paper of some student that she doesn't like, she sees everything.

Now that I've said all this, you ask again, "Is there any hope for my son?" Well, there may be. I do have a theory about student-teacher preferences, and it does work for me. I believe that one of the reasons I don't like someone is that I don't know that person well enough. So if I have a student that I am having trouble getting to like, I just spend as much time as I can with that student, getting to know him in a personal way, and I almost always grow to like him a little better because of it.

In your case, you might help the situation by finding some way to get your son and the teacher together in a close but friendly circumstance. What would you think of inviting the teacher over for dinner or at least after-school snacks some day? Who knows? It might help.

I suspect that some students know this strategy. I have seen junior high students deliberately get themselves assigned to after school detention so that they can spend more time with a teacher. Sometimes, if the student is particularly sharp, he could wind up as the teacher's pet if he spends enough time in detention.

Of course, if this doesn't work, your next course of action should be to try to turn this into a learning situation for your son. Now is a good time for you to teach him the valuable lesson of learning to get along with all kinds of people, of working through difficult situations, of working hard even though you don't feel like it. Actually, this could be a profitable year for your son if both of you are willing to work at the lesson to be learned.

Tom's mother knew that Tom didn't like his sixth-grade teacher, and knowing Tom, she also suspected that he was capable of showing his dislike in a variety of ways, all designed to frustrate the teacher. But she really didn't have any reason for undue concern until one day she got that dreaded letter in the mailbox. You know the one I'm talking about, that ominous letter that comes mailed to you—that just screams, TROUBLE—even before you open it. Well, Tom's mom quieted her trembling hands enough to get the letter open and read the bad news. Over the past three weeks, Tom had failed to hand in eleven homework assignments—eleven assignments in three weeks— enough to lower his quarter grade almost to the depth of oblivion. Tom's mom couldn't figure out what in the world had happened. The kid went to his room every night, locked himself in as if he were doing homework, and stayed locked in long enough to read *Moby Dick* and *War and Peace* both. What could he have been doing?

Suspecting something rather serious, she decided to do something she hadn't done in recent years. She decided to go to his room and snoop. She had to get to the bottom of this. She had to know what her son had been doing in his room all this time. The first place she looked was in his desk drawer, and there she found, in a neat stack, eleven fully completed, mostly correct, past-due homework assignments. Tom had been doing his homework, just as he had said. But he hadn't turned it in. Give Tom credit for being a pretty bright boy. He knew how to frustrate his teacher.

Sarah's mother met me in the foyer of the church one Sunday with a complaint about Sarah's third-grade teacher, Mrs. Rogers. The problem was homework, tons and tons of it every day and even more over the weekend. "Was this much homework necessary?" Sarah's mother asked. The little girl didn't have time to live a normal life, and it was impossible for her to do any of her family chores such as vacuuming and helping with the dinner dishes.

Another mother who was eavesdropping on our conversation said, "I'm surprised. My little girl was in Mrs. Rogers' class a couple of years ago and she had very little homework."

I recommended a trip to see Mrs. Rogers, and a couple of days later Sarah's mother called. Her visit with Mrs. Rogers had been revealing. Mrs. Rogers had, in fact, not been assigning all that homework. Sarah had been assigning it to herself because she saw homework as a way to get out of all the chores. That's a pretty sharp girl, wouldn't you say? And she is going to be all that sharper when she gets finished with all that self-assigned homework.

My son's teacher is terrible. How do I go about getting him fired?

I can't help you. I have no idea how to get a teacher fired, and I am not sure why you want to. I do recognize that you have a difficult situation here, and maybe I can offer some suggestions that can be of more immediate value. Obviously, your son is not getting a good education, and you definitely need to do something about that, but getting a teacher fired is a long, slow, and iffy process, and may not be the answer even if you happen to be successful. Let's see if we can't come up with a more orderly and more profitable way to deal with this problem. I offer the following steps in sequence. I suppose you may vary the sequence a bit, but for the most part, this seems to me to be a good order.

1. Gather evidence to your claim that the teacher is terrible. Just because your son says it's so doesn't necessarily make it so. I am not accusing your son of lying to you (though some do), but he just may have an unusual perspective. So your job is to gather evidence that is accurate and specific. You can include such things as: the teacher wastes classtime; the teacher creates so much tension in the room that the students can't learn; the teacher can't control the class; the teacher doesn't correct student work and hand it back. These are some traits of teachers who aren't getting the job done.

2. Find out if the teacher is successful with any of the students.

Sometimes a teacher is quite good with most of the class but isn't effective with one or two specific people. In this case, the teacher doesn't need to be fired. That would deprive all the other students of good teaching. But we do need to find some way to help that specific student who isn't getting anything from this specific teacher. There are a couple of possible solutions: the teacher and the student might be able to get together and see if they can work out their differences, or the student needs to be moved to another class or even to another school.

3. Visit the teacher. Explain your concerns honestly but nicely. Listen to the teacher explain his side of the situation. Listen well. You may detect personal problems or family problems which are frustrating this teacher at this particular time. Remember that teachers are human too, and none of us does our best work when we have personal problems or anxieties or family crises. If you detect something like this in your son's teacher, offer your prayers and concern and your understanding. Your teacher needs love at this point and not judgment.

4. If the teacher tries to apologize for something he has done or is doing, accept it. Teachers often make decisions and actions in the midst of the battle. Some of these decisions might have been wrong at the time, but a good teacher is the first to know it. If the teacher is already repentant, accept his apology.

5. If it is obvious that your son and the teacher have unresolvable differences, go see the principal and ask about the possibility of moving your son to another class.

6. Remember that the good news of the Gospel is that people can change. Go into every situation with a teacher expecting a change.

If I tell you something, will you not tell my boss? In my job, I have to work very closely with a wide range of high school teachers from about twenty different high schools. Often, I have to ask them favors, and sometimes I have to make demands. I make it a practice of attending as many ball games, plays, and concerts as I can. For one thing, I like ball games, plays, and concerts, but another reason that I make an effort to go is that I accomplish a major portion of my business with those teachers at those extracurricular activities.

Usually, the teachers themselves are more relaxed and more cheerful than during the school day so we can have a more relaxed and cheerful conversation. Also, they seem to be more appreciative of me because I have attended a school function.

Don't kid yourself. Student participants know who comes to the functions, and the teachers know too. Your attendance does make a difference.

Our daughter is going into fifth grade and we have some choice as to which teacher she will have. But how do we choose?

First, let me commend you for the question and let me commend your school for the responsibility it has placed on you. I am so happy to see parents have some choice about where and with whom their children are educated. Just the fact that you have the choice is going to make you a little wiser parent and that in itself will help your daughter get a better education.

But as with all blessings, there is always a responsibility. Now that you have something of a choice, you have the task of knowing something about your daughter, knowing something about schools, and knowing something about what you think an education is.

Let's look at each one of those separately. In order to make an intelligent decision, you first have to know something about your daughter and her educational needs. What kind of learner is she? What are her strengths and weaknesses? Does she function best with structure or with more freedom? What challenges her? How mature is she for her age and class? What kind of a teacher challenges her, one that is friendly and quick to praise or one that is a bit more reserved? All these factors are significant in your deciding which teacher would be best for her. To find the answers to these questions, you can trust your own judgment based on your past experiences with your daughter, particularly if you have helped her with homework and other academic matters. You can ask some of your daughter's former teachers. They should have some further information which will help you, but in addition, they will probably know the fifth-grade teachers so they can give some expert advice. Finally, you can ask your daughter. Don't be afraid of this. By this age, she should have some idea of what her likes and dislikes are, and she should be able to give you some good help. Don't be dismayed if it seems like she may be making a preference based on which class her friends will be in. It isn't altogether bad to be in class with your friends so that you look forward to going to school every day.

After you have thought seriously about what your daughter likes and needs from a teacher, your next step is to gather information about the teachers available. You can do this by consulting parents who have children in classes, or even talking to students who used to be in classes. If you do seek this kind of information, go into the interview prepared. Make a list of specific questions you want to ask so that you get pertinent information. Don't rely on such reports as, "She is very nice," or, "He really loves children." Those kinds of responses don't really tell you much.

Before you make your final decision, you need to go see the teachers yourself. If you are too embarrassed to ask specific questions, at least you can get some idea of the teacher's personal style. If you can, visit the teacher in the classroom. If you know how to look, you can gather much information with just a quick glance around the room. If the teacher's desk is in front and the students' desks are arranged in neat rows, this teacher probably enjoys structure and order. On the other hand, if the students' desks are in circles or in little pods scattered about, this teacher probably relies more heavily on student interaction in the learning process. If the bulletin boards have been designed and constructed by the teacher, this teacher probably places a high degree of emphasis on structured and factual learning. On the other hand, if the bulletin boards display students' work, this teacher probably places a high degree of emphasis on creativity and original thinking.

Now that you have gathered this information, you have one final task—to decide what an education is. What do you really want your daughter to get out of the fifth grade? What do you expect to happen to her during that year? What do you want her to be able to do at the end of fifth grade that she couldn't do when she started?

If you will take the time to back off and ask yourself those questions before you make the choice, you will be in a much better position to help and encourage your daughter so that any choice you make will be even better because you have gone through the process of making the choice.

I have some free time and enjoy children. Could there be some way I could help at my child's school?

I really hope so. Some schools, in fact, a lot of schools, have various kinds of volunteer programs which go by a variety of different names;

and I hope your school is one of those because some of those volunteer programs really contribute to the quality of education students get.

Some of the kinds of things which volunteers would do include: working with individual students, working with small groups, helping in the library, assisting teachers or administrators with necessary paperwork, supervising lunchrooms or supervising play activities. In other words, the list of tasks is broad enough to include anyone who is willing to spend an hour or two at school every week.

So regardless of your talent and your training, if you have some time to spend, hurry down to see the principal and volunteer. Even if your school doesn't yet have a program for volunteer service, just your eagerness and enthusiasm may encourage the principal to start one.

But I do give you one final warning. Volunteers do need three definite characteristics. Let me list them.

A. Dependability—Remember that the teachers expect you to be there on the day and the time you have agreed to. They have rearranged schedules and even made some promises to children. If the school is expecting you, you must be there. (Have I been emphatic enough with this?)

B. Dependability—Remember that the children are expecting you. A child functions best when his world is predictable and dependable. If he expects extra help with his math at 11 A.M. on Thursdays, it is important for the volunteer tutor to be there at 11 A.M. on Thursdays. Your failure to show just once could undo all the positive achievements of several weeks. (Have I been emphatic enough with this?)

C. Dependability—(Have I been emphatic enough with this?)

How can I meet my child's teacher?

Thanks for that question. Bless you. You have just asked my favorite question of all times. If you hadn't asked the question, I would have had to lecture to you, but now I can just answer the question.

The first rule for the parent of any school-age child: NEVER, NEVER, NEVER send a child off to school, any school, unless you know the teacher, if not in the beginning, at least within a few days. Is that emphatic enough? Do you think they heard me?

The reasons are obvious and many. First, you will know who your child is talking about when he talks about his "teacher." You will be able to connect a face to a statement. You won't dread teacher conferences quite so much because you won't be dealing with a perfect stranger. The teacher will have a face to connect with the term when your child talks about his mother or daddy. And perhaps most importantly, the teacher will know how you feel about issues, what your values are, what is important to you. Thus, the teacher just may do a better job of helping you in this awesome task of educating your child.

Now to answer your question. Meet your child's teacher the same way you would meet anybody else. You can try the direct approach or you can resort to more devious methods. Either way, the teacher will know what you are trying to do so you will achieve your purpose. My advice is for you to go see the teacher sometime during the first few days of school. In fact, I think this is so important that I recommend that fathers and mothers go together even if one or both have to take off work that day just for that purpose. (I told you this is important.) It is so simple. Go to the school at the end of the day and tell the principal or whoever is in charge that you want to pick your child up from the classroom. Then go to the classroom. Take a look at the setting where your child is meeting the world of academics. Then, with your child looking on, introduce yourself to the teacher. You don't need to make a big issue, but just meet the teacher. Remember that at this point during the day, the teacher is probably a little haggard and tired, so don't make a nuisance of yourself. Just say hello and go away.

Now, the hard part is over. You have had the initial meeting. Now keep the relationship alive with all sorts of communication. Write positive notes commending the teacher. Call and ask her out to lunch. With teaching salaries what they are, most teachers will do almost anything for a free meal.

Take every advantage to meet the teacher and view the school. Go to teacher conferences. Attend open houses. Volunteer to be a school aide in some capacity. In other words, give your child the best opportunity for good teaching you can. Meet his teacher.

She was a relatively young teacher, a veteran of three or four years. She had been in school enough to know what to expect but still not enough to be comfortable with everything that happened during the year. Sometime during the doldrums of February, she came into the lounge, snapped the top off a big strong caffeine drink, took a couple of swigs, got a contemplative look on her face, and announced to no one in particular, "You know, I just do a better job of teaching them when I know who their parents are."

Why do I dread those teacher conferences so much?

Let's count the reasons. If one or all of them apply, we have at least started down the road to a little better attitude and maybe even a more pleasant experience.

1. They come at inconvenient times, are a nuisance in your schedule, and the teacher acts bored when you do finally get there.

2. The teacher always makes you sit in a student desk, and that in itself is one of the most humbling experiences now available to us in the Western world. When your children are small, teachers make you sit in those little, tiny chairs where you have your knees right up under your chin. But when your children get older, it is even worse, because then you have to sit at one of those contraptions you have to put on. Then you sit all through the conference with at least one piece of your mind constantly thinking, "Am I going to be able to get out of this when the conference is over or do I just wear it home?"

3. You haven't established a comfortable relationship with the teacher and you are afraid the conference is going to be confrontational rather than positive and helpful.

4. Going into a school building, and particularly a classroom, reminds you of all the bad experiences you had when you were a student, and you yourself feel like a little child again being called in to be reprimanded.

5. You are afraid that you are going to have to hear something that you don't want to hear. You do know those two things almost every parent hates to hear. (a) "I'm sorry, but your child is not normal." (This one is first on the list. Most of us live in mortal fear of having to come face-to-face with the fact that somehow our child is not typical, average, normal.) (b) "I'm sorry, but your child is merely normal." (This is a close second to the first. All of us want our children to be simply normal and exceptional, both at the same time.)

I came home rather late one evening to find a terse note on the refrigerator door. "Call your friend Helen. URGENT." Since my friend Helen is an intelligent, calm lady who, as a professor in a teaching hospital encounters life and death emergencies every day, I realized that if she said it was urgent, then the matter was urgent. So I called her at 11 P.M.—long distance at 11 P.M.—my nickel.

Well, it was urgent. That day, her daughter in second grade came home with a note stating that she had been assigned to a newly formed Chapter One reading program. Since the Chapter One program is discussed in another place in this book, I will only say here that it is a federally funded program to help give some special help to students who may be having a problem with the reading group in the normal classroom. Usually, the instructors are specially trained and class size is small enough to permit some one-to-one teaching.

But how does a parent, an intelligent, calm, caring parent like Helen, feel when her daughter is assigned to a special class. Well, that night I found out—on my nickel, I found out. For the first thirty minutes, I got Helen's best "I'm a horrible mother" routine. "What have we done wrong? We read to her. We took her to the library. We bought books. We read in front of her. We listened to her read. Oh, where have I failed?"

After we got through the guilt trip, we took thirty minutes to talk about how terrible teachers, and particularly testers, are. "Well, what do they know?" she asked me several times. "I don't think their tests are any good. We listen to her read. I know she can read. They just ought to listen to her. Maybe she chokes up on tests. Some people do that you know. Those people don't know what they are doing. They just put her in that special class without giving her the tests to find out."

Finally, after we had thoroughly discussed that train of thought—all on my nickel—I asked the telling question. "But how does your daughter feel about that special class?"

"Oh," Helen said, still in her critical voice, "she loves it. She talked about it all night long. She likes the teacher and she really enjoyed the special attention."

"So why was that mother so upset?" you ask. Because someone had just told her that her daughter was not normal. Do you know what else? That would hurt me too.

Why does the school only call me when my son is in trouble?

I have heard the coyote howl as I tried to sleep out in the open. I have heard the rattlesnake shake his tail not two feet from my boot. I have heard the tornado rumble its freight train of destruction outside as my family huddled inside. But despite all of that, the most dreaded sound of all, the most fear-producing sound of all is the sound of that false, pleasant voice announcing, "Good morning, Mr. Schimmels. This is the school calling." When you hear that sound, you know you are in for a bad time.

Why does the school only call us when our child is in trouble? Well, I suppose they are too busy calling the parents of the students in trouble to call the parents of the students who aren't. They don't call us for the same reason that the newsmen never announce at 6 P.M. all the people in the city who did not kill somebody during the day.

I suppose that must be the reason, but I am not happy with it, and I don't think you should be either. Call the school. Go up and see your child's teacher (or if your child has many teachers, see your child's favorite teacher) and just inform that teacher that you are a sensible, caring parent who will cooperate in every way. Now, in simple return, announce that you would like to hear some good news once in a while. After all, you have a lot of emotions at risk in rearing that son. The school should respect you for that. And I think they will.

Leroy was a good friend and a good custodian. He kept the building clean; he managed the help; he repaired things quickly; he responded to teachers' complaints; but most importantly, he listened to students.

Of course, not all of the students talked to him, but some did. These were the people who were seeking an open ear anywhere they could find it; and they found Leroy, cleaning bathrooms or carrying out the trash or sweeping the halls after the lunch traffic had messed things up. Some students found his ear so valuable that they would memorize his schedule and ask for a bathroom pass just to catch a few minutes with Leroy.

On graduation nights, Leroy was always the most popular person in the building. Students would come and shake hands or hug him, and some came back for years just to say hello to the man who listened.

Leroy made my work as principal easier. Students gave him information that it would have taken me weeks to find out. He was the first one to know that some students were planning to run away from home; and with his tip, we were able to help parents and children reach an agreement. He knew who was smoking in the bathroom and wanted to get caught. He knew who was having trouble at home. He knew which student was having trouble in what class with which part of the class.

Whether they are teachers or counselors or principals or custodians, thank God for the Leroys sweeping the halls of our schools and the lives of our students.

Our daughter's teacher came to see us the other night. He really didn't act as if he had any reason except to visit. Is this typical?

No, it isn't typical now, but it may become more so. Educators have begun to believe in the value of establishing a positive relationship between the home and school. One way to do this is for the teacher to stop by in every home for a brief, informal visit.

The educators would hope that three things came from the visit. (1) Your daughter felt good about herself and her school because her teacher took the time to come to her house. (2) You got acquainted with the teacher a bit better so you won't be so reluctant to visit the school for parent conferences or open house and so you won't be afraid to go see the teacher should you detect some problem in your daughter's activities at school. It is always good to have a friend up there. (3) The teacher is now in a better position to help your daughter because he has met her parents and been in her home. When he teaches her, he may use something he saw or experienced as an illustration or model. Also, now that the teacher knows you, he will more readily call you if he should detect some problem your daughter is having.

Frankly, I like this practice. I can't think of anything to help the education of children more than to have parents and teachers meet in an informal setting once in a while just to get acquainted. Perhaps you might have just been a part of one of the most promising experiments that has come through in several years.

CHAPTER FOUR
School through the Teacher's Eyes

If all I knew about the profession of teaching is what I have read in the newspapers during the past five years, I would never be a teacher. Would you? The profession as a whole has been probed and gouged and analyzed and kicked and abused rather thoroughly during the past few years.

In this chapter, we take a look at the teaching profession—at what teachers do and what they work with and against. Some of the questions have been asked by teachers themselves. Others have been asked by parents about teachers.

It is not my intent to say in this chapter, "Pity the poor teacher." Since I have never really been anything but a teacher, I am not really sure whether teachers are more overworked or more stressed out or more unappreciated or more underpaid than any other profession. I suspect that we all could use some sympathy. But since teachers and parents must work so closely together and since, in fact, teachers are special helpers to parents, we do need to understand as much as we can about each other and our roles. Teachers need to understand how parents feel, but at the same time, parents really need to identify as closely as they can with teacher emotions, stresses, anxieties, joys, and triumphs. This kind of understanding will help our children learn.

This is the purpose of this chapter. I have intentionally included questions from teachers as well as questions about teachers to try to encourage us, as much as possible, to put ourselves in the role of a teacher and try to see life through the teacher's eyes, or in the words of the old adage, "to walk a mile in their moccasins."

My daughter's teacher is teaching for her first year. Should I take my child out of her class?

I don't see any reason for that. In fact, your daughter may even profit from the situation. I realize the value of experience, and teaching is no exception. Good teachers learn something every year, learn something every day in fact. There is only one way to get that experience; yet it is so valuable. As a rule, the experienced teachers, at least those bright enough to learn as they go along, get the job done more efficiently and probably make fewer mistakes than the first-year teacher.

But on the other hand, there is something to be said for enthusiasm too. Since this is the first class that young teacher has ever taught, she isn't making any comparisons. For right now, these students are her life. She is giving them all her attention. They are getting the best she has to offer, and students profit from that enthusiasm. They sense it and they enjoy it. For this young teacher, this class will probably always be her very favorite group of students. On that point, teaching is a little bit like falling in love. The first will always be the most special.

Though a young teacher may not know all the old tricks of the trade, she does know the most current, so what she lacks in experience she will make up for with current research. She may even be able to help some of the old veterans learn something.

Also, put some of your confidence in the children. They are rather resilient. They know it's her first year; but if she is trying and they sense that she likes them, they will learn for her if for no other reason than to make her look good.

No, don't panic. Give the young teacher the benefit of your belief, and when you watch her doing something right, send her a note immediately. She really needs your support while she is learning to become experienced.

I am a first-year teacher and I feel constant stress. I am not sure I can live with this. What can I do?

Become a second-year teacher and the quicker the better. I am really more serious than I may sound. Making the transition from college to working life is tough on anybody, and beginning a new career is always filled with stress and anxiety. No one can escape it. As a beginning teacher, you are probably suffering a double dose. Let me see if I can help you identify some of the sources of your stress.

First, there is always more work to do than you can finish. Every night you go to bed without being thoroughly prepared for the next day. You have papers in your briefcase which should have been read two weeks ago, but with staff meetings to attend and lessons to prepare and parents to call, you may never get to those papers.

Next, the day itself wears you out. You don't have one moment to relax. Your mind is always on fast forward. Not only must you be alert to the present, but you also have to be thinking into the future. By the time the day is over, you just want to scream twice, go home, and sleep for six weeks.

You are also bothered by the amount of supervision you are or are not getting. When you do stay up until midnight preparing something special, no one seems to notice or appreciate it. When does the reward come? When does someone stop you and say, "Nice job"? You don't have a single adult friend so you find yourself sharing your opinions of world events with seven-year-olds.

Besides all that, you feel that you are just dragging the students through life by their heels, and they are coming, kicking and protesting all the way. You have such neat goals for them, so you plan such important lessons to help them meet the goals you have set for them. And they don't even care. In fact, they fight you and your dreams for them all the way.

What is a body to do? I don't have all the answers, but let me make a couple of observations which may help you. I'll make a list of these so they might be easier to pin up on your bathroom mirror should you need to have them in front of you at the beginning of each day.

1. Know who the boss is. Right now you are trying to please a principal, twenty-three sets of parents, and an unknown force called the public. That is simply too many bosses. You can't even serve two masters. Focus on one boss, and in this case, make it your students. Plan your time, focus your attention, and evaluate yourself by how well you have taught the students. If you can go home each day and say, "I taught them well today," then that is good enough.

2. Always remember that one bad day doesn't ruin your career. I have been at this business for thirty years. Some days I succeed and some days I fail. Big deal! Twenty years later the students won't remember either kind of day. By then I will be only some indistinguishable glob in their memories. Don't worry about a bad day. Laugh about it and go on.

3. Make the students responsible for some of the learning. As a beginning teacher you are probably trying to do all the work—preparing the lessons, reading the papers, doing the research, and teaching every moment. That may not all be necessary. Make the students do the research. Have them prepare and teach some of the lessons. Let them proofread and check some of the papers. The more you activate them, the less work for you and the more they learn.

4. Learn to take small hints as great rewards. If some student asks, "Already?" when the bell rings, take that as your having just won the Nobel teaching prize. That is the best you are ever going to get. Or if you listen carefully, you may catch some student saying under his breath, "This is fun." Wow. What an award.

I am a second-year teacher and I am lonely. I enjoy my friends, and I enjoy my prayer companions from church, but I really need to have some contact with people who are both teachers and Christians. How can I get in touch with other Christian teachers?

First, let me commend you for the question. At this stage of your career, it is important for you to share your ideas, experiences, and anxieties with people who have similar ideas, experiences, and anxieties. As a teacher, you have some unusual problems and perspectives, but as a Christian who happens to be teaching, you have a particularly unusual perspective to your work and life in general. I do hope you can find some Christian teachers with whom you can share.

Let me suggest activities which I would definitely recommend. First, research your own church and churches in your area. If there are no Christian teachers in your own local church, call some other pastors in the community and ask them if they have Christian teachers in their churches. Don't be bashful here. If you are lonely for fellowship, you can assume that there are other teachers somewhere in your area who are suffering from the same kind of loneliness. They will want to hear from you. In fact, you may even find that there are some Christian teachers very close by.

The second activity I would suggest is that you join a national organization of Christian teachers called the Christian Educators Association International. This is an excellent group based in Pasadena, California and headed by Forrest and Judy Turpen. Forrest is himself a former elementary principal so he knows the problems and joys of teaching.

The group publishes an excellent little paper called "The Vision" which any teacher could profit from, and they also conduct one of my favorite educational conferences every summer. Write to the Turpens at Christian Educators Association Int., P.O. Box 50025, Pasadena, California 91105. You will find them to be warm, friendly people who are interested in you as a person and a teacher.

Our son's fifth-grade teacher spends so much time on math and reading that she cheats the students out of science and social science. How damaging is this going to be?

This is now and has been for a long time one of the major discussion areas among teachers, educational theorists, and parents. There just isn't enough time in a school day, or any other day for that matter, to get everything covered that everybody wants covered. Everybody wants all students to learn math and science. Some have a strong belief in spending most of the other time on writing; others would demand more science; others would like more foreign language. Personally, I could get excited about more of such things as art and shop. Obviously, the school curriculum isn't going to please everybody. In fact, the teacher can't get in everything she wants to get in. Someone has to make a choice.

In your son's case, the teacher has chosen to spend more time and be more thorough in math and reading. Some people would applaud her decision. In fact, this is what some people would call a back-to-the-basics curriculum. The argument is that if the students are grounded and skilled in the basics of reading and computation, they can master all those other subjects when the time comes. After all, no one will ever master history until he has learned to read. It is as basic as that.

On the other hand, others argue that the students could develop their reading and math skills while studying social science and science. Students at this age need to be exposed to a wide variety of studies to fit their wide variety of interests.

Since I am obviously not going to settle this argument with my own personal opinion, I would rather examine this situation from another perspective. The factor of the teacher's choice of curriculum may not be as significant as some other factors. Are the students really making significant progress in developing their math and reading skills? Are they enjoying the class and school in general? Do they see the value of what they are doing? These are the questions which will determine whether this fifth grade is a profitable experience for your son and his colleagues.

Mr. K. is not only the biggest assistant principal at the high school where he works but he also has the biggest voice, so he gets some of the toughest assignments—such as supervising the lunchroom. Even on good days, watching a herd of high school students eat is not one of the most pleasant tasks on earth. They tend to be rather sloppy and sometimes they can be quite creative in using various kinds and colors of food as an art medium to decorate the lunchroom.

As a supervisor of such activity, Mr. K. was always on his gruffest alert. One day, he watched a particular young man miss his mouth and pour a whole carton of milk down his chin, down his shirt, on to the table and on to the floor. Rather than shouting, Mr. K. waited for the young man's reaction. The young man promptly got up from the table, walked over to a towel rack, dampened some towels and came back and cleaned the mess he had made.

Somewhere between surprise and appreciation, Mr. K. went over to the young man and asked his name since it was a student the assistant principal had not really seen before. With that, Mr. K. thought that if it became convenient, he might call the student's parents later in the day and just relay the incident.

But during the afternoon, one emergency after another erupted until Mr. K. had spent all his energy and time, and he didn't make the call. In fact, he hadn't really thought about it until he was walking out the door to leave for the day. As he remembered the incident, he grumbled under his breath a bit for the liability of having a conscience, but he went back to his office and placed a call to some unknown parent of some unknown kid whose only claim to fame was cleaning up a milk mess without being told.

When the mother answered the phone, Mr. K. introduced himself, heard the usual gulp that always comes at such times, and then relayed to the mother the incident of the noon hour. After a few moments of silence, Mr. K. heard sobbing. When the mother gained control, she thanked him profusely for his call and told her story. Three years before, the father had left her to rear the son, and she was scared of the whole endeavor. To hear such a piece of information was one of the significant moments of her life.

Do parents care about their children? I think so, even though it may be hard to see at times.

Not long ago, I had dinner with a very well-known and highly respected school consultant. This man goes across the nation doing research and conducting seminars training superintendents and principals in how to do their work more effectively. He is very good at what he does, and his training sessions surely have some influence and bearing on the quality of education for children in this country.

This consultant's sixteen-year-old son joined us for dinner that evening, so the conversation was more family oriented than professional. During the course of the evening, I asked the son, a high school junior, who his principal was.

"Mr. Epcott," the son replied immediately.

"What does he look like?" I asked, half expecting the answer I received.

"I have no idea," the son replied.

"What do you mean, you have no idea?" the father/school-consultant roared. "You have to know what your principal looks like."

"Nope," the son stuck to his story. "I have never seen the guy."

I shall not soon forget the look in that father's face. It was somewhere between serious pain and a sense of total failure. Here was a man giving all his energy to making education better for children by training school managers. Yet, his own son had never seen the local high school principal.

But that is the way it works in a student's life. That young man was a fairly good student, but his contact with the school was through the classroom teachers and not through the school officers.

That may be good news for some. When I was a high school principal years ago, I used to stay awake at night and wonder what the students were thinking about me. Now I discover that they weren't thinking about me at all.

Our daughter tells us that one of her teachers picks on Christian kids, so she is afraid to let him find out that she is a Christian. What can we do to help her?

Pick out some friendly and casual reason to go see the teacher. If necessary, invent some little reason, but get in to see the teacher. After you have covered your casual conversation, say to him in almost Columbo afterthought style, "We hear people say that you pick on

Christian kids," and smile as you say it.

Hear from him what he thinks of that charge. There could be at least two possibilities. Sometimes students perceive that a teacher picks on one special group, such as Christian kids. And the other possibility is that he really does pick on Christian kids.

I find that teachers who do pick on Christian kids do it for a variety of reasons. Some teachers are just looking for a good discussion (translate "argument"). Since Christians have been trained to be expressive about their faith and since Christians know what they stand for, they are always good participants in a classroom discussion. Since the non-Christian students in the class usually don't know what they believe and can't express it, the teacher is almost always caught with holding up the dissenting side. In this case, the Christian students would perceive that the teacher is picking on them.

Some teachers use little personal bits and pieces as a way of getting to know their students. We would hope that the most personal piece of data about a Christian student is his faith, so the teacher might allude to the faith just as an attempt to get to know the student a little better. With another student, he might allude to sports or a car or a girlfriend. For the teacher, the reference to Christianity might be an innocent attempt to help the student feel comfortable, while the student sees it as a put-down.

On the other hand, some teachers may have a strong dislike for Christians which just comes out. If this is indeed the case, I would recommend that you go see the principal. By law, a teacher cannot discriminate against (pick on, embarrass) any student for religious reasons. The teacher needs to be reminded of his obligation to fairness.

In the meantime, I recommend prayer. I am rather enthusiastic about what the power of God can do in a human life. Wouldn't it be great to see God's redemptive power working in this teacher?

I have been teaching for eighteen years, and I just can't keep up with all the changes in curriculum methods and procedures. How can I cope?

This is one of the major plights affecting all conscientious teachers. Somehow, we have the idea that we have been successful with our students in the past; we are comfortable with what we are doing; the students seem to like being in class. Then one day someone comes along and tells us that we have been doing it all wrong. Small wonder teachers are often discouraged.

What makes it worse is that we make some adjustments to accommodate the new ideas, and next year those same experts tell us that the old way was probably better. Now our heads are really spinning. Since this is the only profession I have ever been in, I don't know whether it is more faddish than others or not, but it does have to qualify for one of the top five. I don't know why this is true for sure. Of course, we are always learning something about human nature which may help us a bit, but basically our subjects (children in schools) and our purposes haven't changed all that much in the last couple thousand years.

And this observation becomes my recommendation for you to begin to develop some skills for coping with all the new theories and systems which come along. Establish early on some firm convictions about young people and how they learn; and regardless of what comes along, stay with those convictions. You may be able to adapt and modify as new theories tend to make sense to you, but stay close to those convictions. Those will serve as an anchor in the turbulent sea of constant changes, some good and some not as valuable.

Also, focus on what you have done. You have been in the profession long enough to know what your former students are doing. Every time you get a chance, meet one of them. Talk with them. You will find that your own former students may be the most refreshing and reassuring therapy you can find. As you interact with them, you may even begin to see some of what you taught them begin to come out in their conversation, in their habits, in their lives. Then you can reassure yourself of what you already know about this profession as the new ideas come and go.

My third suggestion is for you to remember that some of what goes by the name of educational research is really rather poor research. The proponents of change are fond of saying, "Well, the research shows us. . . ." Sometimes that may be a conclusive statement, but sometimes it may represent a quotation from a piece of work completed by some assistant professor who wants to be an associate professor and has to do so much "research" to get there.

Finally, don't lose sight of the wisdom of common sense. If what you do makes sense to you and you can see the comprehension in the eyes of your students, you are probably doing it about right already. Don't feel compelled to change just for the sake of changing.

As a teacher, I don't want to be antisocial, but I just can't go along with everything the NEA stands for. Should I join?

That may be one of the toughest questions a Christian teacher faces these days. Should you or should you not join and take an active role in the union and union process?

Obviously, I am not going to answer it for you. It is too complex and too personal. But let me offer a few points on both sides of the issue for you to consider as you make up your mind.

First, you must realize that many of your colleagues in the profession are committed to the NEA—the state branches and the local organizations. Teacher unity has produced some positive contributions to the education of children in this country. If through their show of unity, the teachers in the organization win some gains for the schools or for the teaching profession, you will get to share in the gains whether you belong or not. But if you don't join, your colleagues will probably always consider you something of a freeloader.

Some Christian teachers have answered your dilemma by not only joining the organization but becoming part of the leadership of both local and state organizations because they want their influence and suggestions to make a difference.

On the other hand, sometimes organizations of people do not collectively represent all the feelings of all the members of that organization. Such is the case with you and the NEA. I know how you feel because I am presently a member of a large religious denomination which as a body does not always represent my convictions.

Your question is how to register your protest. Not joining and not participating is one possibility. Joining and taking an active role in trying to set policy you can agree with is another. It is a tough question.

As a Christian teaching in the public schools, will I be censored often?

What a complex question! First, we don't even know for sure what is legal and not legal for a teacher to do. When young Christian teachers ask me what they can and cannot do in the classroom, I, in mock seriousness, tell them to divide a sheet of paper into two columns. Label the left column, "Things that are legal to do" and label the right column, "Things that are illegal to do" then write anything in the left column. But if someone tells you that is illegal and takes you to court, and the court rules it is illegal, mark that piece of business out of the left column and move it over to the right.

Do you get the idea that all this is indefinite? It would be so much easier if everything were cut and dried, but it isn't. So the key for any teacher and, particularly for the Christian teacher, is to use good judgment and sensitivity. If you are genuinely and sincerely interested in students and their learning and if your chief form of witness is your commitment to their learning, there is a good chance that you will never be even questioned about your Christian witness.

I know dozens of Christian teachers who witness every day by being fair and effective teachers who are considered by parents, administrators, and fellow teachers to be the best around.

As a classroom teacher, my biggest problem is that parents don't care. What can I do?

I don't know where you teach, and I don't know the circumstances, but I can understand why you feel as you do. When we hear stories of how parents work while children go home to empty houses, of how you make assignments and children don't have the encouragement to work on them, of how schools hold open houses and other parent meetings for no more than 20 percent of the parents, we do get the idea that parents don't care.

But a couple of years ago I quit believing that. I don't have any new evidence to prove you wrong, but I just decided that believing that parents don't care was not a very profitable attitude. Rather, I have decided that they do care but don't know how to demonstrate it.

Since you ask for a suggestion, that is the one I am going to give you. Try operating with that for a couple of years. Just decide that every student you have comes from a home where parents care and care deeply, parents who are starved for helpful information about what their child is doing and how they can help their child reach his maximum potential. Then supply the parents with that information.

You can begin simply enough. Take ten minutes each day to write a few friendly notes home to parents telling them something specific and nice their child did that day. It may be as simple as a child doing particularly well on an assignment or helping you erase the chalkboard. It doesn't really matter. Sometimes the little things are as encouraging as the big ones. In those notes take a positive attitude. Say nice things about the students and encourage the parents. This is not the place to be negative or corrective. Now don't expect immediate results. You may have to work at this for several weeks, maybe months, before you begin to get a response; but I believe with all my heart that most parents will begin to respond. You will not only start getting some encouragement back, but you will also begin to get some support for assignments and school projects.

If you want to take a really bold stand, go visit the home. Again, this doesn't have to be elaborate, but just drop in for a few minutes to visit the home of every student in your class. You don't have to spend more than ten minutes so you could get to several during one evening. Again, just be friendly and encouraging. I am going to venture the strong assumption here that if you take your time to visit a child's home, that parent will take his time to come see you the next time you offer an invitation.

Well, you asked for my opinion and you got it. This business of educating children is too complex and too involved and too risky for one agency to do it alone. If you are going to do a good job of teaching their children, you must have the parents' support. You already know that. But to get that support which is necessary for you to be effective, you may have to make the first gesture of goodwill. Try it. Let me know how accurate my guesses are.

Our state has begun giving all teachers a standardized competency test. Will that improve the quality of teaching?

Probably not. How's that for a rather cynical answer? But I believe that these tests are probably overrated in their ability to predict or especially to improve teachers.

Let's consider for a moment the four characteristics of good teachers which we have talked about earlier. (1) Good teachers care about students. (2) Good teachers are confident of their abilities. (3) Good teachers know the subject matter. (4) Good teachers know something about the methods of teaching.

At the very best, these standardized tests which are becoming popular may tell us a little bit about how much a teacher knows about the subject matter and maybe a bit about what the teacher knows about teaching methods. In no way can those tests tell us which teachers really care about students enough to stay up late at night and prepare lessons, will check material quickly and will hand it back, will be flexible enough to allow individual differences in the classroom or in short, who will stand the rigorous life of teaching.

What the test will do is tell us which teachers cheated their way through college without learning very much and now doesn't know enough to get the job done. So far, that represents no more than 2 percent of the teaching candidates who are taking the tests. In other words, more than 98 percent of the people who take the tests pass and go on to careers in teaching. So the tests are actually achieving a couple of positive results. They are telling us that most of the people who go into the profession are fairly competent and they are helping us identify those few at the bottom who shouldn't have been in the profession in the first place. The tests weren't designed to help individual teachers get better, so that won't happen. But the tests are still probably making a contribution to education overall. The question is whether the gain is worth the anxiety those tests create in the really good teachers in the profession.

What is a certified teacher?

Usually, state departments of education control teacher certification, and what is required differs from state to state. However, there are some general principles which tend to hold true in most places, so we can understand something of the process by looking at those. Basically, the requirements are in terms of college courses the people have completed. In other words, the state department of education requires that the teacher candidates have completed so many courses in the subject matter they wish to teach and so many courses in educational theories and practice. Though these vary, almost all require some kind of internship which requires the student to spend some time in a school observing and working with an experienced teacher. This is called student teaching, practice teaching, or even teaching internship.

After a person has completed all these course requirements, he applies to the state and receives a teaching certificate. At regular intervals, he has to renew the certificate, so he has to go through the process again. States do vary on the length of those intervals. Some states require that the certified teacher continue taking courses or attending workshops or indicate some assurance that the teacher hasn't died on the vine but is continuing to stay current both in subject matter and teaching methods.

Since states do vary so much in what courses they require for teacher certification, I would suggest that you write a letter to your state department of education and ask.

Teachers complain all the time about being overworked, but I can't see it. They only work about six hours a day, and they have those long vacations. Could I be missing something?

Yes, I suspect you are. I learned a long time ago not to bad mouth the difficulty of someone else's profession until you have tried it yourself for a while, so I am not going to give a long sermon about how tough teaching really is as compared to other professions. But let me assure you that it is a tough way to make a buck. Since I cover much of this in discussing the issue of burnout, let me make one more suggestion. Ask your favorite Sunday School teacher how long he prepares in order to teach one hour every Sunday morning. Now, take the figure the Sunday School teacher offers, multiply that times 30 (the number of hours the average teacher teaches per week) and see the preparation time. Next, ask any baby-sitter how much more difficult it becomes the more children one has to sit with. Now, multiply those problems by 30 (the average number of students in many classrooms) and you will begin to get some idea of what the average teacher goes through.

Of course, as in any other profession, the good ones go through more work and more stress than the weak ones do, but it is still a lot of work.

What are the advantages and disadvantages of teacher tenure to my child's education?

Thanks for the question. It is exactly the kind of question which should be asked of every district, school, state, or federal educational policy. How is this going to help my child get a better education? If we could keep all questions of school policy at this level, perhaps our policies would make more sense.

Now, let me answer your question briefly and directly.

ADVANTAGES OF TEACHING TENURE

1. Your child will be assured of having at least some experienced teachers during his school career. We could probably debate the value of experience. As the old joke goes, "Some teachers teach forty years and some teachers teach one year forty times." Nevertheless, good

teachers do learn from experience. They learn how to be more effective with students and they learn how to handle the pressures of the job. Schools need a good blend of seasoned veterans and young teachers.

Since teacher salaries are based on the number of years a person has taught, those veterans do get more money and are more expensive on the school budget. If we did not have a system of protected tenure, an insensitive district could dismiss those veterans and keep their classrooms stuffed with less-expensive beginners. This wouldn't help your child much.

2. Teachers are not necessarily intimidated by personality conflicts with administrators. Teachers need to go into their classrooms with some confidence. Sometimes administrators, such as principals or department chairs can be unrealistic in some of their demands. Tenured teachers don't have to cave in to those unrealistic demands. Thus, tenure gives them the assurance to teach with confidence. This should help your child get a better education.

DISADVANTAGE OF TEACHER TENURE

Incompetent teachers can hide behind it. That's the rub, the whole issue. Now, your task as one interested in the quality of education is to decide how to have a system that protects the capable, effective veteran but doesn't protect the incompetent. If it's any consolation, you have several different people helping you with this—state legislators, school administrators, and even teacher groups themselves are directing a great deal of time and energy to this question of what to do to evaluate teachers and what to do with those who simply are not effective in the classroom.

How does a school choose its teachers?

Though this procedure varies somewhat from school to school, state to state, and situation to situation, let's discuss some of the more common aspects which are usually true.

Usually, teaching candidates—certified teachers—begin the process by making an inquiry to a local school district about the possibility of vacancies. At that time the candidates send a resumé and perhaps fill out a district-prepared application. This material is put on file, to be held until a vacancy does occur.

When a vacancy does occur, the district then advertises for prospective candidates in such places as college placement offices and educational newsletters. Hopefully, more candidates apply for the posted vacancy. How many people apply for a specific position depends on what the vacancy is in and where the school is. For some positions, the district may have hundreds of applications to screen. For others, they may not have much of a choice at all.

Then some official at a school reviews the applications. Who that official is depends on the school. In some places it is the department chair or team leader. It may be a building principal; or in some districts, that process is handled at the superintendent's office.

The designated school official analyzes the paperwork considering such things as past employment records, experience, recommendations, grades, interests, and makes a decision to invite a few of the candidates (usually between three and five) in for personal interviews. Who and how many people are involved in the interviewing process again depends on the school. In some situations, the candidates are interviewed at the district office. In others, they are interviewed by department chairs, principals, and sometimes even by other teachers in the department or school building. In some cases, the prospective candidate may even have an opportunity to teach a class while he is at the school. Thus the students can be involved in the process in a small way. Usually, the candidate who is most impressive during the interviewing process is offered a contract.

In the last thirty years, I have applied for dozens of teaching positions in several different states. During that time, I have grown to have a good deal of respect for the process. I think that, in general, schools are doing a good job of screening, processing, and interviewing candidates. Obviously, the system is not foolproof, but the people involved in the process are aware of its significance and they are constantly working to make themselves as proficient as they can be in finding the right person for the position.

Of course, there are always a variety of factors which affect the final decision. Schools do have to consider such things as: the amount of experience the candidate has (since teacher salaries are based on years of experience, a teacher with fifteen or twenty years of experience is going to cost more than a rookie; the district has to determine whether it can afford the added expense); what the district needs in addition to a classroom teacher (if a school needs a coach or a yearbook sponsor, the candidate with expertise in that area will get some preference); the balance of staff (some schools may give some preference to one sex or one ethnic group or one age-group in an attempt to keep the staff balanced. For legal reasons, the school can't advertise those preferences, but they can still be present).

How does a teacher union work?

At the national level, there are two major organizations representing teachers, the National Education Association (NEA) and the American Federation of Teachers (AFT). Both organizations have representative state and local organizations.

In a specific local school district, teachers choose to join one or the other of these two organizations. If one of the organizations has more than 50 percent of the teachers in that district in its membership, then that organization represents the teachers in the bargaining process. In other words, a certain school district may have 80 percent of its teachers in the NEA and the state and local organizations of the NEA. Perhaps some of the teachers in that district may even belong to the AFT and some may not belong to any union at all. But since the majority are in the NEA, the NEA organization will represent the group in all matters pertaining to the group as a whole.

Teacher unions provide a variety of services for the members. Both organizations demonstrate a great deal of interest in improving the quality of instruction so they provide inservice training, prepare instruction manuals, and offer general educational assistance. Both organizations provide other kinds of help such as insurance, legal counseling, investment counseling, and purchasing tips.

Both organizations exercise a great deal of government lobbying efforts both at the state and national levels.

And finally, both organizations provide bargaining strength at the district level. Since this is the activity that affects us the most, this is the one we know most about. Again, the district bargains with the organization that represents most of the teachers.

What districts and unions bargain about varies from place to place and year to year—class size, assignment of teachers, teacher retirement programs—but the big issue is still salary. Sometimes the district officials and the union officials reach a quick and amiable agreement and everyone is happy. Sometimes they don't reach any agreement at all and the teachers go on strike.

Since the local teachers have the state and national organizations behind them, they do have a good deal of expertise and strength in the bargaining process, and they have made an impact on how educational decisions are made at the local level.

Please keep in mind that this whole explanation is brief and somewhat generalized. For example, the NEA still sometimes protests that it is not a union but a professional teachers' organization that has been around for more than 100 years.

Another point that we need to keep in mind is that for the most part, school administrators do not belong to the union, so union activities represent teacher interests only.

What exactly is teacher tenure?

This is a rather difficult question to nail down because the concept changes from state to state and even in places from school to school; but in general, teacher tenure is a status or degree of recognition passed on to teachers who have proved that they are capable of teaching. Actually, you can look at it as a kind of promotion in one way.

When a teacher begins teaching in a specific school district, that teacher is under probation for a given period of time—usually two or three years. During that probationary period, the teacher is usually evaluated frequently, maybe required to attend inservice training sessions, and is reviewed and analyzed before a new contract is issued. During this probationary period, the teacher can be more easily dismissed. For example, the school could conceivably get rid of a non-tenured teacher just on the grounds that they think they can find a better teacher somewhere for that position. Also, if the district loses students and consequently loses teaching positions, the nontenured teachers are the first to go. (This process, commonly called RIF [reduction in force] is not, however, limited just to nontenured teachers. In some areas where the number of students has decreased significantly, veteran tenured teachers have been riffed.)

After the teacher has spent the required probationary period and is granted a new contract for the following year that new contract automatically grants tenure. In other words, the teacher has proved himself worthy to teach in that district. Usually, there are now fewer evaluations and if the teacher is to be dismissed, the school district will have to show specific reasons for the dismissal. In other words, the district can't fire the teacher simply because they think they can find a better one somewhere. The teacher has to goof up in some way to be dismissed.

There is a common misconception that tenured teachers can't be dismissed. That isn't true. They can be dismissed, but the district has to prove the reasons for dismissal.

Is the teaching profession attracting the best possible people? If not, why not?

I am sure we have all seen some statistics recently which indicate that the college students with the best grades are not enrolled in education courses and are not preparing to teach, thus leaving the profession to those people whose grades are not as good.

From these statistics we are supposed to make two assumptions. First, we are supposed to assume that the students with the better grades are more desirable prospects for employment so they are holding out for professions that pay better than teaching does. The second assumption that follows logically is that the teaching profession is only getting the leftovers.

Though there may be some truth in both these assumptions, I think we need to be cautious about accepting either at face value. First, I am not convinced that the students with the best college grades are naturally the best employment prospects. I would like to think that there are other factors to be considered—such things as well-roundedness, courtesy, and even independence. I am not sure I know where these things are going to show up on a college transcript, but without these qualities a person simply isn't going to be a very effective teacher in American schools. I am not opposed to good grades, but I am just not convinced that grades tell the whole story. Thus, I am not willing to accept those grade statistics as a reason to panic about the quality of people entering the profession.

I suppose I ought to use this opportunity to make an argument that teachers, particularly beginning teachers, ought to be paid better; and I do believe that. But I have been working with college students in teacher preparation, and I am frequently overwhelmed with the commitment some of these young people have to becoming teachers. This past semester one of our students quit a $30,000-a-year engineering job to study to become a teacher. Another took a full year off from his business as a cement contractor to study to become a teacher. Another finished college with $11,000 in debts and immediately signed a contract to be a third-grade teacher for $17,000 a year. Do these people qualify as the best possible people available? I think so.

What is accomplished by teacher strikes?

I don't know. It's too early to tell. To answer the question we would have to ask, "How do teacher strikes improve the quality of education in this country?" And in my opinion, we haven't been in this negotiation process long enough to determine that.

As most of us remember, teacher strikes were pretty much unknown until about the mid 1960s. In fact, I remember in 1964 when our local representative to the state branch of the NEA came back and reported that he sensed unrest at the meeting. I was a little shocked at the time, but I convinced myself that regardless of what happened, teachers would never strike. I have never been much of a prophet.

At this point, I still am not sure what has been accomplished by striking. Some of the issues which became topics of negotiations and subjects of strikes are noble enough—class size, free time for teachers, yes, and even salaries. If teachers feel good about themselves, if they feel that the public appreciates them, and if they are paid enough to provide for their families, they will be better teachers, and students will get a better education. If these are the true issues, then teachers do have the best interest of the students in mind.

On the other hand, I would like to think that the school boards and administrators—those people whom the teachers actually strike against—have the best interest of the students in mind too.

I suppose, then, that the conflict is a difference of opinion about priorities and methods to accomplish an aim.

Now, the question is, "How do we settle that difference of opinion?" If a school board believes that it is in the best interest of the students to spend surplus funds on a new water main and the teachers believe it is in the best interest of the students to spend those funds on hiring aides to help in the classroom, there has to be some process of settling that difference of opinion. I really don't like teacher strikes, but at the same time, I don't see much of an alternative.

If our teachers go on strike, it will be right in the beginning of the school year. What should we parents be doing with our children at this time?

Since that is the most common time for teacher strikes, your question is appropriate for most parents facing a strike situation. I also guess from the way you ask the question that the schools will remain closed during the length of the strike.

The easiest answer would be for me to tell you that the strike is just an extension of summer vacation. But that isn't true. Too many things happen at this time. The friends in other districts all go to school. You have already bought the new jeans and lunch boxes. The air has taken on a fall feeling. The swimming pool has closed. There is just something inside your child that tells him it is time to start school, and here he sits at home all day, idled by something totally outside his control.

I do recommend that you get your children involved in some kind of activity different from what they have been doing all summer. They need a new schedule and a new routine. You may not be able to duplicate the feeling of school, but you can at least offer an alternative.

This would be a good time for your church to use its facilities and personnel to conduct a camp or a Christian education week or a daily Bible study—something that would bring children together in something of a formal setting. In fact, I would recommend that the church keep an emergency plan for such a project just in the event that the strike could occur. This is not only an ideal time for the church to provide a service for its members, but it would be a good outreach ministry as well. The program would not have to be as formal as school and it would not have to be as long as the school day, but it needs to provide a formal structure for students to gather and socialize.

If your church is not in a position to offer that kind of service, perhaps some mother or group of mothers in your neighborhood could offer something like that for all the children of the neighborhood. Again, this doesn't have to be school, nor as structured as school, but it needs to be a place where children are organized and supervised in play and learning activities.

If you are further worried about your children losing ground during this time, you can supplement their education during the evening or other blocks of free time. Don't worry about teaching what is in their books or curriculum, but offer them review and drill. The first few weeks of a school year are spent on review anyway.

Of course, the major problem here is for the poor young person who is involved in an extracurricular activity which has to be suspended. Athletes do miss part of their seasons; band members are hampered in practice time, etc.; and there isn't much concerned parents can do about that.

Our teachers went on strike. The schools opened with substitutes. We didn't know whether to send our children or not. What do you think?

Wow, what a tough question for parents everywhere! There just isn't an easy answer, but let's see if we can look at the question in a logical manner so that you are at least in a position to make a decision.

First, there is probably only one basic reliable fact here, and that is an unfortunate one. Unless the strike is a long one—at least a month or more—it will probably not hurt your children educationally to hold them out of classes. Though the substitutes may be quite capable teachers who spend the time covering lots of material, the striking teachers are going to cover the same stuff when they get back. Very few veteran teachers would ever trust someone else to begin their classes and take students through worthwhile material.

Of course, if the strike goes on past a month, then the striking teachers will have to rely somewhat on what has been accomplished during the strike. So your first problem is to try to discern how long the strike is likely to last.

The next factor to consider is what your children are going to get other than educational material. Starting school is an exciting ritual, at least for most people. It is the time to get acquainted with your classmates, check on what everyone did in the summer, meet new friends, find out where you belong on the playground and in the lunch room, learn how to open your locker. Usually, students learn all these rituals the first three or four days in the school year. To miss that would definitely set a student back, not just in mastering the procedure, but in adjusting to the socialization process.

The third factor to consider is what you think of strikes. If you are in favor of the teachers, then I think you should have a conference with your children, tell them your position, and honor your convictions. (Again, you always run the risk that the strike is going to last awhile.) On the other hand, if you don't favor the teacher's point, you will want your children to attend school.

I hear about a teacher shortage. Is there such a thing?

The answer to that question depends on what year you ask and what year I answer. I have been in education since 1959 and there is always a teacher shortage or glut; but regardless of which it is, we are never more than four years away from correcting it. In fact, these things almost always correct themselves. Let me illustrate.

I am writing this answer in the latter part of 1988, and the picture is bleak. Some experts predict that at least 50 percent of all teachers will retire in the next six years. The average age of a high school science teacher is well over fifty. Even the best schools can't find really good applicants in such fields as foreign language, math, science, and even recently P.E. One college dean reported last month that just to fill the retirements alone his state needs 19 percent of all college students preparing to teach. They have only 4 percent.

Yes, these figures do indicate a shortage. But on the other hand, correction has already started. I teach education courses at a small college. In the last ten years my methods course has averaged fifteen students per semester. This year the average is twenty-nine. We haven't put out any great cries for the need for teachers, but somehow the word filters down, and young people begin to prepare themselves for the profession. Thus, a teacher shortage is not really an issue which merits any great panic because it can correct itself so quickly.

What we do need to worry about at this time, however, is to keep the standards high as we fill the retirements and other vacancies. Even during the era when there was supposed to have been a glut of teachers, most administrators complained of how few really fine applicants were available for any given position. The concern is always quality and not quantity.

Why are teachers always changing the way they do things?

If I knew the answer to that, I would be a genius. I suppose all the world is changing rapidly and everyone must change, but it does seem that education is especially subject to the blowing winds of change.

Maybe it's because those of us who help children grow (or at least stand around and watch while they grow) are an insecure bunch. We want to do the best we can for children. We want to help them. We are frightened of making mistakes. We are never quite satisfied with the job we are doing. So in our efforts to do our jobs better, we grab at the next new thing as if it is the key to making us brilliant.

Maybe teachers change so often because there is so much research out in the field. Every year thousands of people conduct thousands of research projects about children, learning, schools, and all sorts of things. Usually, these research projects conclude that this new way is better than the old way. Someone then reads the research project, thinks of some way to implement it into the classroom, and presto, the teachers and the students are faced with yet another change.

Yet, all this might be profitable. In spite of the seemingly endless stream of changes, schools look pretty much like they did when Nero was a boy (except we have since added girls). The process is about the same. Every once in a while, we get a new idea which is going to make a drastic difference, and for a year or two every one is championing the new idea. But soon it fades away like a good old soldier. Yet, there is always some residue. Every idea that comes and goes leaves a little ash in the process and school is never quite the same, different ever so minutely, yet different. And that is how we make progress.

It was the saddest day of my life, just behind the day my father died. I was chairman of an English department of a small high school during the mid-1960s. Though I had no definite proof, I had a gut sense that we were going a good job. Students wrote well—all of them, in fact. They seemed to enjoy coming to class. The teachers were, for the most part, content.

Then we went through North Central Evaluation. When the visiting experts came, I suggested that we go into the classrooms. They asked to sit in the office and look at the paperwork. When they asked how we taught English literature, I reported that we approached the topic chronologically, starting with Beowulf and ending with John Masefield. They glanced at each other, said, "Tsk, tsk, haven't you heard of thematic units?"

When they asked how we taught grammar, I reported that a noun is a noun and a verb is a verb and we expected our students to know the difference. They glanced at each other and said, "Tsk, tsk, haven't you ever heard of transformational grammar?"

When the report came back, the words were strong and damaging. "The chairman of the English department," they had written, "is twenty years behind the times and is retarding the education of the students. We recommend that he be retrained or dismissed."

As I said, it was the second saddest day of my life. I did go back to school to study what they had recommended, but I changed little.

Now, twenty years later, almost all schools teach English literature chronologically from Beowulf to John Masefield and teach nouns and verbs. Good news. I wasn't twenty years behind the times after all. I was twenty years ahead.

When I was in school we used something called the "magic circle." Is this still in practice?

Oh, yes, the old magic circle. I remember it now. Popular in the late '60s and early '70s when it was important that people found themselves, it was something of an elementary student's version of an encounter group.

At regularly scheduled times or sometimes when the need arose, the teacher would assemble the class or some part of the class in a circle, sit down in the circle with the students, and have everyone listen as each explained his or her day including the events and the feelings and reactions to those events. The rules were that everyone should listen and no one should evaluate or judge, or criticize, or interrupt. The implication was that everyone was entitled to his feelings and should not be ashamed of them if they were honest and genuine.

The magic circle was never really a common practice in schools and really didn't last too long even with the teachers who believed in it. There were too many problems. Some students simply are reluctant to share their feelings and felt that the conversation in the circle was an encroachment on their right to privacy. Sometimes overeager teachers didn't have enough control of the class to manage the discipline problems which arose. Some people were opposed because the circle took away class time that could be used for something else. And the big problem was that there was no overarching sense of right and wrong being taught.

So the magic circle is now just a part of a past, given way to other educational theories. But as I watch the steady stream of new and great innovations and ideas come and go in schools and teaching, I always wonder if we perhaps learned something from each one. For all of its flaws, the magic circle might have taught us something valuable about children. Children, at least some children, really do need to have some outlet for expressing themselves. They need some adult who will not lecture so much but will listen more. They need to have a sense that someone hears them cry out. The student who has at least one teacher who will listen is indeed fortunate.

Just the idea of a circle itself has some value. Based on my attempts to play student in recent years, if I had to be a student all the time, I would really like to sit in a circle and look at faces rather than backs of heads.

Those two goals and some others are now being met in a new educational practice called the Great Books seminar sessions. In these, students sit in a circle and discuss their reactions to a classic book they have read. I saw one of these discussions the other day in a high school. The next day, I saw a similar one in a second grade. Both were profitable.

I hear about teacher burnout. What is it and how big of a problem is it?

As best as I can tell, teacher burnout is a rather common human malady. People get tired of what they are doing. Since I have never been anything other than a teacher, I don't really know whether it is more of a problem in education than in other fields, but there are some unusual characteristics of teaching which do tend to wear out the nerves in a hurry. Again, I don't want to sound as if I am saying, "Pity the poor teacher. We have it worse than anyone else." I am sure that people in all professions and careers have problems too. But I do think that it might help a bit if parents and students did understand some of the factors which cause teachers to grow tired, disillusioned, frustrated, and sometimes depressed. Let me list some of those.

1. There aren't many promotions in teaching. I have four brothers-in-law who are quite successful businessmen. About every time we assemble at some family reunion, we spend most of the time talking about everyone's new promotion—from stock boy to salesman to sales director to regional manager to vice president to chairman of the board. On the other hand, I started as a classroom teacher thirty years ago and I am still a classroom teacher. I am not sure I mind all that much until my mother-in-law asks in all innocence, "When are you going to get a promotion?" That's the question which causes me to suffer teacher burnout. Actually, the only promotion would be for me to move into administration (become a principal) and that isn't a promotion at all but

a change in careers. Being a principal is an altogether different profession from being a teacher. In recent years some school districts, and even some states, have instituted some kind of career ladder or merit recognition program for teachers. I don't know all of what these programs are intended to accomplish, but at least maybe they will provide some semblance of a promotion.

2. Teaching has few inherent finishing points. When you write a book, you will, if you persist, someday finish and ship it off to the publisher—finished forever. If you plow fields for a living, or make sales, or build automobiles, you have the same kind of point to look forward to. But these points are rare in teaching. A teacher never really sees a point where he can say that he is finished. About the best thing the teacher has to look forward to is the end of the year. Teachers aren't really finished then; they just quit because they ran out of time. This feeling of always working on projects in progress has a way of becoming a source of frustration after a while.

3. A good teacher is never caught up. Every day, good teachers go to bed with the feeling of not being finished for the day. There is always something more the person could have done to be a better teacher the next day—call a parent, read some papers, find some more background material, worry, think. Consequently, a good teacher is never totally satisfied with the job he or she has done. There is always the feeling that it all could have been better if there had been more time.

4. Teachers must associate with people during some of the most difficult and trying times in their lives. Learning is not an easy task. It too is demanding and often frustrating; and frequently, learners rebel against the pressures. Now the teacher not only has to deal with the material to be learned, but has to deal with the rebellious people they are trying to teach. If you wonder about teacher burnout, try inviting thirty third-graders to your house and play lots of games with definite winners and losers. It is interesting to note that there is a much higher rate of attrition in certain teaching assignments such as special education than in other teaching areas.

5 Teachers must get positive reinforcement vicariously. If a salesman does a good job and wins a big contract, he sees the immediate result and he is emotionally reinforced. He feels good about his achievement. On the other hand, if a teacher does a good job, the student wins the award and the teacher gets the reinforcement secondhand.

Again, let me emphasize that I am not trying to make a case for poor, downtrodden teachers. I am simply listing some characteristics of the profession that exhaust teachers and often cut short their careers. If you sense that this is a problem—that good teachers are burning out and quitting the profession too soon—you perhaps can help by offering those people as much encouragement as you can.

CHAPTER FIVE

Teaching Methods and Instructional Practices

T here are those who tell us that how we teach a lesson is more important than the lesson itself. Though this could be an over-statement, there is enough truth in it to remind us that teaching methodology is an important field, not something to be taken lightly and never something to assume "naturally." All teachers study teaching methods, and good teachers make deliberate, sound decisions about how to approach a concept, how to approach a class, and how to approach a single student. In fact, that may be one of the most significant differences between good and mediocre teachers. Good teachers are those who have thought seriously about what they are doing and how best to do it.

The problem with studying teaching methods is that the field is in a constant state of revision and updating. About every other day, someone comes up with a new curriculum or a new technique or a new piece of equipment which is going to revolutionize the way we teach reading or writing or arithmetic. The underlying assumption is that we have been wrong for at least 2,000 years, but someone has finally discovered how to do it. From now on, every student will be infinitely wiser and better educated and a better reader and a better mathematician and a better writer.

Just to show how rapidly these new ideas come into existence, much of this chapter is spent answering questions about methods and techniques of the last five years, and this only scratches the surface. Everywhere I go, someone asks me about some new technique that the local school has just implemented. However, if you take a closer look at some of these new methods, you may get the strange feeling that we have been here before. Sometimes the new technique is little more than taking an old idea and putting a new name on it. So studying methods is about as much language study as anything else.

For all of our changes and innovations, schools still look a whole lot like they did when Nero was a boy just beginning to learn to fiddle.

Let's take a test. Question 1. Quickly, remember the name of your favorite teacher—elementary, junior high, or high school. It doesn't matter. Just remember the one teacher who qualifies as your favorite.

Wasn't that easy? Now for Question 2. Name three specific things your favorite teacher taught you. Now, how are you doing on our test? I'm going to guess that you found that second question a little tougher and perhaps even impossible.

We remember the teacher. We remember the person. But we don't always remember the specific lessons. That's the wonderful ministry of teaching. The best lessons in life are those people who teach them.

I went out to watch a "Writing as Process" seventh-grade class in action. To understand better what was going on, I consulted an expert, a student sitting next to me. "What is this 'Writing as Process' all about?" I asked.

"Well," he told me as he was thinking through his answer, "it seems to mean that no matter how well you write it the first time, you are going to have to revise it anyway, so you may as well goof off on the first draft."

There you have, straight from the expert, the newest theory of teaching composition.

I think it was Winston Churchill who once made this commentary about education: "It doesn't matter what you teach a boy, so long as he hates it."

Unfortunately, there is still some residue of that kind of thinking around. To be good, schools must be hard and tough and miserable, if necessary. To become educated, we have to suffer and buckle down and pay the price.

Now that we have extended the school experience down to include five-year-olds and four-year-olds and even three-year-olds, that kind of thinking frightens me more than it used to.

Forget the buckling down and paying the price. Surround me with children and teenagers and adults who inquire and probe for the sheer excitement of inquiring and probing, who study because they want to know, and who love learning and love life because to love life we have to love to learn.

Our first-grade son's teacher just sent home a discipline sheet which states the class rules and the consequences of each violation. What is this about?

Scary, isn't it? This is one of the new theories of classroom control called assertive discipline. In practice, it is really not as frightening as it may sound.

The theory is that class time is too valuable to waste on classroom management procedures. No student should have the power to disrupt the educational process. Thus, the teacher, or sometimes the teacher and the students working together, come up with the class rules. To keep matters simple, there should never be more than five rules. These rules and consequences are either posted in the room or distributed to students and sometimes parents. The teacher then decides on the consequences of violation. If a student violates a rule, implementation is automatic. For example, if a student talks without permission, the teacher simply goes to the board and writes the student's name there. The teacher doesn't break stride and doesn't interrupt the lesson. She just goes to the board and writes the student's name there. Since the class had already gone through the rules and consequences together, that student knows that he has been warned. If he violates a rule again that day, the teacher will slip to the board and put a check by the name. Usually, that means an automatic punishment of some kind, such as a detention. If the student violates a rule again before the day is over, the punishment increases.

According to the theory, the system is quite fair because the student always knows where he stands and is never facing surprises or inconsistencies.

I have seen this system work wonders in some classrooms, particularly among younger teachers. I have heard parents praise the system for what it has done for a child's classroom. But the success depends on the teacher's commitment to such a system and on the teacher's ability to use it.

What is a curriculum guide?

A curriculum guide is a paper or a manual prepared by a committee from a local school district or even from an individual school which describes what concepts and ideas and information is to be covered in a specific subject matter at a given grade level. For example, a curriculum guide for science would detail the information, concepts, and experiments which students will cover in seventh-grade science, eighth-grade science, ninth-grade science, biology, chemistry, physics, etc. This information is to help teachers design lessons and units so that there is some uniformity and to avoid gaps and overlaps in the presentations.

In some places, the curriculum guide is a rather simple statement which merely provides the teacher with the information and gives the teacher some clues about what to do. In other places, the curriculum guide can be quite elaborate and prescriptive—detailing and prescribing what a teacher will teach almost day by day. Some curriculum guides even contain the tests which all teachers will use; thus holding the individual teacher responsible for even the basic facts taught at a given time.

The purpose behind these elaborate guides is to ensure some kind of uniformity. It is important for teachers, parents, and administrators to know exactly what students studied in ninth-grade science, regardless of who the teacher was.

Our daughter has a teacher who tells us that he believes in using "individualistic instruction." What does that mean?

Though the term sounds rather self-explanatory, it really isn't because there are different types and methods of individualized instruction.

The concept is based on a simple but profound human observation. No two students are alike. They don't have the same abilities, the same past experiences, and consequently, the same needs. Thus, we need to develop a program which not only uses the individual resources but meets the individual needs. How we achieve that is subject to argument.

Some teachers would argue that they meet individualized needs in the day-to-day operation of the class. For example, when the teacher assigns students the task of writing what they did on their summer vacations, they will write from their own experiences and according to their own abilities; so this would be an individualized assignment.

Others would argue that this isn't good enough. Since students work at different rates of speed, it would be foolish to expect all students to write the same number of pages in the same amount of time. For them, individualized instruction would be having each student working on his own packet of materials and his own projects at a rate of speed with which he is comfortable. The faster workers might complete two or three assignments in a day while the slower one is completing only one.

Others would protest that this isn't good enough. Since students not only work at different rates of speed—but they also have different needs and interests, individualized instruction would provide each student with his own specific assignment, either one that he chose or was assigned to him by the teacher or even in some cases a computer.

Thus, in a class of thirty, every student would be working on something different.

In teaching, it is popular, in fact almost necessary, to say that you are doing something to recognize and provide for individual differences. But that is a bit like saying that you go to church to worship. The operational definition could be about anything.

Our child's report card has an item called "Time on Task." What is that?

Time on Task is just a fancy phrase for how much time the student spends studying rather than staring out the window. In recent years, this has become one of the significant factors in evaluating teachers, evaluating instructional methods, and evaluating students.

The inference is that good teachers know how to keep students on task, listening or reading or doing the assigned work. Motivated students stay on task. They are able to concentrate longer and spend less time in transition between learning activities.

Obviously, the more time a student spends on task, the more he should learn. At least, that is what the theory suggests.

I would guess that the reason this is on the report card is that it will help you understand what kind of study habits your child has. This information may even help you understand some of the reasons for what is on the rest of the report card. It now becomes your task to decide how important this is to you and your child. For example, a dreamer isn't going to get too high of a mark on time on task, but some dreamers can be quite effective as students. It is your task to decide the worth of the information, just as it is your task to decide the worth of any information on a report card.

Our daughter is learning something called D'Neillian penmanship. What is this?

D'Neillian is a form of printing which looks more like cursive writing than the old block printing styles did. The theory behind using this as children are first learning to hold the pencils and make letters is that it will be easier for these children to move into cursive writing when that time comes.

The teaching of penmanship is actually a fascinating topic. I teach college seniors who have spent sixteen years in schools. As many as one fourth of them print rather than write on such things as essay tests where their work needs to be neat and legible. I am not sure I understand the reason for this, but I find the fact interesting.

My daughter is in a second-grade class of twenty-seven students. Isn't that too large?

Now you've done it. You have absolutely asked the wrong question. There is no way that I can be objective or even calm about this. You are going to get my opinion, and in as strong a language as I can state it.

Yes. That is too large. (I told you that I was going to be blunt.) In fact, that is probably about twice too large. There is no way in the world that any teacher can effectively teach twenty-seven second-graders.

With that paragraph I have probably angered every school superintendent and school board member and most principals in the nation. But I can't understand why this issue is so controversial. It seems to me that it is so evident.

Based on everything I have seen and experienced in schools over the past forty years, I have formulated a plan for educational reform. Listen to this. I think it has some merit. Let's pass a national law that no primary class (grades kindergarten through three) should ever have more then fifteen students and no other class should ever have more than twenty students. (That applause you hear is coming from teachers—not from school boards or even taxpayers.)

Though I do see the impracticality of my suggestion, I am serious about the implication. Let's try this plan for ten years and see what happens to all the educational problems—classroom management, dropouts, test scores, and even drug use. We've tried several other expensive projects. Let's try this for a while to see what happens.

The opponents to my proposal argue that I don't have the research to support my contention, and they are right. Research really doesn't give us much clue to appropriate and effective class size. But I argue from the standpoint of common sense. After all, we still make a lot of decisions about educational procedures and policies without having research to back our experiments. I just don't understand why we demand so much research for class size.

If I had one piece of advice to offer parents who wish to campaign for more effective schools for their children, I would recommend that all of us unite behind the efforts to control class size.

A few years ago when my daughter was in the seventh grade, I developed a strong urge to play a little catch out in the backyard with the softball. Together, we went to the store, bought two new gloves and a good ball, and built a mutual excitement about the father-daughter relationship which was about to begin.

But when we got to the backyard the excitement died quickly. That seventh-grade girl didn't know how to catch a ball; she didn't know how to throw a ball; she didn't even know how to place her feet. In short, it was a dismal mess. I decided at that point to be angry. After all, she had been in organized physical education classes every day for the past seven years. What in the world do they do in those classes? Why can't my daughter play catch?

By this time, I had built up enough anger that it made me courageous, or stupid (with me the two look about the same), and I decided to go down to the school and register my complaint.

When I got there, I went straight to the gym, ready to lash out at the first person I saw. But at the gym I didn't see a person—instead I saw seventy-two persons—seventy-two junior high persons playing volleyball, screaming and running and shouting—seventy-two players and one P.E. teacher with the soar of a hawk and the eyes of an eagle, keeping some order to this whole mess.

I didn't say a word. I just went home, took my daughter out to the backyard, gave her a little individual attention at catching and throwing, and within three days developed a sore hand from catching the balls she threw so hard.

There are two lessons here. The first one is a big one. All the instruction in the world falls flat without a little bit of individual practice. Quite often the little bit of individual practice can work wonders. The second lesson is that the teacher may not have the time to get around to everybody.

A few years ago I spent some time in a high school French class. The teacher was one of the most effective I have ever seen. She had planned how to use every minute of class time. Nothing was wasted. The students were always busy and the activities were designed to accomplish the goals of the lesson. Besides that, the teacher had the energy to make it all work. She moved about the class. She stayed on top of things. She knew each student and she monitored each one's learning progress.

I have never seen a teacher work harder or achieve better results. Those students were certainly fortunate to have this lady for their French teacher.

There was only one problem. She had thirty-five students in the class. Because of that high number, the students couldn't speak French as often or as much as she would have liked, and they simply didn't master oral French as quickly as they would have had there been fewer students.

I hear people argue that good teachers can teach large classes. I agree partially. I would rather have a good teacher in a large class than a sorry teacher in a small class. But common sense tells me that this teacher would have been far more effective with twenty students than she was with those thirty-five.

Why do teachers put students in alphabetical order?

For two reasons—students have to sit somewhere, and the teachers need help in learning the names. Other than that, I can't think of a single reason.

I do understand and appreciate the teacher's need to learn the names. Some teachers have as many as 150 students a day, and just managing some kind of recognition handle for each one is a major assignment. They have to have that seating chart, and the alphabetical order just makes looking up the names easier.

I am concerned about no-name students—those people who sit through classes hour after hour and day after day without any kind of personal recognition. You can spot them easily, but the dead giveaway is when the parent calls to check on the student's progress. If the teacher has to look at his seating chart to see which class the student is in, you begin to understand why the student is having some difficulty learning in that situation. Learning is a lonely activity at best, but those students who are isolated even further by a teacher who doesn't know their names have even greater hurdles to leap over.

I realize that sitting in alphabetical order may be a nuisance to some students, but I recommend that they comply. Having the name recognition outweighs the handicaps. In fact, if you promise not to tell the teachers I said this, I will make a further recommendation. I recommend that all students at whatever level develop some problem early in the term which requires the teacher's personal attention. You are left-handed so you need a left-handed desk. Someone tore a page from your book. You are too near the board. You are too far from the board.

Develop the problem and go see the teacher. You don't have to be dramatic, but just establish eye contact and make sure the teacher knows your name. The next time he calls his roll from his alphabetical list, he will pause at that name, look up and grin. Then, that person has become not just a name but even a personality, and learning won't be quite so lonely.

Our fourth-grade daughter's teacher says she is operating a democratic classroom. What does that mean?

It probably means that this teacher has taken seriously her task to prepare young people to live in a democratic society. Most schools and most educational philosophies list this as one of the primary goals of American education. It is a lofty and noble sounding ideal—something worth striving toward.

On a more practical basis, the ideal is rather difficult to implement. Frankly, most classrooms are not democratic at all. Someone makes most, if not all, of the decisions, at least the obvious and significant ones.

However, some teachers still make an attempt to put the students more in charge of what happens. They try to give the children the opportunity to participate in the decisions which are going to affect them. They ask the students to help write the class rules. They have students vote on classroom activities and such things as due dates for homework. They ask students to decide on bulletin boards and other classroom decorations.

Despite all those efforts, the classroom is probably not a true democracy. If the classroom is functioning smoothly, I would guess that the teacher is still very much in charge, but at least the students get some experience with their own decisions. It isn't a bad learning experience.

Why don't they separate girls and boys in the P.E. class? I'm afraid my daughter is going to get hurt.

Well, first there is a legality involved. There is a federal law which prohibits discrimination between sexes, and one of the ways which schools must interpret this is by conducting coeducational P.E. classes.

These classes have been common for about ten years, and probably the quality of physical education has improved some during that time. It seems to me, as a general rule, that physical education classes are a bit more serious about what they are doing, that they provide a wider variety of activities for the students, and that they spend more time on what they call lifelong sports, those things that the people will continue to play after they get too old for competitive football, basketball, and baseball.

Such activities as golf, tennis, jogging, bowling, and yes, even folk dancing can be quite successfully handled in coeducational classes, and there isn't much danger of anyone getting hurt. Of course, sometimes boys are expected to hold hands with girls and some junior high boys find that experience rather painful, but they do get over it. So far, coeducational classes make sense.

However, P.E. teachers have to be sensitive to the fact that there are some physical activities where size and strength become natural discriminators. Everytime I watch a junior high P.E. class playing softball, and I see some big eighth-grade boy playing shortstop and some small girl playing first base I shudder with the same thoughts you have. We can just hope that teachers are sensitive to the possible dangers and make some kind of adjustments.

Why do teachers humiliate children in front of the class?

They get angry. They get exasperated. They lose their tempers. They allow themselves to become defensive with students. They don't have any better strategies for controlling the students and the class. Or maybe they just have a mean streak.

Do you remember when you were young saying something like this, "When I become a parent, you'll never catch me. . . ." How many times have you broken that promise to yourself? Shame on you. Why did you do it? I suspect that was the same reason we teachers sometimes resort to this despicable method of getting some students' attention.

We know better. At least most of us do. This isn't any way to treat another person, and it isn't even a very effective way of dealing with misbehavior. The problem with humiliating a child in front of his colleagues is that you put him into a no-win situation. If the child is timid, he will probably shrink from this kind of treatment and become even more shy. On the other hand, if he is an aggressive person, he will probably find some way to fight back. He may throw a temper tantrum right on the spot, or he may just act subdued for the moment and lay back and wait for his chance to get even. Either way the teacher has just put himself into a bad situation.

I am not opposed to speaking to children about their misbehavior or their lack of effort or their daydreaming or whatever. But the wise teacher, and the wise parent, will always look for the most opportune moment where we will not put a child into a position where one of them has to lose face.

Why do American educators use so many standardized tests?

That is an excellent question, particularly when it suggests that we compare American schools and testing procedures with the same procedures in other countries. I don't know whether we use more or fewer standardized tests, but we definitely use a different kind, and we use them for different purposes.

One of the rather unusual characteristics of American education is that we use tests that have one-word answers, or better yet, we test a student's ability, knowledge, or aptitude by having him circle a letter which is the correct response. Then we can throw all those sheets into a little machine and in within a matter of seconds have all the answers

119

marked, know how many each person got right and missed, and know where everybody stands in relationship to everyone else.

With the American emphasis on both quick knowledge and rapid reporting, we don't have much use for essay questions such as, "Why do you think the North won the Civil War? Support your contention."

Some other countries in the world would find our system not only strange but a bit inadequate. They wonder how we can find out what a student knows by just having him circle a correct response. They would rather put their emphasis on a student's being able to express himself on why he knows something than on just what he knows.

Perhaps this peculiarity of American educational methodology breeds more testing.

Another interesting characteristic of our emphasis on testing is that after we have gone through the process, we really don't do all that much with the results. Again, in other countries, students are frequently screened into one school or another by test results. In many European countries, students are tested at about the junior high level, and are put into either academic or vocational programs based on the results of those tests.

In this country, we might put some students into special classes based on their test scores, and some colleges use test scores as one of the requirements for admission, but as a rule, we don't make significant decisions based on those scores.

While other countries use the scores more to prescribe educational programs, we tend to use tests scores to describe, to tell us what is going on, both with individual students and with the educational process in general. Frequently, we test several thousand students across the nation to determine if we are being successful in teaching math or science or English, or some other subject of study. If the test results aren't what we like, we then begin to make proposals to change our educational programs.

I don't know whether we test more than other countries or not, but we do use the information we learn for different purposes.

If a child is labeled as having a learning disability, does that mean that he will have to do manual labor for the rest of his life?

No. We all know that the answer to that question is no. We have heard enough illustrations of people who learned to compensate and work against the odds. In fact, we probably all know someone with a learning disability who is quite successful. Yet, when it happens to our own child, we have a way of forgetting all those great role models, and we convince ourselves that the world has just lost its luster, at least for that person and his family.

Let me be just one more reassuring voice in the midst of all the other reassuring voices. I teach college seniors. These are the people who were successful enough in high school to get admitted to college and they were successful enough in college to get to be seniors. Most of them will go out next year and become successful teachers. Every year, I have one or two students who have some kind of significant learning disability. I may have even more and not even know it, but I do get close enough to some that they will tell me about it. So I know about them.

I have had students who confused letters in words. In other words, something was wrong with their perception ability so that they saw letters in a different order than they really appeared. By compensation, these students learned to read and read well. Some of them never learned to spell, so they just compensate by using a dictionary. Now they make great use of the word processing spelling program.

I have had students who would jumble events in their memory. They couldn't remember that a class was to start at 9 o'clock rather than at 8. Again, they just learned to keep tons and tons of notes so that they got where they were supposed to be when they were supposed to be there.

I use these two examples to illustrate my point again. A learning disability is a little extra burden, but it in no way implies that a person can't learn or is destined to failure.

The task for the parent of a student with a learning disability is to keep that disability from becoming an unnecessary burden. Despite his difficulty, the student must keep some kind of level of self-confidence. When his self-confidence fails him and he tells himself he doesn't have a chance, then the disability will wreck his life. It isn't the learning disability that frightens me, it is the child's response to it.

My son is a late-night person who gains steam as the day progresses. Yet, the schools always give those year-end achievement tests during the morning. Why?

They give the test then simply because the school officials assume that most students are the opposite of your son. They are people who go to bed early so that they can be on their best early in the morning. (Notice how many advanced math and science classes are offered during the first three periods of the day.)

Since the test schedule is designed to accommodate the majority of students, I doubt that the school people will change it. In fact, several years ago, this very topic was the subject of a great deal of research, and this schedule is the one which was found to be most satisfactory for the largest number of students.

For this reason, I would recommend that you help your son adjust his clock a bit to prepare for the tests. About a week or two before the tests are scheduled, have him begin to go to bed an hour or so earlier. He may get into the habit and be fairly good at a little earlier retirement at test time.

I notice that our school has an overhead projector in every classroom. Is that really that necessary?

The overhead projector is an excellent teaching device on one condition. To be an effective tool, it must be used. It must be plugged in and turned on. In fact, if the overhead is to be really effective, the teacher needs to have some transparencies worth looking at.

The researchers tell us that we retain a very small percentage of what we hear. (I am not going to give that figure because the researchers themselves disagree about what it is. Some say we retain about 35 percent of what we hear and some say as little as 6 percent.) But when we both hear and see something our retention doubles or perhaps goes even higher.

We really don't need researchers to point this out to us. Since we learn at least some of what we know through the senses, the more senses we employ in the process, the more we should learn.

Wise teachers know this, so they use all sorts of methods to involve as many senses as they can. The overhead projector is one of those methods.

My son almost refuses to do his homework when he gets home from school. We waive it until after dinner, which ruins his chance to participate in any family activity. How can we get him to do his homework earlier?

You may not be able to. I don't want to hurt your feelings, but I am going to take your son's side. If he has good teachers throughout the day, his mind is probably fried at the end of the day. All he wants to do is to go home, eat everything in the refrigerator, relax his mind, and take a nap.

Frankly, I think he is entitled to it. I am sorry that homework destroys the family activities. I realize that is a costly price to pay, but the average student is bombarded with so much new material, so many new ideas, and so many new theories and concepts that his mind is too full at the end of the day to take in much more before a break in schedule.

"We teach the way we were taught," the old adage assures or warns us, depending on your perspective. We may want to protest and rebel a bit, but I'm convinced that there is more truth here than most of us wish to admit.

The way we learned something, the way we got our mind around it, the way we first came to understand it becomes more than a method of learning, but it becomes a part of what we have learned as well.

Not only is this important for teachers to understand about themselves, but it is also important for parents to understand as well.

Most of us make educational decisions and evaluations based on a standard I call the "glorified I." We say, "I remember how I learned, and since I am almost perfect, everyone else must learn the same way."

This may help to explain why schools don't change all that much. We parents like for our children to be taught as we were taught, and we teachers teach as we remember being taught.

Our fourth-grade daughter is in a new experimental program, and she is a mess because of it. She isn't learning anything, and she is upset most of the time. What can we do?

I could suggest a very professional approach. I could suggest that you go to the school. Learn as much as you can about the new program. Find out how it is supposed to work. Read books on the subject. Meet the teachers. Have discussions with other parents. Then after you have done all that, work with your daughter trying to help her understand how the new program works so she can live with it comfortably.

That's what I could suggest, but I am not going to. New experimental programs are often designed by people who may understand programs and learning theories better than they understand children. Your daughter is simply not fitting into this program, and I doubt that any amount of coercion or instruction will change all that. Let's all face the reality. Not all programs are for everybody. The people who designed the program and implemented the program in your school should understand that.

Assuming that you have given your daughter time to try to adjust to the new program, I am going to recommend that you go to the school. I suggest that you start with the teacher. But go with a smile on your face. You are not out to abolish this new program from the face of the earth. You have just had time to see that your daughter doesn't fit. It is now time for her to get into another program or even another school if necessary.

I would suspect that the school officials will welcome your observations and your daughter's reactions. They know the program is experimental, and they are looking for evidence of the success or failure. They really need to hear from you, and they should welcome the opportunity to work with you.

Since the effective schools research and the effective schools movement seem to be one of the most significant new developments in education presently, I recently attended a statewide conference on effective instruction.

I approached one of the sponsors and asked her to give me a clear definition of what effective instruction in schools was all about.

She thought for a moment, and answered carefully, "I went to a parochial all-girls school," this forty-year-old veteran teacher said, "and as best as I can tell, effective instruction is what those nuns did when we were students."

Teaching doesn't change all that much. We just develop new names for it.

What is homogeneous grouping and what does it mean to my child?

Homogeneous grouping or ability tracking or whatever it is called at your school is the practice of putting students with similar abilities in the same classroom. In other words, the good students will be with good students and the weaker students will be with weaker students.

Usually, there will be somewhere between three and five different levels of ability grouping. In a three-level system, those groups will be called something like basics, regular, and accelerated. Sometimes the educators will camouflage the issue by calling those groups something like bluebirds, redbirds, and white birds, but those are names for the teachers and administrators. The students know that they are basics, regular, and accelerated. You don't fool them with fancy names. In a five-level system, there will be a group below the basics and a group above the accelerated.

The proponents of homogeneous grouping argue that there is an advantage to students and teachers alike. Since teachers direct their instruction and time their lessons to somewhere in the middle of the abilities, homogeneous grouping allows the teacher to go as fast or as slow as needs be to meet the specific needs of all students. Students themselves profit from being in classes with people of their own abilities because they can find reinforcement from their peer group. The better students will be challenged by the people in the room while the slower students will feel more comfortable with other students of similar abilities.

On the other hand, there are a couple of problems with the system. Some students are slow learners in one subject area but ahead of the game in another. Deciding where that student belongs is a major dilemma.

Another problem is the student who has the ability but isn't highly motivated. If he is put in a class with slower students based on his past performance, he will find a comfortable spot and settle in doing as little as necessary. This student really needs the challenge of the other students but doesn't have it.

What is mainstreaming?

Mainstreaming is the practice of placing students with physical or learning disabilities in the same classroom with all the other students. About twenty years ago, the operating principle was that children with

125

special problems should be separated from the other students throughout the school day. This was both for their benefit as well as the benefit of the other students.

Somewhere during the last twenty years, that principle has been modified a bit. Now the idea is that these students should be with the other students as much as is educationally feasible. Thus, these students are mainstreamed into classrooms.

Sometimes the special students are mainstreamed for all classes. Sometimes they are only mainstreamed for specific classes, depending on the nature of the class and the nature of their disability.

The idea of mainstreaming is sometimes referred to as the principle of the least restrictive environment.

CHAPTER SIX
Reading

When I first began teaching, I understood my mission to be teaching literature to high school students. Soon, I realized the task to be too enormous, so I decided I would be content just to teach poetry. Soon, I realized the task to be too enormous, so I decided that rather than trying to teach poetry, I would teach students how to read literature. This change in careers brought some satisfaction, but I did not find complete happiness until I set as my mission the task of teaching students to read poetry.

This complete mystery called schooling is really rather simple when we reduce it to its common denominator. Students come to school and spend thirteen or even seventeen years in the process of learning to read. Now, of course, they learn to read poetry and math and social studies and science, but all the while they are basically learning to read.

It is essential that parents and teachers understand this because we need to realize that we simply can't teach everyone everything. Somewhere in this process, we have to come to view an educated person not as one who knows a lot but as one who is able to read and keep learning.

This is the theme of this chapter.

How early should a child learn to read?

Obviously, this is one of the hottest topics of debate in educational circles around the world. Everybody has an opinion, and that is all right—except no one agrees with anyone else. What is a parent to think? One expert says start them at two. Another says start them at eight. So which one do you listen to?

I am not sure I have the right answer either, but I do have an observation.

Teach your child to read when he wants to read. How's that for begging off the question? But it really isn't. If you watch your child he will tell you when he is ready to read. In fact, a lot of children teach themselves to read before any adult even knows about it; then one day they surprise the world by revealing their accomplishment. Most parents are usually embarrassed at this point. They celebrate the achievement, but they feel a bit guilty that the child learned something on his own without having to be taught by the parent. Aren't children wonderful?

But if you listen carefully, my suggestion requires a rather difficult thing from you—honesty. If you let the child start to read when the child wants to read, you have to make sure that that is when the child wants to read and not when you want the child to want to read. There is a big difference between those two.

But let's suppose your child doesn't show any interest in wanting to read until he is six years old or so. What do you do then? Well, frankly, I am still not all that disturbed. Most of my friends who are college professors with all sorts of impressive letters behind their names and frequent references such as scholar, learned to read at six. They seem to have done all right in the academic world with that late a start. Actually, I am far more impressed with people who read at fifteen years of age than I am with the people who read at five years of age.

Of course, if you adopt this attitude, you will need to stay away from those super-parents raising those super four-year-olds who take in the *New York Times* on a daily basis and are working their way through Encyclopædia Britannica before they get too busy with kindergarten.

On the other hand, if your child shows signs of wanting to read at three or four or five, don't be afraid to encourage him. There are some little fun ways to get him involved in the process. You may want to do such things as making name tags for the items around the house, Your child will already know the names for such things as stove or table so he can easily pick up the written symbol for that item. (Remember that reading is the process of interpreting symbolic language.) You may want to help your child learn to recognize the sounds of language. Help him discover the sound in a specific word. Then you can introduce him to hand-drawn flash cards with those sounds on them. With that, he learns that reading is the process of putting sounds to letters. Again the age to start this is when the child seems to be interested. You can prime, but I see no real value in forcing. But never lose sight of the fact that reading is a language activity. The more comfortable a child is with language, the more aggressive he will be in making the language work for him. You are actually teaching your child to read when you are talking with him, listening and encouraging him to talk, and letting him participate in your discussions.

Why don't they teach phonics anymore?

Well, some people still do. There are more reading experts in the nation than there are racehorses, and as best as I can tell, every reading expert has his own unusual and somewhat different theory which he believes is the one and only and absolute way to teach a child to read. As classroom teachers and other educators sort through those theories to try to make some sense of all that diversity, some bet on one theory and some bet on another—about like a racehorse. Sometimes it might appear that the phonics theory is not winning the race, but confidentially, I see more phonics work in classrooms than some of the experts would like.

Actually, the argument boils down to two factors—mechanics or interest. Some reading experts believe that children must learn the mechanics of reading before they can ever begin the process. This, of course, is the traditional position. Throughout the history of schools in this country until about fifty years ago, reading was taught as a mechanical activity. Students first memorized the letters and the sounds; next they memorized significant combinations of sound or syllables; then they got to words; and eventually they began to read from the printed page. Of course, this technique for teaching children to read has an illustrious history with its roots in first-century Rome. Latin was almost always taught this way, and that makes sense because Latin is a phonetically consistent language. In other words, letters always sound and mean the same thing. Unfortunately, English is not that reliable. Try, for example, writing the sentence, "Would you wait for Harry?" and think of all the variations of each word.

Obviously, this process for learning to read is laborious at best and boring at worst; so about fifty years ago, reading experts began experimenting with teaching theories which would arouse the students' interest. They hypothesized that if the students were interested in the content of the material, they would more readily learn the mechanics of the process of reading it. As usual with any new educational theory, some people went overboard with this new idea and quit teaching the sounds altogether. To this day, the debate rages on. Most sensible people agree that the solution is somewhere in the middle; but unfortunately, that compromise is sometimes hard to find.

If you believe that learning phonics is important to a child's language growth—reading, spelling, and perhaps even speaking—you may want to spend some time with your child yourself. It's really rather easy. Make some flash cards with the letters (or use blocks) and when the child makes the sound, hand him the card (or the block.) It makes an interesting game. I have seen three-year-olds play this game in the back seat of a car for hours.

If you want to get more advanced, make flash cards with phonetically consistent words on them and have the child pronounce the words by sounding through each individual sound.

Through the two rather simple illustrations, I want to make the point that teaching a child phonics is not really a major endeavor which requires years and years of tedious concentration. It is really a rather simple affair which could easily be turned into a fun family game.

Will watching too much television destroy a child's desire to read?

Do you know what? That's not as easy a question as some people would have us believe. The most popular answer would be a resounding yes. Television destroys the desire to read because it is passive while reading is active. Watching television does not require the mental concentration it takes to read. Watching television takes too much time. The list goes on. And I think all of it is true, or at least could be true.

On the other hand, some of the most dedicated adolescent readers I have known have also been dedicated television watchers. That really doesn't present as much of a mystery as it may seem. I am not sure there are too many people who really enjoy the activity of sitting on a hard chair, holding a book with both hands with the nose pointed at the printed word. No, the desire to read is the desire to know or the desire to be entertained or the desire to be broadened; and sometimes that desire sends interested persons into all sorts of investigations, including television. In fact, quite often the better read a person is, the better he will enjoy the process of watching TV. Some television requires a rather broad background for full appreciation.

Now, for whatever reason, some people—children, adolescents, and even adults—have a greater desire to know than others. Frankly, I have met some adolescents who don't seem to have any interest whatsoever except to take the next breath, and they don't even seem to be too interested in how that process works. Give me a television watcher any day. At least we can carry on a conversation.

Now, let's review what I have said. The presence of a TV in a family home does not necessarily indicate an intellectual vacuum. The real danger is when it isn't controlled, and that's what parents are for.

I take my children to the public library regularly, but there are so many books to choose from. How do we make a choice?

Picking a book to read is just one of the little risks of life that makes it all so enjoyable and such a challenge. Picking a book for someone else to read and enjoy is particularly risky.

There are a few guidelines to help this process. You could begin by soliciting the opinions of other mothers in your neighborhood who have children about the same age as yours. Actually, this could be an interesting way for mothers in your area to get to know each other a bit better. You could meet once in a while just to discuss what your children have read and what they have enjoyed.

You could also consult various published lists. The children's librarian at your public library will be able to provide you with a rather comprehensive book recommendation for children at various ages. Since this list will contain little blurbs about each book, you and your children should be able to get some idea about what they would like.

If you don't mind an investment, Dr. Elaine McEwen's book, *How to Raise a Reader* (David C. Cook), is available at your Christian bookstore. In this book, Elaine has put together a rather thorough list of books for children of different ages. I have found it quite helpful.

In addition to all that, you also need to consult your children. Even if they are old enough to read for themselves, you will need to spend some time with them to discover what they enjoy and why. You will also want to read their books so you will know what is in them.

My favorite pet peeve is those teachers who assume that everyone reads as well as they do. If you can remember your student days at all, you know exactly what I am talking about. How many times have we heard the teacher say, "I read this myself last night and it just took ten minutes. So don't complain. This is a simple ten-minute assignment." Then we spend an hour and thirty minutes of the best television time of the week plowing through a ten-minute assignment.

The teacher's mistake is actually a common one. Most of us do assume that everyone reads as well as we do. When we read a piece of material, we assume that everyone else sees the same images, receives the same messages, and gets the idea as quickly and easily as we do.

Probably the opposite of this assumption is closer to accurate. A good teacher who studies his area of expertise thoroughly will probably never have a student who reads the material as well as he does, for the simple reason that every body of material reads differently.

History reads like history, poetry reads like poetry, and nuclear physics reads like nuclear physics. A person who is knowledgeable in the field and reads that kind of material often is just better at reading that kind of material. Personally, I do all right with an educational philosophy book because I know what all the words mean and I recognize the allusion. But you ought to see me with a chemistry book.

Our high school is considering adopting the "Saxon math" curriculum. What is that?

Saxon is a math educator who has written a curriculum with all the textbooks based on the idea that students need a great deal of practice with every concept they learn. So the Saxon book introduces fewer concepts each day but gives the students many, many practice problems and review problems.

In other words, students who go through the Saxon curriculum will probably know fewer concepts at the end of the year, but they should know what they know quite thoroughly.

As with all new ideas, the Saxon approach is highly controversial. Some people, math educators and lay people alike, feel that this approach is the most sensible approach to teaching math. Others contend that this approach waters down the curriculum, removes the challenge from the brighter students, and does not produce the kind of thinking math classes are supposed to produce.

Since your school is considering the Saxon curriculum, I would recommend that you ask to take a look at the books yourself.

What is a B.D. student?

A B.D. student is a behavior disorder student or, in other words, a student who, for whatever reason, simply can't fit into a normal, structured classroom.

Usually, these students are identified and labeled after several weeks or months with counselors, teachers, and even parents working together to try to find some method for helping these people adjust to the typical classroom.

Some of these students have various kinds of physical problems which prevent them from sitting still or keeping quiet or being kind. Some have dietary problems; some have temporary personal or family problems which upset them; and some may just be rebellious people.

Many schools have a special classroom for these students where they spend some or all of their time. These classrooms usually have fewer students, fewer pressures, and fewer distractions than the normal classroom, so the student learns to manage himself better and not be so disturbing to the other students. Often, these students are able to move back into the normal classrooms after spending some time in the B.D. special class.

My child is five and shows little interest in learning to read. How can I help him get started?

It is my opinion that children should learn to read when they are ready to learn to read. (Notice how I avoid these problems.) Obviously, some are ready earlier than others. I am not sure that we know everything that goes into the process of readiness, but we do have some ideas about some of the aspects of readiness.

For one thing, learning to read requires that a child has mastered a certain level of language skills and is comfortable with how language is used. Rather than actually tying a book to the end of a three-year-old's nose, perhaps we could do him more of a favor by involving him in intelligent conversation with good words and acceptable sentence structure. When he gets comfortable hearing and using oral language, he will develop an interest in the mysterious world of symbolic language.

Another factor in reading readiness is simple physical maturity. Some children grow a little sooner than others and are physically more capable of holding a book, sitting still, and even seeing words and carrying the images to their brains. The timing of this physical growth seems to be a characteristic of the will of God and has little to do with proper parenting.

Another factor in reading readiness is, in blunt terms, the factor of the child's propensity to imitate. Children do imitate what they see the adults in their lives do; and if the adult models read, the child will probably move into reading a little earlier.

Now that I have listed those known factors which contribute to reading readiness, let me go on to say that there is still a giant unknown factor which makes this whole process a wonderful mystery which we will probably never understand. Let's just call it a secret pact between the child and God which outsiders to that pact may never understand.

I frequently visit a preschool of three-, four-, and five-year-olds. The school is a wonderful place. The equipment is designed to fit children; the teachers are excellent, bordering on brilliant at times. The students are happy and love to learn. Some three-year-olds have already begun to read. On the other hand, some five-year-olds aren't reading much even when they leave the school. The director, a woman that I admire for her knowledge of both children and the process of learning, doesn't seem to be at all concerned about this difference. So I take my cue from her. If a three-year-old wants to read, I suggest that we encourage him, but on the other hand, if a child decides to wait until he is six or seven, I don't see any need to rush him.

Frequently mothers say to me, "Oh, my son is reading at three years of age." Frankly, I'm not all that impressed. I'm definitely not as impressed as that mother is.

Sometimes a mother says to me, "My son is thirteen and enjoys reading." I'm beginning to get impressed.

Once a mother said to me, "My son is forty-three and he reads all the time." Wow! Now I am impressed.

I'm impressed because, though I don't know what it is, there is still some connection between three years of age and forty-three years of age; and I'm impressed to see a mother who understands that.

We listen to our daughter read and she pronounces all the words all right, but we don't know whether she comprehends. How can we tell?

What an excellent question. What is happening in someone else's mind is always a mystery. How can we ever know for sure? If I could answer that, I could solve most of the educational problems of the universe.

On the other hand, since you have your daughter in a one-to-one situation perhaps you can get something of an idea. The simplest way is the most direct. Ask her. Use direct questions. Get her to retell you the story in her own words. Ask her what the accompanying pictures represent.

As she is reading, watch her facial expressions and listen for vocal inflection. Sometimes these will give us clues as to how much the child is really comprehending.

If you want a more scientific view, you may want to try a cloze test. (See the model below.) These are actually easy to prepare and can tell us quite a bit about the reader. Make a copy of a passage of 250 words omitting every fifth word, regardless of what it is—proper noun, preposition, or even an article. Then have your daughter read the passage, supplying the missing words. If she can get more than 35 percent of the words correct, this is a good indication that she is using the context of the material to help her comprehend. In other words, she is comprehending fairly well. If she is able to provide more than 55 percent of the missing words, the material is too simple for her.

That morning I woke ___1___ really excited. It was ___2___ our second week in ___3___ camp, and already our ___4___ was going to take ___5___ float trip down the ___6___. I yelled more than ___7___ during the cabin cleaning ___8___.

I was in a ___9___ to go.

When the ___10___ came, we piled into ___11___ truck and rode to ___12___ river. Soon we had ___13___ boats unloaded and into ___14___ water. We loaded up, ___15___ to a boat. In ___16___ boat

I had Chris, __17__ son of a famous __18__; John, the son of __19__ company president; and Mark, __20__ son of a millionaire __21__.

I noticed a metal __22__ on the bottom of __23__ boat which advised, "Don't __24__ during an emergency."

The __25__ part of the journey __26__ simple, quiet, still water, __27__ serene.

I paddled while __28__ boys played in the __29__, splashing about and jarring __30__ serenity. I enjoyed the __31__, but I was excited __32__ getting to the fun __33__, the rapids. After about __34__ hour, the river tapered into __35__ narrow channel, and the current __36__ swifter. For the first __37__ all day, I didn't __38__ to row. I liked __39__. But too soon the __40__ grew angry, moved over __41__ the bank, and rushed __42__ great force. We ducked __43__ avoid the low-hanging branches __44__ hovered near the bottom, __45__ my passengers soon grew __46__ of taking the easy __47__. At the same time, __48__ stood up. The boat __49__. I immediately dropped the __50__ into the river.

1. up 2. only 3. summer 4. cabin 5. a 6. river 7. usual 8. ordeal 9. hurry 10. truck 11. the 12. the 13. our 14. the 15. four 16. my 17. the 18. physician 19. a 20. the 21. oilman 22. plate 23. the 24. panic 25. first 26. was 27. almost 28. the 29. water 30. the 31. quiet 32. about 33. part 34. an 35. a 36. grew 37. time 38. have 39. that 40. current 41. toward 42. with 43. to 44. and 45. but 46. weary 47. route 48. each 49. rocked 50. paddle

---

I read to our little girl every night, but she always wants me to read the same story—"The Three Bears"—night after night. What should I do?

Read it to her. Read it well. Read it with expression and emotion as if it were the first time you ever saw the story. Stop once in a while to see if she has it memorized yet herself. And love her for being a child.

Actually her choice is not so difficult to understand if you think about it. You listen to the same songs over and over again. You go to familiar restaurants. You travel the same streets on the way to work. Children like the familiar too. They carry around the same old blanket (sometimes for years and years). They play with the same toys, and they enjoy hearing and rehearing the same story night after night.

But this is not only just comfortable to them, it is also healthy. Through hearing the same story over and over again, they become familiar with language patterns. They begin to see the way a plot is developed. They learn to pick out intricacies of character development. They are learning to read. More importantly, they are learning to enjoy reading.

I have a confession to make. I have never read *Tom Sawyer*. Isn't that terrible? Mark Twain is probably my favorite writer. I read *The Adventures of Huckleberry Finn* about once a year, but have never read *Tom Sawyer*. Let me tell you why.

In March of my first-grade year, we went to town and bought baby chickens. That was always a thrill for me and is still an interesting memory—the square boxes about three inches deep with all the little chicks poking their heads out through the air holes punched in the side.

But no sooner had we got the new chicks home and placed them comfortably in the brooder house than a terrible, late-season blizzard hit. The winds howled and the snow blew and the old brooder house was not a match for the elements. Surely the chicks would die if we didn't do something. So we gathered them up and carried them to the cellar, which we heated with kerosene lanterns. There the chicks were comfortable from the cold, but they had a tendency to crowd around the lanterns until they were in danger of suffocating. So we three children spent two full days sitting in the cellar keeping the chicks from bunching together. Our mother came down, turned an old pail upside down, and in the dim light of the kerosene lanterns she read read *Tom Sawyer*.

During the past forty-four years I have chosen not to reread the book. The memory of where we were and what we were doing and the love that went into the reading is too powerful in my appreciation for the story that I don't want to run the risk of ruining the memory.

If you do it right, reading a good book provides two memorable experiences. Of course, there is always the experience of the book itself, but the experience of reading can be a powerful memory as well.

We talk about reading quantity—reading lots of books, reading in free time, reading into the wee hours of the morning. But I hope in the midst of all this, we don't lose sight of the value of the quality of the experience.

We have always read to our daughter. Now that she has begun school, and she can read for herself, should we stop reading to her?

Never! There are so many reasons why reading to a child is a positive experience. It teaches the child to value the printed page, of course, but it also brings child and parent together in one of the closest bonds of the relationship. The children who have parents who read to them just have some happy memories of childhood that other children don't have. For those reasons alone, never stop reading to your children. Those pleasant memories will be valuable to them throughout their lives.

On the other hand, the process may change a bit as your daughter learns to read for herself. Learning to read is one form of gaining independence. You will notice that independence, particularly if she is language-oriented. In the past, she would climb up on your lap and surrender to you entirely to help her interpret the symbolic world of language. Now that she can read for herself, she may not need to be so dependent on you. She may even choose to flaunt her newfound independence a bit for a while, and it may get difficult to get her on your lap. But don't despair. Make sure she knows the invitation is still open and in a few weeks something will happen in her world to make her seek the security of your reading to her again.

You may also want to change roles a bit. Now that your daughter is learning to read for herself, the two of you can take turns reading to each other. That way, reading becomes a sharing relationship, and that is when it is the most valuable to us.

Our daughter doesn't like to read and doesn't read too well. Will this be a problem for her as she enters junior high?

Yes, I am afraid it will be. In fact, it could be a rather serious problem in a variety of areas. Throughout most of elementary school, the aim of the curriculum and instruction is to teach students the basic skills of learning—computing, organizing, and writing. Of course, the most important of these and the one that gets the most time is the skill of reading. In other words, the greatest emphasis of elementary school is to teach students how to read.

In junior high school, there just isn't that much intensity in teaching students how to read. Instead, students are expected to use that skill of reading to master the other subjects. History teachers, science teachers, English teachers, health teachers, and even math teachers assume that students already have mastered the skill of reading and should now be able to use that skill to master the content of the subject. Actually, teachers probably expect too much of even the best readers. Unfortunately, most teachers make the false assumption that everyone reads as well as they do, and that assumption dictates the amount of homework assignments, the expectations of the students, and even the kinds of tests given.

Anyone who comes to junior high without being an average reader is going to struggle some. Your daughter will have to read in order to do the other assignments. And it will take her longer to read them than it will the other students. That is an unfortunate dilemma—she will spend more time studying and get fewer rewards. Somehow it doesn't seem fair.

That's where the other problems begin to arise. She may develop a strong dislike for school. I can't say that I blame her. I wouldn't much enjoy a place where I had to spend most of my day doing something I don't do well. You may find a real chore in just keeping her enthusiasm up.

But what is even worse, she could develop a strong dislike for herself. This happens far too often with junior high students who don't read well. Though it is not often cool to be an egghead or a nerd, it isn't cool to be stupid either; so even such things as popularity and friendships are too often tied into reading ability.

Now, if I could be permitted a sexist observation, this seems to be more acute in girls than in guys at this age. For whatever reason, reading is something of a feminine activity. Eighty percent of all books are bought by women. Mothers sit at home and read while Daddy sits at home and watches TV. The girl at puberty who struggles with reading seems also to struggle with identity problems. I don't tell you this to frighten you, but I do think your daughter's difficulty with reading will have an impact on her success and personality development during junior high. It is very important for her to know with certainty your support during this critical time.

I would further suggest that you may want to look around your area for a private reading clinic, somewhere your daughter could go for special diagnosis and help with her reading problem. I have seen many of these which are just excellent in helping these young people not only improve in reading but deal with their struggles as well. Of course, it is going to cost you some money, but it could be a sound investment in the long run.

I am not sure I know how much I want to emphasize this business of modeling by parents, but I do know it's important. Personally, we have three children. Each spent childhood at our house during a different era of my life. The oldest daughter spent her childhood during the period when I wanted to be a writer, but wrote very little. She herself writes very little and finds the process difficult. Our son spent his childhood during the time when I wrote professional articles. He now writes expository, professional material. Our younger daughter spent her childhood at our house during the period when I was writing novels. She writes all the time. She keeps a daily journal. She publishes in the school newspaper. She aspires to be a professional writer. And above all she writes for therapy.

Natural talent and special gifts? Parental genes? Models? I'm not really sure I know.

I want my children to be good readers. What can I do to help?

Let me just jump right into that one. According to all the authorities, there are some definite things that parents can do to help their children learn to read—not just learn to read but learn to love to read.

1. Read! How's that for putting the pressure on you from the beginning, but I am convinced that this is the best piece of advice I can give you. Regardless of all the new pedagogical theories and research, the most effective teaching technique is still modeling. That's logical because children are for the most part imitators. Watch them at play and you will see them imitating grown-ups, so show yours something wholesome to imitate. Let them catch you reading and enjoying it.

2. Read to them. When do you start? As soon as they are born. When do you quit? I don't know. I have a daughter who is almost thirty and I still read to her once in a while.

Now, I know for some people this is tough advice. You have heard someone say this before, and you are convinced that you need to do it, but you have problems working out the mechanics. When do you get the time when the two of you are together? What do you read to him? What if you can't keep his interest?

Well, let me start with one reminder. You are reading to your children. You are not trying to imitate school. In other words, there aren't any rules. School says they have to be sitting quietly when someone reads, but you don't have to ask for quiet at home. Read to your children while they are playing with their toys or trying to fall asleep or fighting among themselves. Don't underestimate a child's mind. They may be absorbing more of this than you can ever imagine.

As far as selecting material, don't worry about being an expert. If you look hard enough you can find a list that someone who is supposed to know such things has put together; but until you get the list, read whatever you have—newspapers, magazines, the backs of cereal boxes. I know one family that read the dictionary through over a period of a couple of years. They complained that the plot wasn't much, but they did enjoy the frequent changing of topics.

And don't tell me there isn't enough time. You can read to your children when you are traveling in the car or when you are at the restaurant waiting for the pizza to cook. Or sit on a stool in the kitchen and read to them while they wash dishes. That way both of you will learn something.

3. Surround your children with reading materials. Buy newspapers and magazines. As soon as they can walk, introduce them to the local library. I have discovered some of the finest reading experts in this nation working as librarians in the children's sections of public libraries. Take your children down there and see what is available. You may find a cooperative, supportive expert. Make sure there are always books lying around the house should the urge hit.

4. Listen to your children read. Let's get this straight now. If your child only reads at school, he will never be a good reader. When children are learning to read, they need someone to listen to them. Since the teacher has twenty-five students to listen to, she can't give your child as much time as he needs. Do both of them a favor. Listen

to your child read. And you don't need to quit that just because your child gets through the Primary years either.

Why is the rate of illiteracy growing in this country?

Oh, that is a complex question. It does not have a simple answer, and the implied problem that arises does not have simple solutions. I am sure you have heard some of the typical responses. The schools are not doing as good a job as they need to. We have quit teaching phonics. Our immigrants aren't interested in learning the language. Too many people are dropping out of school. We are teaching too much phonics. There is a national conspiracy. The statistics aren't accurate.

I don't want to ridicule any one of these answers, but I do want to say, that taken by itself, each is too simple to offer much help. But as we think about the situation, we do need to consider two almost contradictory facts.

First, millions of children are still learning to read and learning to read well in all kinds of schools throughout the nation. We do hear about the ones who don't, and we are concerned about those, but there are far more who are learning to read, and who are enjoying reading than those who don't. In trying to determine why we are failing with some, we probably should begin by investigating why we are succeeding with others.

The other fact is more sobering. We are simply not as much of a reading nation as we would like to tell ourselves we are. All across the nation, newspaper circulation has diminished, forcing many publications out of business. Johnny Carson speaks to about 20 million people every night; yet if an author speaks to 50,000 through a book, he feels he has a successful volume. Far more Americans use a public swimming pool than use a public library.

Since modeling is still the most effective teaching technique we know, this national trend to get our knowledge and our entertainment from film rather than from the printed page could become the major educational issue of the future.

Our son is going to middle school next year, and he is a bit behind in his reading. Will this be a major problem?

It could be. I am sorry to tell you that, but the reason is rather logical. During most of the elementary years, school is basically about developing skills—skills such as arithmetic, writing, organizing, and reading, especially reading. Much of the work of the early grades is designed to help children develop reading skills, and the students spend a lot of time every day on the skill of reading.

But middle school is different. There, the teachers expect the students to have the skills, so the focus is on having the students use the skills to learn subject matter. In other words, students are expected to use their reading skills to learn such things as history, science, or literature. Since the teachers assume that students already know how to read, the weaker readers quite often get trapped in that assumption and really struggle academically, not only through middle school but through the rest of their school careers.

In fact, they get a double whammy. They have to work harder and longer than the other students do, and often they make worse grades.

Most middle schools do recognize this dilemma, and they have special classes to help these students—classes in such things as spelling, reading skills, and reading lab. Frequently, these classes even help some, but still it is almost impossible for the poorer readers to catch up completely. While they are working on a basic skill of reading, their classmates are progressing more rapidly with the regular subject matter.

But there is another problem which also develops too frequently with these middle school students who have difficulty with reading. Somewhere in the process, they lose their confidence. They aren't doing as well in school as their peers. They are working harder just to complete assignments. They may be enrolled in basic skills classes which carry something of a stigma. Because they are not successful in classes, their social standing changes. For whatever reason, many of them decide to give up on academics at this point.

This may sound like a totally sexist statement, but from several years of observation, I have come to believe that this is even worse for middle school girls than it is for guys. For some reason, reading is perceived as a feminine activity. Mother reads books while Daddy sits in his undershirt and watches the ball game on TV. The early adolescent girl who struggles with reading struggles also with establishing an identity.

Now, before all this becomes too frightening, let me see if I can offer some suggestions which could turn this whole thing into a positive experience for both you and your son.

1. Regardless of what you do at this point, work hard at helping your son maintain his self-concept. He needs your help now more than any other time in his school career. Help him find something at which he can succeed because he isn't going to get too much positive reinforcement from his schoolwork. Give him more responsibility. Assure him often that you are pleased with him as a person.

2. Don't make him feel guilty about his reading difficulty. In other words, don't give him books for presents.

3. Check to see what kind of special help is available to him. Visit the teachers of the special classes in the school. See what they do with their students. If you feel that this is not enough emphasis, you may want to consider investigating the possibility of a special private reading clinic in your community. Several communities do have such a place, and some of them are quite effective in working with students of this age.

4. If the problem is serious, if you are really frightened, or if your son is really upset about the whole academic process, you may want to consider having him take fifth grade again. If this were handled properly, it would allow him to spend one more year on the skill of reading, and perhaps he could catch up with his colleagues. I have seen this happen. But if you consider this option, you will need to make some special provisions. If at all possible, you may want to move him to another school for the repeat year. This way, he will be able to do his work without the added burden of explaining his presence to all the rude people, adults and students alike, who will surely ask.

5. Work hard at helping your son maintain his self-concept. I know I said that before, but since it is the most significant piece of advice I have given, I will repeat it.

I first met Lawrence when he was a student in my senior speech class. Though he was not one of the outstanding students in class, he was solid. At that time, he was working after school for an electrical contractor; so he often gave speeches about such things as wiring a house or making a lamp or replacing a fuse—the kind of stuff that I could use even when I didn't find it interesting.

When the doldrums hit in February (as the doldrums always hit in February in schools) I decided to give this bunch a break, so we started to work on a poetry reading unit. It was simple and required almost zero preparation. The students were to stand in front of the class each day and read a favorite poem. Of course, most of them stopped by the library on the way to class, picked up a book with something that looked like a poem, hurried on down the hall, and fulfilled the assignment. It was a fun game we played. I acted as if I didn't know what they were doing; they acted as if they had fooled me completely; and we both derived some satisfaction from our own little secrets.

But one day Lawrence's tenth-grade sister stopped me in the hall and attacked me with a plaintive plea. "When are you going to get off that poetry reading thing in Lawrence's class?"

I could tell she was upset. No, maybe haggard is a better description. "Why?"

"Well," she said, "that poetry thing is about to wear me out."

I chuckled when I began to realize the scene that I had created. This macho young man could not dare to appear to like poetry so he had enlisted his sister to help him search for daily selections. Isn't that a pleasant image? Two high school kids, brother and sister, poring through the family literary collection, the old textbooks, and *Reader's Digest* condensed versions to find a piece of poetry. At that point, I was proud of myself.

But then, the sister went on with her explanation. "I don't know whether you know this or not," she said, "but Lawrence can't read. Every night he brings that stupid poem home and I have to read it over and over again until he memorizes it for your class. And I am tired of it," she proclaimed with an air of finality, and went marching down the hall.

I tried to remember everything I had observed about Lawrence since I had had him in class for more than six months. What were the signs? Was I so stupid that I could not tell that this young man could not read? How had I missed it?

The next day, I observed more closely as he "read" his poetry in class. Sure enough, it was memorized. This young man was a rather successful senior in high school, yet he still could not read.

Lawrence, now in his early forties, has his own electrical contracting business in the same little town. He is quite successful. He has a nice wife and almost-grown children. He is a leader in his church and the community. He has a reputation for being one of the best chess players in the region. From all indications, he seems to be happy and content. But he still can't read.

I heard that some books read at fifth-grade level. How is that determined?

That is an excellent question because we do love to banty that kind of information about as if it is important. Newspapers read at eighth-grade level, etc., etc.

Actually, the formula is rather simple. Reading level is based on two factors—the length of sentences and the length of words. Though there are several different scales or models of the formula to determine reading level, each eventually comes back to some kind of an interpretation of these two factors. Thus, let us pick a common one for an illustration: The Frye Readability Chart. In using Frye, you simply count 100 words; you then count the number of syllables in that 100 words for one of the variables. Then you count the number of sentences for the other. You plot these two variables on the Frye chart and find the reading level of that piece of material broken down in grade level and month. In other words, a book that reads at 5.2 reads at fifth-grade level, second month. Isn't that simple?

Of course, in order to get a good idea you need to check the reading level at several different places throughout the book. Sometimes things like a cluster of proper nouns in a passage will alter the reading level a bit, but the multiple checking usually yields at least an educated guess of the reading level of a specific piece of material.

Usually, the authors of school textbooks recognize reading levels and write with that in mind. For example, a good fifth-grade book will begin at something like the 4.9 level and will end somewhere in the middle of sixth-grade level.

Incidentally, if you would like to become an expert on determining reading level yourself, go down to your local library (if your public library doesn't have the book, the library at the nearest community college will have), find the Frye book in the section on reading instruction, make yourself a copy of the chart, and presto, you are in business.

How can students progress through school and not be able to read?

They learn to hide. No, that's the wrong word. They learn to cope. I know the purpose for that question. "How do all these functional illiterates get through our school system and graduate?" is what you are really asking, and I think it is a question that needs to be asked. Are the schools doing everything they can possibly do to make sure every student has every opportunity to develop his God-given talent, whatever it may be, to the fullest? We need to ask ourselves that question every day in hard terms. And we don't ever want to take no, or even maybe, for an answer.

But back to the original question. Though reading is an important activity in our schools, it is quite possible for a student to pass through the system and not master the skill too well. This is true now, and I suspect it has been true for years in this country. I personally know people in their fifties and sixties who completed several years of school and never learned to read.

Principals rarely find quiet moments during the day, and when they do, they cherish them. One rather dependable spot comes during the lull that occurs about ten minutes after the morning bell. The typical principal has been up since 5 A.M. and has been in school since 6 A.M. He has dared to call in unknown quantities from the substitute teacher list. He has met the buses and refereed all the fights that occurred there. And he has heard about ninety entertaining and incredulous reasons why people didn't come to school yesterday. But now, with classes started, the halls empty, and all the little urchins at work on academic matters, the nimble principal might steal a few moments of quiet, at least on some days.

As a principal, I had reached this point one day; and feeling confident that I had earned my lull, I escaped into the seclusion of my office, slammed the door, and found Chuck sitting behind it.

Though Chuck and I were not necessarily friends, we at least knew each other. In other words, we had had frequent discussions in the seclusion of my office during the course of the school year. Chuck was not necessarily defiant, but he was active; and his activity was frequently misunderstood—by his teachers, by his peers, and especially by me.

The look on Chuck's face told me that this was not to be a pleasant encounter. More depressed about losing my lull than having a miscreant in my office, I demanded, "Chuck, what has happened now?"

"I don't want to talk about it," he responded without changing the sullen expression on his face.

"Well, what do you want to talk about? You aren't going to sit here in my office and waste my lull and not talk about something."

He grinned a huge grin and said, "I want to talk about lemmings." And we did.

That is the first time in my life I had ever heard about the lemmings. For a while, I thought he was making it up, but he convinced me that he wasn't. His interest had been stirred when he had seen something on television. (Chuck watched a lot of television. In fact, I think he stayed up every night to catch Johnny Carson, and that is one of the reasons he had trouble in school.) But after seeing the television program, he had gone to the library and found six books on lemmings which he had read and digested. He knew that topic.

To this day, my life is richer because of our discussion about lemmings. I have really profited from his knowledge. I fill many empty spaces with thoughts about lemmings.

(If you don't know about the lemmings, go to the library and find out. You are really missing some delightful news about God's creation.)

CHAPTER SEVEN
Boards and Policies

Schools are the products of common people taking positive action. This is the theme of this chapter. Perhaps it is a little naive and perhaps even a bit too enthusiastic, but one of the basic American principles is that the local schools are just that—local schools, operated and controlled by local people for the education of and service to local communities

If the schools don't work that way, then we must assume that citizens somewhere are letting down on their duties. So this chapter has two functions. It is meant to inform but it is also meant to persuade. As you learn more about how the system works, you should become even more excited in seeing how the system can work for you and your children. As a veteran educator, I am convinced that the more people know about and understand their school systems, including school politics and management, the better the systems will work and the better education it will provide.

To achieve this, you need to consider becoming acquainted with the system in several areas.

1. You need to know something of the history of the system. How did things get to be the way they are. What are the laws and regulations which control decision-making policies; and how did those laws come into being.

2. You need to know who is responsible for decisions which are made. Some decisions are made at the local level either by administrators or school boards; other decisions are made at the state level; still others are made at the federal level. You need to know where the decision originated.

3. You need to know the officials in charge. It is a start to know something of the local administrators and school board members, but

that is just a start. You also need to know the educational officers at both the state and national levels.

4. You need to know how your fellow citizens feel about policies and practices. The public schools must represent the best interest of the public. If you think something needs to be investigated or even changed, it helps to make sure you represent a group instead of a majority of one.

5. You need to know how much it costs. Let's start with a simple test. How much did it cost your local school district to provide educational services for your child last year? I am not going to chastise you for not knowing the answer, but I do want to point out where you need to start your study.

How much uniformity is there in what students study in different schools and even in different states?

Since uniformity is a relative term, measuring uniformity is impossible. Some would say that school is school and basically the same regardless of where you are. Others would say that school is an entirely unique experience, not only from building to building but from classroom to classroom.

Different districts and different states have different requirements. For example, states differ on what they require for high school graduation, and since that is something of the ultimate standard which dictates all policies leading up to it, the whole program would differ. Some states require four years of P.E. and some require very little. Some states require foreign language and some don't. Some districts may have requirements that other districts don't, so the class offerings do vary some.

In states where students take statewide examinations, these exams dictate what and how students are taught. Teachers will probably protest the statement, but it is true. If a teacher knows that the students are going to take an exam, that teacher is going to base at least some of his instruction on what is on those tests.

Trends in instruction tend to be rather regional and provide some variety in what and how students are taught. For example, in the Midwest, a California educator named Madelyn Hunter has had a tremendous and widespread impact on instructional methods through the whole decade of the 1980s. In some areas, she is the ultimate quotable source. When teachers get together to discuss what they are doing, or what they should be doing, someone can put a closure on a discussion by simply quoting Madelyn Hunter. Yet, in some areas of the country, the teachers haven't even heard of her. This does provide for some variety.

The purpose of education produces some uniformity. Regardless of where you are, school is still about learning to read and write and compute. The techniques to get there may vary a bit, but purpose alone gives a common direction to the task.

Textbooks also provide uniformity. Regardless of what some teachers say and what some teachers do, we are still rather heavily textbook dependent in this country. A student using a specific history book in California is going to get about the same history course as the student using that same book in New Jersey.

Depending on your perspective, there is diversity and uniformity. Some educational thinkers are telling us that the nation is too small and the population too mobile to have too much diversity. They would suggest national policies and standards to bring uniformity to the curriculum, requirements, school year structure, text materials, and even instructional techniques. On the other hand, some thinkers are telling us that the unique strength of American education is the local school which provides for the educational needs of the students in that specific community. Thus, they protest any suggestions for more uniformity.

It is an interesting point for debate.

Shouldn't parents be given some choice in how their children are educated?

Well, of course they should. That is one of the trends in American education which excites me. In the last twenty years we have developed many avenues for parents to have more choices and more say in how their own children are educated. Just for starters, let's look at some of those ways that you have to exercise choice.

1. Types of schools—Parents can choose to send their children to public schools, or to private Christian schools, or to private non-Christian schools. Or they can even choose to keep their children at home and teach the children themselves. Praise God for the choice of different kinds of schools. This isn't a freedom in all the countries of the world.

Of course, the problem with exercising this choice is how to finance it. All parents must support the public schools; so when they choose to put their children in private schools, they wind up paying for two school systems. Many are protesting that this isn't fair. Some educators, some parents, and even some political figures have proposed measures to alleviate the double taxation burden on parents. For example, some have proposed a voucher system where parents would receive an educational voucher which they could spend at any school of their choice, provided that school met the required standards.

2. Choices of schools within one public district—In the past, students living in one school district have usually been assigned to a specific school building based on the place of residence. In recent years, some districts around the country have begun to relax these assignments a bit and give the parents their choice of school buildings within the district. This is a particularly valuable trend in districts where some buildings are attempting to conduct experimental programs. For example, some students could profit from a highly individualized approach to instruction while others need a more teacher-directed approach. If a district has one school with an individualized program, that program has a greater chance of succeeding if parents are given some choices about being assigned to that school. As we have said before, a school has a much better chance of being effective when the students really want to be there.

3. Parent advisory programs—This is becoming common in many districts. If your district hasn't started such a program, call your school board members and recommend it. Some districts have a parent advisory committee for every school in the district, and in some places these committees have been invaluable. They have helped schools resolve such difficulties as transportation and parking problems, textbook selection, new programs (particularly in some of the more sensitive areas such as sex education and AIDS education), attendance policies, etc.

Frequently, responsible parents are in a good position to offer valuable suggestions. For one thing, they are in a position to listen to the students, and since they are not in schools every day, they do have the opportunity of being objective.

As I said earlier, I am encouraged by the recent trends to give parents more choices and more responsibility in determining how their children will be educated. We aren't perfect yet, but we do seem to be moving in the right direction.

Of course, there is one problem with this. If parents are to have more choices and more input, they need to know something about schools. Just making significant educational decisions based on what happened to you when you were a student or based on what you read in some newspaper or based on what your neighbor says is not good enough. If parents are to have some choice in how their children are educated, they need to know what education is about and some of the ways to accomplish it. In other words, they have to become students of the educational system.

How do school board members get their jobs?

In some isolated districts (such as some big city districts) the boards are appointed, but in most school districts throughout the nation, individual members of the boards are elected by the people at large. In those districts, anyone who is an eligible voter may file for the school board and conduct a campaign. If he or she is elected, he then serves on the board for a number of years (the number of years differs from district to district and state to state.) Usually school board members are not paid for some of the hardest, most thankless work any person has ever done.

Some people who run for school board have political ambitions and see the school board as one way to get involved in the process of government. They see the school board as the way to get established. On the other hand, a vast majority of people on school boards are people like me or you who have an interest in the education of young people and volunteer their time selflessly.

Regardless of how much we gripe or complain or criticize, the local school board still represents one of the things right about this country and about American education. If you don't like what is going on or if you do like what is happening, you have a place to express your feeling. If you want a really stronger voice in the process, you can file an application and try to convince your peers that you can make a contribution.

The local school board represents the principles of American democracy as well as any institution in this country.

Our local newspaper published some statistics on the school's A.D.A. What is that and why is it important?

A.D.A. stands for Average Daily Attendance which is the actual count of how many students are in school on a given day. For most educators and bureaucrats, this is the figure which is the true measure of the size of a school rather than A.D.M. or Average Daily Membership, the number of students on the roll on a specific day.

For example, if a school is receiving part of its funds from the state government, those funds are almost always allocated on A.D.A. rather than A.D.M. Thus, it is important for a school to have as many students in attendance every day as it can possibly get.

I am pleased to hear that your local newspaper has published those figures and brought attention to that aspect of schools. In recent years, A.D.A. has become at least one test to measure the quality of the educational program. The assumption is that the higher the percentage the A.D.A. the more attractive the school climate and curriculum. Anything above 90 percent is considered good enough to brag about. In other words, if 90 percent of the students enrolled in a school are in attendance every day, there is a good indication that something positive is happening at that school. Students enjoy coming or feel that the program is worthwhile, so they get up and come even when they have possible alternatives. Have you ever noticed how having something enjoyable to attend works wonders on a small headache?

I am also happy that parents in your community are also becoming aware of the importance of the statistic. Parents need to know that A.D.A. is the figure which determines the amount of funds from the state. In other words, if your school is receiving state funds based on A.D.A. any student absence actually costs the district money. You need to consider that the next time you think of keeping your child out of school for a day to go on a family outing or help with the chores.

In many states, the A.D.A. figure is based on half days, so attendance is counted twice each day, once before noon and once after. That may explain why some administrators dismiss school on the day of the giant blizzard right after the afternoon bell has rung. If students are counted after lunch, they are in attendance for the whole day.

Is corporal punishment now illegal in schools?

According to the most recent court decisions, there is no federal law prohibiting the use of corporal punishment in schools. Some states have statutes seriously limiting and even prohibiting the use, and many school districts across the nation have district policies banning corporal punishment. If you have a question about your own local district, you really should call the school superintendent's office and ask. Your school district probably has a printed policy outlining the place of corporal punishment, and someone will be happy to read you the policy or even send you a copy. That way you will know for sure.

As you know, the use of corporal punishment is a highly controversial issue right now, much like the issue of capital punishment in society in general. Most would agree that the only justifiable reason for the use of corporal punishment is as a deterrent, and there is a big argument about how effective it is as a deterrent. Probably some of us know by personal experience how effective a little bout with corporal punishment could be in eliminating a certain kind of behavior from our repertoire. However, it doesn't work that way with everybody. So the question is whether there are more effective ways of dealing with misbehavior. If so, what are those ways?

The other question is when does corporal punishment cease being punishment and become abuse. Some school districts, in response to parental fears about abuse, have established a policy that teachers should never touch a child for any reason. I can see their rationale, yet the experts tell us that casual touching is one of the most effective means of communication. I know of teachers who are seriously limited in their effectiveness as teachers because of their fear of touching children. Obviously, this question does not have an easy answer.

As a parent, I may be like the mother who brought her child to school the first day and explained to the teacher, "Johnny is such a sensitive little boy. If he gets out of line, just slap the kid next to him and I am sure Johnny will shape up for you."

Who actually decides what goes on in our schools?

The list of possible suspects could be endless and the real culprit may be close at hand. Let's first look at the possibilities.

1. Federal judges—In recent years federal judges have been rather conspicuous in their efforts to influence day-by-day educational opera-

tions. They have ruled in such matters as who goes to what schools in the name of desegregation; of teaching Creation or not teaching Creation; of giving students some choice in what they read; of what can be printed in school newspapers; and how students may or may not dress.

2. State legislators—These people make laws which cover such things as required uniform curriculum, textbooks, length of school days and years, and qualifications of teachers.

3. Local school boards—Theoretically, the local school board is supposed to have the biggest say in policy formation by dealing with such things as the school budget, class size, curriculum matters, etc.

4. Parent groups and special committees—In many districts, the parent committees or curriculum committees have some voice in designing academic programs and activities.

5. Textbook publishers—If a teacher uses a textbook, that textbook publisher has a great deal to say about what the students actually learn in class, when they learn, the sequence of learning, and the depth of study.

6. Individual classroom teachers—From most students' standpoint, their only contact with school and school policies is the classroom teacher, so that teacher represents almost a sole authority of what goes on in school. Since there is no other empire on earth quite as self-contained as a teacher in a classroom with the door closed, that teacher becomes a significant factor in deciding what goes on in school.

If we want to keep the system strong or even improve it, maybe we ought to focus our efforts there.

The number of students has decreased while taxes have increased. Why?

There are simple answers and complex answers to that question. If you look at those answers from a taxpayer's point of view, you might say there are good answers and bad ones.

The most obvious answer is that expenses have increased. As you know, utilities are increasing every year. The schools are particularly hard hit, and there is even an interesting paradox. It would sound logical for me to say that it takes just as much heat in a half-full building as a full one, but actually, the full building may need even less heat because bodies help provide some of the warmth.

With recent court decisions, liability insurance has become a major expense rather than just another expense. Paper, gasoline, textbooks, and all sorts of supplies have undergone major price increases.

But the big increase has been in the area of salaries. Not too many years ago, school budget experts would tell us that a district would need to spend 50 percent of its budget on teacher salaries. Now, that figure is closer to 80 percent. (And I am still not convinced that teachers are paid as much as they deserve.)

In the meantime, the money provided by the federal government to local schools has diminished, leaving the local property owners to dig even deeper to finance schools. As the population grows older, more and more we are asking people who no longer have children in schools to finance the educational system. It is all very complex.

We would also probably argue that schools haven't always been wise in long-range planning. This is obvious when we see huge school buildings complete with gyms and parking lots and playing fields sitting empty and unused. As many districts have discovered, there isn't too much market for used school plants.

But long-range planning for schools is a difficult, if not impossible, proposition. We just don't know how many students we are going to have in a specific district in ten years. Based on what we see, we make guesses; but we miss about as often as the weatherman does in his predictions. As he can tell you, circumstances change.

For example, a few years ago the population experts looking at the birthrate of the women in their twenties decided that there could be a rather rapid decrease in school population. Those women just weren't having as many children as women that age once had. But those women fooled us. They began having children much later than the last generation did. Some women have begun to start their families in their mid-thirties and go on to have three or four children in school. The experts simply hadn't counted on that.

Not too many years ago, a school district in our area watched a large section of the district open to housing development. Not wanting to be caught off guard, the district went in and built a new building right in the middle of all the development. But the homes which were built were more expensive than the average home in the area and were purchased by people who had already reared their families. Now that new building operates about half full.

Obviously, we haven't always made good decisions, but planning is difficult. I would still maintain, that dollar for dollar, the taxpayer is getting as much from his money spent on schools as any other government function. As they say in Pennsylvania, "It's cheaper to keep a young man at Penn State than at the state pen."

Our high school just went through something called a North Central evaluation. What is that?

In an attempt to do a better job of educating students and in an attempt to achieve a broader level of credibility, many schools around the nation have chosen to participate in a voluntary program of accreditation and evaluation. To help schools in this effort, there are six of these nongovernment voluntary regional accrediting agencies in the United States. The North Central Agency which you mentioned is the one which covers a wide swath right out of the heart of the United States from Canada to Mexico.

These regional accrediting agencies accredit colleges and universities, high schools, junior high schools and, in recent years, even elementary schools. To be accredited by the voluntary regional agency is to say that this particular school meets certain criteria of performance such as library requirements, teacher education and assignment requirements, student expectations requirements, curriculum requirements, etc. This gives the school and its graduates a broader degree of acceptance and accreditability.

Once a school meets the standards and is accredited by the North Central Agency, it must continue to maintain those standards. To insure this, each school goes through an evaluation process each seven years. The first requirement of that evaluation is that the school go through an extensive self-study which requires teachers, administrators, parents, and students to come together in committees to discuss what the school is doing and what changes it ought to make.

After the school completes the self-study, it then calls in a team of visitors, consisting of administrators, teachers, and educators, to come to the school for a few days, basically, to check to see if the self-study is accurate and to make further reports about the programs and progress of the school.

Though these evaluations procedures require a lot of work, I have always felt that work was worthwhile because it focused on what was happening in a specific building rather than trying to evaluate education on some grand scale.

Do school board members get any kind of special training?

The simple answer is, not really. Though there are a few exceptions, particularly in some major cities, for the most part across the nation, school board members are people just like you and me—housewives, pastors, farmers, laborers, merchants, businessmen—who have a special interest in education, young people, and serving the community.

Once a person gets elected to a local school board, there are often opportunities to learn something about the nature of the job through workshops, training sessions, and journals and publications. Many do take advantage of these opportunities, yet some don't. Nevertheless, I would think that anyone who has ever served on a school board got a rather good education during the process.

On a deeper level, this question has provoked much discussion recently. With the complexities of tax structures, court decisions, and labor negotiations, school board work can be exacting, demanding, tedious, and highly professional in nature. In many districts we are asking a great deal of private citizens with other full-time jobs to choose to prepare themselves adequately for all the difficult decisions and maneuvering that boards are sometimes required to do. The question that comes is whether we should require some kind of formal training for prospective school board members.

Where do public schools get their money?

The obvious answer to that question is simple. Schools get their money from taxes. But that system of taxation is rather interesting and a bit complex.

Across the nation, about 50 percent of the funds for public schools come from the taxes of local school districts. Usually, these taxes come from property assessments. (Sometimes called *ad valorem* taxes.) In other words, property owners pay the bulk of the school funds.

Across the nation somewhere between 35 and 40 percent of the funds for public school come from the states. States distribute these funds to local districts in a variety of programs. Most states have some kind of equalization program where the poorer districts get help from the state for day-by-day budget expenses. States also help with such things as transportation expenses and textbook costs.

Across the nation, about 10 to 12 percent of the funds for public schools come from the federal government through such programs as hot lunch programs, special programs to help special segments of the society such as the students from poorer families or students with handicaps and learning difficulties, and sometimes special programs due to national emergencies. For example, in the early 1960s following Russia's launch of Sputnik, the federal government, through a program called the National Defense Education Act, provided funds to build and equip labs, to give special training to teachers, and to help selected college students with college expenses.

In recent years, the federal government has provided fewer funds directly to schools, which has caused the local districts to pick up the slack by increasing taxes and tax rates at the local level. That is one of the reasons why there have been so many tax levy or bond levy referenda across the nation during the last few years.

The idea of providing an education for everyone without a direct cost to the student is something of an American notion, far more popular here than in other parts of the world. The idea of taxing local property to raise the funds to provide this educational opportunity goes all the way back to the days right after the federal Constitution was ratified. Various states tried various plans to finance the ambitious educational expectations of the new republic. These included such things as lotteries and even endowments. But in a few years these all failed for one reason or another, and states turned to the idea of real estate taxes.

In 1874, the Supreme Court ruled in the Kalamazoo case that local districts could even tax local property to finance high schools.

Where does the idea of the local school district come from?

In this country, the idea of local school districts goes all the way back to seventeenth-century Massachusetts. As you recall from your American history days, the people first settled at Plymouth in 1620. In 1635 those same people, hearty and tough with a thirst for knowing, started Boston Latin Grammar School. In 1636, they started Harvard College. With this same determination, in 1647, they passed one of the first pieces of school legislation in this country. This act, popularly called "The Ould Deluder Satan Act" warned of the spiritual dangers of an illiterate and uneducated populace and specified that when any community grew to at least 50 households, that community would employ a teacher to provide a basic education for the children of that community. Further, if the community grew to 100 households, it had to provide a grammar school for even higher education.

This was the beginning of the idea of local school districts. By the time the national Constitution was written in the 1780s, almost all of the New England states had a strong commitment to the practice of establishing and maintaining local school districts. During the days of the writing of the Constitution, there was some discussion about the need for a national school system to provide the education necessary to make this new republic work, but this discussion produced no significant consequences, and the American Constitution makes no mention of the establishment or control of schools, leaving it rather in the hands of the states.

Can a private citizen ever have any say in the way schools are run?

I am just naive and simple enough to believe that private citizens have almost all the say in the way schools are run. In spite of all the talk about federal court decisions, in spite of all the talk about state legislation, in spite of all the talk about the power of educators and administrators, I still believe in the power of the local school board, and in most places that board is composed of private citizens.

Except for perhaps some isolated places in large cities, there is no need for the private citizen to ever feel powerless about the way things are going in his school. In other words, if you don't like it, do something about it. If you don't want to run for the school board, at least you can go to the board meetings. Except in very special cases when they are talking about matters of personnel, all board proceedings are open to the public. And don't be deceived. School board members make special note of who comes to those meetings.

If you don't like the way things are going, volunteer for parent committee work. Get involved in the P.T.A. Take some time to get acquainted with some teachers and develop friendships with them.

If the issue is larger than the local school, write letters to your congressman. Make your thoughts known.

By history and intent, the public schools are meant to serve local communities and to be run by the private citizens of those local communities. If you feel that your school is not being responsive to the needs of the community, perhaps it is time for you to go to work.

What ever happened to the "schools without walls" idea?

That was another one of those ideas of the 1960s which was going to get schools and students and teachers ready for the twenty-first century.

Called the "schools without walls," or open schools, the theory was attached to architectural design. We could put all the students in one giant room with individual class pockets located around the periphery and a large learning center in the middle. Architecturally, the idea had some merit. Without going to the expense of building inside walls, a school district could save as much as 40 percent on new construction costs at a time when many districts were needing to build new buildings to accommodate the postwar baby boomers. Some educators and boards were sold on the idea for that reason alone.

The educational theory was more complex and difficult to implement. The theory proposed that the learning center which was more of an activity center rather than a library would become the center or the hub of learning. The students would go into their individual pods for some simple instruction; then they would move to the learning center for activities, applications, and reinforcement drill. It was a great plan, and in some places it worked well. Unfortunately, there were some unexpected glitches.

For one thing, the theory had a built-in assumption that all students would be highly motivated and would quietly throw themselves into those learning center activities. This didn't always happen. The loud ones were loud and the quiet ones were distracted.

The theory assumed that the teachers would not spend hours instructing large groups of students, but would talk briefly and softly and send everyone off to some individual activity. This didn't happen either. The teachers still talked to entire classes; and as the noise level in the building increased, they increased their volume as well, until everyone was shouting or sounded as if they were shouting.

The theory also assumed that those people in the learning center would come equipped with roller skates and endless energy. This didn't happen either.

The theory also assumed that all of us involved in the process of education—teachers, students, and parents—could make adjustments to a new theory. This didn't happen either.

Because of this, the "schools without walls" idea has about disappeared. Most of those buildings built in that era are now equipped with cardboard interior walls which provide some isolation for the individual teachers and classes. Some schools have even gone so far as to paint those cardboard walls to make the place look something like a traditional school. Some haven't painted the walls yet, leaving everything a brown cardboard which rather reminds me of being inside a refrigerator shipping crate.

On the other hand, I do know of one school which is still using the schools without walls concept. The classrooms are still around the outside with free opening into a well-equipped, pleasant resource center. I really like the school. The students are happy, and they seem to be learning a great deal, as much as any students I see. Yet, the building is staffed with some of the finest teachers I have met and one of the finest principals I have seen.

This leads me back to another observation. The quality of education is something more than the shape of a building.

I don't agree with the requirement for so much P.E. for students. How do I protest?

I am going to begin by assuming that the P.E. requirement which you are protesting is a state requirement rather than a requirement of the local school district. Most curriculum requirements do come from the state. Thus, you must direct your protest to the state.

To start, you will want to identify the branch of state government which decides curriculum for the schools. This may be the state department of education or, perhaps, even the state legislature.

Next, you will want to develop the reasons for your protest in clear, concise, and provable terms. Opinions aren't worth much, neither are accusations and strong language. Develop a sound and reasonable argument.

Now, I would suggest that you try to find other people who agree with you. You must realize that the P.E. requirement is a political maneuver by someone. Someone got it put into the curriculum in the first place by playing political games according to the rules of politics. If you are to lodge an effective protest, you must play the same political games. In politics, numbers talk; so solicit as much support as you can. If you write a letter and sign it yourself, you will probably get a polite, but formal, answer as to why your suggestion is unworkable. But if you write a letter and get 400 people to sign it, you will get more response than a simple, polite note.

There are two principles here which you must remember if you wish to influence school decisions. (1) Know who made the decision so that you can know where to launch the protest. (2) Remember that many decisions affecting schools and the education of children are political decisions made by cigar-chomping wheelers and dealers through the fine art of political compromise and greasing the squeaky wheel. If you propose to change one of those decisions, you will need the political clout of numbers on your side.

Who decides what a student must have for graduation from high school?

Usually, some branch of the state government such as the state board of education or the state superintendent of schools or state law passed by legislators specifies the minimum requirements for graduation from a state accredited high school. In some places, local school districts may add to this list with additional requirements.

These are two sources of official graduation requirements. Sometimes there are some unofficial ones as well. For example, if the officials of a state university place the requirements for admission into the university higher than the official requirements, many schools will adopt those added requirements for all students as a safe measure to guarantee university admission and creditability of a high school diploma.

There are those who would propose that the process of establishing graduation requirements and, consequently, high school curriculum is not as systematic and thoughtful as it could be. Often the list of requirements has grown through a number of years, and the people now involved in the government agencies responsible for the process weren't around to hear the rationale. Sometimes they even forget what is already required. Usually, if there is any change in graduation requirements, it is adding to. Rarely does a state drop a requirement. We can just go on with this trend so long until the students run out of time and nobody graduates.

The solution to this would be to throw out all requirements and start again from scratch to determine what does constitute a good high school education. But the problem with this proposal is how to implement a change in structure of an ongoing program. During the transition, students would all be working on a different set of requirements.

Who decides who can ride a bus and who can't?

Usually a state law controls this. Most states have what is called the mile-and-a-half law which specifies that any student who lives farther than one and one half miles from his school building can receive free transportation to school. Those living within a mile and a half of the building must get to school the best way they know how.

To back up the law, the state officials require that the school supply statistics naming those students who can ride the bus. The state then reimburses the local district for at least some of the expense of transporting those students.

If a local school district has extra funds, it may then choose to bus the others as well; but this cost will have to be carried by the local district.

If you live within that mile-and-a-half area and feel that you are being cheated out of your right to transportation, there is little need to talk to the local school officials. Their hands are tied by state law. Rather, write directly to your state congressman.

It is important to know which government agency covers which aspects of school operations.

Whatever happened to the modular scheduling idea that was so popular in high schools a few years ago?

Aha, the old modular scheduling that rode into our schools to shake us out of doldrums and propel us into the twenty-first century. I remember it now. We divided the school day into fifteen-minute segments; then we shuffled those segments into stacks so that students had a little longer stack in "important" courses such as science and a little shorter stack in those other things such as art and/or P.E.

That modular scheduling experiment was one of the bolder innovations during that era of the '60s and '70s when we were going to reform education by messing around with the school day. Does anyone still remember the floating period schedule where we lengthened all periods to seventy minutes and made it through the day on time by omitting a different "floating" period every day? Or maybe someone still remembers the double-period maneuver where we had two-hour periods and students took only three courses a day for double periods for one semester, then took a whole new set of courses for double periods the next semester.

I am not trying to be cynical. Those were all valid experiments, and

165

we probably needed to go through that era to remind ourselves of what changes need to be made and what changes aren't necessary. Obviously, we learned something from all the experimentation. Maybe we learned that teachers and parents and even students are more traditional when it comes to schools and learning than we might want to believe. If it was good enough for Calvin Coolidge, it is probably good enough for us. Or maybe we learned that something is more vital to quality education than how we shuffle the day around. So the old traditional, six or seven fifty-five minute periods are now the model for the future. Is that progress? I think so.

Why does our daughter have to have P.E. the first hour of the day? She is sweaty for the rest of her classes.

Obviously, your daughter has P.E. the first hour of the day because someone has to have it then. For most of the school day in most of the schools both the facilities and schedules are full and students often have classes and special events, such as meals, at unusual times.

It is simply unfortunate that any student has to have P.E. the first hour of the day. But I do appreciate your asking the question. At least, your daughter's plight has your attention. I am pleased that you are aware of part of the hassle of her day. It isn't much fun to get up in the morning to hurry off to a P.E. class where you don't have time to primp properly when it's over.

This is just one more of the frustrations which students face and live with. I admire them for how well they make it through.

Our son signed a petition asking for a pop machine in the cafeteria. The principal said that it was against the law. Whose law?

Believe it or not, it might be against the federal law. I know that this sounds like a case of a principal not wanting to take action, so he offers some lame excuse and blames it on someone else, but he is probably telling the truth.

The hot lunch programs in most schools are supplemented in funds from the United States Department of Agriculture. To qualify for these funds, the school must provide facilities, equipment, and a menu that meets federal guidelines. Though these guidelines are federal, the interpretation of those guidelines vary from place to place. In some places, junk-food vending machines can't be placed in the cafeteria.

That is a rather simple answer to your question, but it does represent a larger idea. If you would like to see some changes in a school practice or procedure or policy, it sure helps to know why the school is doing it that way and what government agency has made the policy. Some school policies are established by local boards. Some policies are established by state guidelines, and some school policies are established by the federal government.

CHAPTER EIGHT
Textbooks

As the typical American, I had always thought that textbooks constituted the basic core of any education. But a couple of years ago, I had the privilege of traveling to Kenya where I was able to visit several schools in that country. My first shock came when I discovered that many students in that country don't regularly have textbooks, and some go through their entire school careers without ever seeing a book.

About the time I had learned to live with that shock, I encountered the second wave; and this one still has me in a state of imbalance. Not only did those students not have an abundance of textbooks, but some of them were very bright people.

Based on that observation, I have concluded that we Americans are a bit spoiled. Because of the abundance of books, we have been able to put the textbook at the center of the educational experience. The school officials—administrators and teachers—spend a major portion of their time selecting textbooks, cataloging textbooks, distributing textbooks, and maintaining textbooks.

Parents, particularly those who are interested in what their children learn in schools, spend a major portion of their interest on analyzing textbooks, worrying about textbooks, and helping the school make decisions about textbooks.

As this chapter will point out, this interest and dedication to the textbook is something of an unusual feature of the American education system. Because they are such a significant part of the whole educational experience, they deserve our understanding and study. However, as we spend our time and concern with textbooks, let's spend some time wondering why textbooks really merit that much of our attention.

Let's take a test. How many of you can remember your eighth-grade math class? That's good. I see those hands. It's wonderful that you have those memories of your school years. How many of you remember your eighth-grade math teacher? Of course you do. If you remember the class, you will in all probability remember the teacher.

Now for the hard part. How many of you remember the textbook you used in eighth-grade math class? That's what I thought. We do remember classes, where we sat, our colleagues, some of the assignments and especially the teachers, but we rarely remember our textbooks when the class is over.

Usually, I don't have any trouble avoiding reading messages printed on T-shirts. Some may contain some worthwhile homespun philosophy, but most are rather uncreative and a bit arrogant.

The other day I spotted this young man of about twelve years of age who was at the time sliding joyously down the banister of one of the more prestigious and reserved museums in our city. I don't know whether it was the totally unrestrained act of misbehavior or the pleasant serenity in his face, but something attracted me to this ball of energy, and I felt compelled to get close enough to read the message he wore on his T-shirt.

I was not disappointed. The message declared in bold letters:
SCHOOL WILL NEVER CORRUPT ME
I DON'T LET THEM TEACH ME ANYTHING

Can parents have any say in what textbooks the schools use?

Yes, yes, and a million times, yes. If you are interested in what textbooks schools use, there are so many ways to get involved that you have no excuse for not making your voice heard. The first requirement is that you need to do your homework. Don't go by hearsay or reports that you have read. Don't even depend on your own child for accurate information. I am not accusing your child of not telling the truth, but sometimes the people who have to study a book don't like any book.

Begin by reading your own children's books. If you have problems—if you feel they are inadequate, provide wrong information or provide wrong inferences—document your problems with page numbers and examples. If you want to compare and contrast the books your school is using with others available, go down to the local school and see if they have some review copies you can borrow. Be thorough. In fact, this is the first rule. Know what you are talking about.

Now that you are armed with all that information, choose your level and get involved. You can get involved at the local level. Most school districts appoint a committee to study what books are available and to make a decision about which to use. If your district uses parents on this committee, volunteer. If not, suggest to the board that they do. Either way, the committee meeting should be open. If you can't be a part of the voting committee, you can at least attend the meeting and make sure they hear the value of your research.

Some states have a statewide textbook selection committee which makes decisions about which three or four different books will be available for students in that state. Again, these meetings are open to the public. Invite yourself and show up. If you have anything to add to the proceedings, check with someone to find the process for getting on the program.

You can also write directly to the publishers. Tell them what you as a parent like and don't like. I think you may be surprised at the response. Publishers are in the business to sell books. They are interested in publishing what people want to buy. If they don't hear from you, they have no idea how you feel about it.

Again, I repeat myself. Yes! You can make a difference in what books your school uses.

How often are textbooks rewritten, updated, and changed?

With as many publishers as there are in the business, somebody is coming out with a new textbook every few weeks. Since the competition is heavy, each publisher is obviously looking for the newest material or the newest method or even the newest gimmick to attract teachers and other textbook publishers. Usually a particular publishing company will issue a new edition of a book about every five years.

The more important question then is how often does a particular school change a textbook in a particular subject area? That varies depending on how much money the school has, the whims of the faculty, the nature of the material (science gets outdated quicker than literature), and the emphasis the school has on a particular area.

I visit some schools which use history books more than twenty years old and other schools which order new books every five years. Some schools are still using literature anthologies first released in 1962. In fact, some teachers in some schools have a more recent set of anthologies on the shelf but prefer the older edition.

One of the big problems school administrators face is what to do with old textbooks after they have been taken out of use. Most books get outdated before they wear out; thus the local administrator has to think of some way to discard those books discretely lest the local taxpayers see perfectly good books not in use and ascertain a case of waste.

Why do publishers include what they do in textbooks?

I'm not smart enough to understand motives, but I am going to venture a guess. I often hear people talk of policies and philosophies which direct textbook writing, and sometimes one would even get the idea that those publishers have some kind of educational objective in mind as they sort through material, hire consultants, field-test model copies, and canvass the nation. Somehow as they coordinate their research with their educational objectives, they make purposeful decisions about what material they include, what they leave out, the degree of difficulty, etc.

All this sounds nice, and I would really like to believe some of it. But deep down inside, I suspect that textbook publishers are almost overwhelmingly committed to one objective over all the others. They want to make money. They want to sell books. So I have a notion that the cardinal test of what does or does not go into a textbook is a simple question, "What'll sell?"

But there are some specific guidelines to even that kind of thinking. The two states in the nation with the largest number of students are California and Texas, so if a publisher really wants to rake in the big bucks and show some dividends they have to sell books in those two states.

In California, the present state superintendent of schools is an astute evaluator and sometime critic of textbooks. Since he is outspoken and honest, the publishers can quickly learn his opinion. However, in Texas, a state committee is appointed to review the possible texts and specific ones which can be bought in Texas schools with state funds. You can bet that every textbook company has a representative at all those meetings.

So the question which directs the choice of text material is not an open-ended "What'll sell?" but a little more specific "Will they buy it in Texas and California?" That is probably the most significant factor dictating what gets into textbooks.

I would like to see what textbooks our school is considering before it orders. Can I do that?

Of course you can. Just call the school principal and tell him what you want to do and why. Be nice. Don't start an argument. Just state your purpose. Parents have every right to get involved in the selection of textbooks. In fact, school districts throughout the nation put parents on the textbook selection committee so that all parents are represented.

If the principal doesn't seem to be too keen on the idea of your seeing the books, contact the superintendent and perhaps even members of the school board. As a taxpayer and as a parent, you have a right to see the books the school selects.

I would recommend that you do some homework before you actually go to the school to examine the books. Make a list of issues you are looking for. Develop some method for evaluating material. Make a list of questions you may want to ask. Remember that these school people are busy. Respect their time by doing your homework first.

If you are not sure you know what you are looking for, let me recommend that you consult the work of Mr. and Mrs. Mel Gabler of Texas. These people provide for parents everywhere a model of the correct way for parents to get involved in the process of the selection of school textbooks. Even if you don't agree with everything they do, they still provide a solid model for how to use the process.

As a final note, I just want to remind you that schools must select textbooks for a wide variety of students coming from a wide variety of backgrounds and interests with a wide variety of educational needs. Frequently a textbook is chosen not necessarily on its merit, but because it is the least offensive to the greatest number of people.

Who pays for the textbooks?

That varies from state to state and district to district. Most states have some kind of funds to purchase or at least supplement the purchase of new textbooks. The local school districts then either have to stay within the budget allowed within the state or pay for the difference themselves.

In some states, some districts pass some of the cost of the textbooks on to the students. For example, a school may charge each student a flat fee for textbook use. Since the book will be used by five or six different students over a period of years, no student has to buy the whole book.

Who writes the textbooks?

There seem to be three dominant sources of authors for textbooks and other text material. First, some books are written by college professors who are considered scholars in the field. Some are written by public school classroom teachers themselves. Usually these people have distinguished themselves in the profession either by achieving an outstanding teaching record or by being actively involved in the national organizations such as the National Council for Teachers of Mathematics or National Council of Teachers of English. Frequently, textbook publishers seek out and contact these people.

On the other hand, some books are written by editors or writers employed by the textbook publishers themselves. Usually, these are people who have had some experience actually teaching in the field.

Perhaps the most common textbook authorship is a combination of two or maybe even three of these. For example, perhaps two high school teachers will work with an in-house editor to develop a new Spanish text.

This cooperative process allows the teachers to make the most of their ideas without worrying about form and style.

We hear about a textbook series. What exactly is a series?

Sometimes textbook publishers will develop books in a specific subject area to be used for several different grade-levels. For example, the publisher may decide to publish grammar books for grades seven through twelve. Since they want to sell their books and since they want to present the material in some kind of a logical development, they will develop a coordinated theme and schedule through the different books for each grade-level. Thus, the publisher has developed a textbook series. If a school district buys that series and the teachers follow the textbook presentation, the students will get a coordinated and developed program of grammar.

On the other hand, another publishing company may choose to present different aspects of the material at different times, so if the school district mixes the series, there could be gaps or duplications of material. That is why choosing a textbook series is a complex, often tedious, and very important task.

The term for the schedule of when the series presents various material is called the SCOPE AND SEQUENCE and is available from the publisher. Teachers and even parents should study the scope and sequence carefully before a series is selected.

Who is Madelyn Hunter and what is her contribution to education?

During the 1980s, Madelyn Hunter has become one of the most powerful forces in American education. I doubt that there has been any one person who has had more impact on what actually happens in classrooms than she. The reason for this is that she is a teacher and she knows how to speak to teachers. When the message comes straight from her and is not filtered through bureaucratic emphasis, teachers find it reassuring, confirming, and educational. Madelyn Hunter has said as well as anyone ever has, "You're doing a good job. Now, let's look to find ways to make it easier for you."

Unlike others who would influence teaching, she didn't create any new theories. She went out and watched good teachers teach. From those observations she has put down her ideas about what good teachers do day by day and how they manage the minor parts of the profession such as motivating students, teaching so that students will remember next week what you covered today, and developing a lesson plan which is educationally sound but won't require you to stay up late at night to perfect. One of her major contributions has been the seven-step lesson plan which serves as a model for how teachers can develop lessons which meet the learning needs of the individual students. Obviously this has had such major appeal to teachers that she has almost become a guru in some parts of the country.

Unfortunately, in some places, Madelyn Hunter has become too popular. Some administrators have listened to her ideas and have decided that this is more than *a* way to teach. They have decided that this is *the* way to teach, the only way, and any teacher who isn't following the suggestions as prescriptions isn't doing a good job. In some places, principals actually require that teachers follow the Madelyn Hunter suggestions every day.

I don't think Hunter herself would be pleased with this. I doubt that she meant for her findings to be that prescriptive and one-dimensional. But this does demonstrate what too often happens to good ideas in education. Too often the students of those ideas become so zealous in their application that the ideas are burned out way before their time.

Frankly, I like Madelyn Hunter's material. I think she makes sense and she speaks the language of the classroom teacher. I think that it is unfortunate that those ideas are becoming overemphasized because I am afraid that we will wear them out and discard them long before they have had the impact they deserve.

I don't approve of a book my daughter is supposed to read in English class. What can I do about it?

You can call the teacher, or better yet, go see him, and explain to him the reason you don't want your daughter to read the book. I would suggest that you know specifically what you are talking about when you call the teacher. Don't deal in hearsay. Don't quote someone else or even worse, someone's second cousin's niece. Know yourself what you don't approve of and why.

Then, ask the teacher for an alternative book for your daughter. It is really as simple as that. Recent court decisions explain the procedure quite clearly. The teacher will come up with a suitable alternative and your daughter will study that book while the rest of the class is studying the other.

At this point, you may want to help the teacher select the alternative. In the course of your conversation, see if you can find out what literary experiences the teacher is hoping to get from the book he has chosen. If he is any kind of a teacher at all, he will have a definite goal he is hoping to achieve from having the students read his selection. For example, many teachers have students read the novel *Catcher in the Rye*, which is about a high school student struggling with adult emotions and situations. Since that struggle is rather common to most high school students, teachers assign the book in hopes that it will help the students understand themselves a bit better. You must commend the teachers for their purpose. Unfortunately, the book is a bit rough around the edges. (Actually, I don't like the book all that much.) Yet, the teachers assign the book with noble goals.

If you discover this kind of thing during your conversation with your daughter's teacher, see if the two of you might come up with an alternative book which will achieve something of the same purpose but is less offensive.

Another question which you must consider now is whether or not your daughter wants an alternative assignment. If the teacher handles the situation correctly, your daughter will not necessarily have to feel like an outcast unless she brings those feelings on herself. Before you start the process with the teacher, make sure that you and your daughter are in agreement about what you are doing and why.

To what degree does the textbook determine what is taught in a course?

Since there are approximately 3 million teachers in this country, there are about 3 million answers to that question. Every teacher uses the textbook somewhat differently. I have seen some classes where the textbook is not only the sole source of information but it dictates organization, teacher methods, and student activities. A few years ago I worked with a biology teacher who had more than a master's degree in biology. One year the textbooks were two weeks late in arriving and the man simply couldn't conduct class. The students just sat without a book.

On the other hand, I know some teachers who don't even order books. They go solely on their knowledge and organization schemes.

As an educator who visits schools every day, I realize the need for all of us to be concerned about the quality of school textbooks, but I am personally more concerned about the sad fact that the textbook quality is so important in the instructional process.

Our sophomore daughter is in a psychology class which doesn't have a textbook. Why is that?

There could be at least two reasons for this. (1) There aren't any books available at this time, or (2) the teacher doesn't want books. Let's look at each of those reasons in more detail.

1. There could be several reasons why there aren't any books avail-

able. Perhaps this is a new course which the school put into the curriculum rather late. Thus, the textbook order went in late, and the books are now on back order somewhere tied up in the bureaucracy of shipping, which is far too common in situations like this. Perhaps the course was so popular that it grew faster than the teacher or administrators expected. Since there aren't enough textbooks to go around, the teacher has chosen not to distribute any books. Perhaps this is an experimental course and the school is not prepared financially to buy expensive books until there is some evidence that the course will continue.

2. There could be several reasons why the teacher has chosen not to have books. Psychology is a broad topic, and there are a variety of areas to cover and a variety of methods to cover them. Perhaps this teacher wants to design the course in his own way, and he doesn't want to be tied to a textbook. If this is the case, he probably has a wide assortment of other readings such as magazine articles and newspaper clippings. Perhaps this teacher just doesn't feel that any textbook covers the subject sufficiently to justify the cost of the books.

Not having a textbook is not a sufficient reason to question the integrity of a course. Actually, I am more concerned about teachers who are too dependent on the book for presenting what is to be learned and when. My suggestion is that you wait and see how this course develops. It could be a highlight for your daughter.

CHAPTER NINE
Educational Alternatives

Perhaps I could be accused of being a little overly optimistic at times, but frankly, I am excited about what is happening in schools. I am excited about what I see in the classrooms. I see lots of fine teachers who not only know their material and how to teach it, but who also care about their students. I see students who work hard at passing their classes and are really getting a good education.

But one of the things that excites me most about American education in the latter half of the twentieth century is the variety of school opportunities now available to most students and most families. For the first time in the history of the country, most families have some choice about how their children are educated and where they go to school.

Let's just look at some of these opportunities. First, we always have the large, extensive public school which is virtually available to everyone between the ages of five and eighteen. But we also have a large variety of religious schools ranging from fundamental Christian schools to Catholic schools to Lutheran schools to Jewish schools. In addition to that, we have independent private schools which are not necessarily affiliated with any creed or cause.

In addition to all the school opportunities, most parents in this country now have the opportunity to choose to educate their children at home if that seems like the best option available.

Of course, blessings always come with obligations, and those choices in schools come with obligations as well. Now that parents have all those options available to them, they have to make some kind of decision. To make that decision, they have to know something about schools, they have to know something about what their family wants and needs from an education, and they have to know something about their own children—each of their own children.

This may sound as if I am putting a great deal of pressure on parents. If so, then so be it. I realize that there are people around who have suggestions about how families ought to educate their children. But those people are smarter than I. I simply don't know enough about individual families or individual students to tell anyone where to send a child to school. That is a decision that only the family can make for itself and has to make for each individual.

But I am happy that families have to make those decisions. In fact, I am convinced that having those decisions to make is one of the factors contributing to the success of the American system of education. Having that decision forces parents to think about education, and that helps them get involved more in the process. When parents become more involved, the whole process improves. Also, having to make those decisions forces parents to spend some time thinking about their children, and that will help the parents and children grow closer together.

Just having the opportunities and options has already begun to improve the quality of the whole enterprise. Only God can see the future.

Recently I had to go out to evaluate a young biology teacher who had just begun her career in one of the local high schools. I was fairly excited about the opportunity, right up until she announced the content of the lesson for the day—the human digestive system. To begin with, I am not much of a scientist, and the human digestive system is not among my favorite topics of conversation.

But this day I was wrong. That young teacher had such a brilliant lesson, and she told the story in such a way that soon I was totally fascinated by what I was learning. She described what happens when we eat a piece of meat; and though she used some of those foreign sounding big words, I could still understand enough to be awed.

According to what she described, when the meat gets to our stomachs, some folks come from somewhere and take some stuff and then go home. Then some other guys come from some other place and take other things and all go home. Soon, these creatures are coming from everywhere, taking what they are supposed to have and going home. There is a real system going on down there, a highly structured and completely compatible community.

I was amazed, and in my amazement, I turned to my colleague, an old veteran science teacher who claims to be an agnostic, and I asked, "Why does that work that way?"

"Because that is the way we are made," the veteran agnostic whispered back.

Praise God. That's the way we are made. Even in a lesson about the human digestive system, we see the beauty and majesty of a wonderful Creator at work.

Every piece of knowledge will eventually lead us to that single insight where we can only sit with our mouths open and proclaim, "Look what God has done." That's what it means to be fully educated.

What exactly is a state-accredited school?

In short, a state-accredited school is one which has been examined by state officials and meets all the state standards. Of course, all public schools must be accredited; however, some private schools, including some Christian schools, aren't.

Those state standards include requirements for such things as teacher certification and assignment. In other words, the state standards require that anybody teaching science must have had some college classes in science and must have had some training as a teacher. The state standard includes some requirements for curriculum. In other words, the state requires that anyone graduating from high school must have passed so many classes in the various subject areas, so the state-accredited school must offer those classes.

The state standards also require that schools spend so many hours a year in session and that students attend those sessions. In most states, that requirement is for at least six hours a day for 180 days per year.

The state standards also require that school facilities meet certain health and safety features to insure that the children can attend without any peril to their well-being.

The state standards also require that schools provide adequate educational facilities and programs for those students with special educational and personal needs.

Since the U.S. Constitution is silent on the subject of education and schools, the states derive this power to establish those standards over local school districts from the States Power article of the Constitution.

The state accreditation does insure that the local school meet certain requirements, and that the students have had an opportunity for an education.

We are thinking about home-schooling our children. Where can we find some direction?

I appreciate the way you have asked your question. Obviously, you have already considered the first point that I will make and make in loud terms. Home-schooling children is such a significant step not only in the life of the children but in the whole family that no family should even enter into the endeavor without first doing extensive research.

To begin such an endeavor without gathering all the evidence first and making a serious, logical decision could work all sorts of difficulties on your children. I would also encourage you to make a logical, thoughtful decision. Some of the literature describing home-schooling is quite persuasive and quite emotional. I appreciate the enthusiasm these people have, but let's always read that material conscious of the fact that home-schooling is not for everyone.

Now that I have issued the appropriate caution, let's consider the positive steps to gather an answer to your question.

1. Get in touch with people who are home-schooling. The best experts on the joys and pitfalls of this whole procedure are the people who are actually doing it. Find some of those people and talk with them. In fact, many home schoolers join local support groups where they meet together regularly. I would advise that kind of activity for you. These home schoolers should be easy to find. Call your local pastors and see if they know some people in your area. If not, contact your favorite Christian broadcaster to see if that company would have some addresses of home schoolers in your area.

2. Get in touch with people who have home-schooled children who are now adults. Though I have met some home schoolers who are completely excited about this form of education, I still think that we need to see a generation of people who have come through the system before we can totally evaluate all of the advantages and perhaps even disadvantages.

Because of this, I put a great deal of confidence in what veteran missionaries tell me about their home-schooling experiences. For the missionaries, home-schooling is not new. It has been around long enough for those parents to make an objective evaluation based on what their children have become as adults. I would encourage you to try to talk to some of them.

3. Read some books on the subject. Of course, the major speaker on the home-schooling movement is Dr. Raymond Moore. His books

should be available in any Christian bookstore. These books are valuable because they not only tell you how to get started, but they also tell you the various state and local laws and regulations. You will want to know these before you go any further.

4. Sit down with your family, and fully discuss every aspect of the situation before you even consider the endeavor. Some questions which you may want to consider are:

a. How much time do both parents have to devote to the education of the children? This is too big a task to be tackled by just one parent. If both parents are not fully committed and if both parents do not have at least some time each day to spend on the home school, the education won't be complete.

b. Who is available to help in the areas where neither parent has the expertise? In other words, who can you get to help teach art or music or tough science if neither of you is capable?

c. What opportunities for social interaction do your children have? Though social interaction may be a bit overdramatized as an educational goal, children do need to learn to play with other children their age. Do you have such opportunities for your children?

d. Is the family prepared to make the financial sacrifice to keep the home school going?

e. What is education and what do you expect of your children educationally?

f. How do you evaluate your children as human beings? Let's be honest. Most of us as parents get some joy and perhaps peace of mind by comparing our children to other children of the same age. If you have any of those tendencies, you will need to deal with those before you begin home schooling lest you duplicate what the students could have had in the typical classroom.

What is A.C.S.I.?

A.C.S.I. (the Association of Christian Schools International) is a worldwide association of Christian schools which provides a wide variety of services to its members.

For a certain fee (based on the number of students in the school) a Christian school that meets the criteria, which includes both theological and educational standards, may join the A.C.S.I.. The services that A.C.S.I. provides include a professional journal for teachers and administrators, professional meetings at local, state, and national levels. different kinds of competition events such as speech and music for the students, standards for accrediting member schools, and standards for the certification of teachers.

In addition to all that, the A.C.S.I. provides its member schools a united voice in speaking out to the government agencies and the public as a whole on issues pertinent to Christian education.

Presently, the A.C.S.I. has a school membership of approximately 2,300 schools, which serve more than 330,000 students. The home office is in Whittier, California.

Other organizations of Christian schools include Christian Schools International, an association of Reformed schools; and the American Association of Christian Schools, which serves another large segment of Christian schools.

Our son says he wants to take some high school courses by correspondence. Where does he find out what is available?

Before I answer the question which you asked, let me persuade you to make sure your son has contacted his high school counselor or principal to tell them of his intentions. There are sometimes good reasons why students want to take courses by correspondence, but they really do need to check with local school officials first.

Some reasons why students might want to investigate correspondence include: the student has been sick and missed a portion of his time at school; a student has failed a course and is now motivated enough to complete a correspondence course; or a student attends a high school which does not offer a course which he would like to have.

If your son does have a valid reason to explore high school correspondence courses, I recommend that you investigate the high school correspondence programs at the University of Nebraska. These courses are the most common throughout the United States and even common with American students in other parts of the world. They are also highly respected by school officials.

Again, be sure to remind your son that he needs to be motivated. These are not simple programs. The courses are well constructed and demanding. Frankly, most high school courses are probably easier to complete than these will be.

Our daughter goes to a very small high school which has many advantages. But she is limited in course selection in such studies as math. What are our options?

I am pleased that you recognize the advantages of the small high school. Let's hope that in this small school, your daughter is able to develop confidence in herself and also learn the valuable lesson of good study habits. Frequently, those lessons are easier to get in a small school than in a larger, more impersonal one.

However, as you point out, there are some disadvantages as well. I would like to say that having a limited course selection is not really a disadvantage. I would like to tell you that if the teachers are excited and competent, their enthusiasm for the subject and your daughter's ability to learn will compensate for not having the more advanced courses. In some situations and with some students, this may even be true. But it is not always. High schools with a good science curriculum simply have more of their graduates majoring in science in college than the high schools which don't put that kind of emphasis on science. The quality of the high school program does make a difference.

Since this is the situation, you and your daughter do have some options. If there is a larger high school within driving distance, you may want to explore the possibility of your daughter driving over to that school for selected courses. Notice that I am not recommending that she transfer to another school, but to check to see if your school could work out some arrangement so she could take those needed courses in the other place. Believe it or not, this is rather common in some rural areas throughout the United States.

If there is a community college nearby, you might want to look into the possibility of having your daughter enroll in those advanced classes at the community college. Frequently, some of those early courses at the college level are about the same as the advanced courses in high school. She may be able to get the same material but with the added advantage of being with older students. She might even be able to get some of those courses during night sessions.

If there is no other option, your daughter might want to explore the possibility of taking those courses by correspondence. (The University of Nebraska has such a program.) In fact, her teachers in her school might even be available to offer her assistance and supervision.

Our son is bright, but he just can't adjust to the structure of a normal classroom. He is now failing most of his courses. Is there some educational program for a person like this?

Yes. In fact, there are a couple of rather promising possibilities for people like this—people who are intelligent but just can't accept or adjust to the stress and structure of a normal classroom.

One of the programs is frequently called the alternative school. Basically, these are schools operated by a public school district or by several districts working in a cooperative. These schools employ teachers who have been trained to deal with these special students. Usually, the classes are smaller and not as impersonal as the normal classroom. Students are often encouraged to work at their own rate of speed and aren't as crowded to meet time deadlines as they would be in a normal high school.

Because there are fewer people, there are fewer distractions during the school day.

Some of these alternative schools have had amazing success rates with students who were just swallowed up in the activity and demands of the typical high school. To investigate this possibility, you might want to check with the officials at your son's school. They could help you locate the one nearest you.

If you cannot find an alternative high school near you, you may want to consider giving your son the option of doing some of his work at home through correspondence courses. Again, check with the school officials about this possibility.

How does a regional vocational school work?

The regional vocational school is usually a cooperative. Several school districts in the same area get together and decide that instead of each school trying to maintain vocational courses for its students, they will combine all their efforts to one central vocational building and program. Thus, the vocational school can offer a much wider range of programs and they can acquire and maintain better and more up-to-date equipment.

The students, usually high school juniors and seniors, then attend their own high schools for part of the school day for such courses as history and English, those things which are required; then they are transported over to the vocational school for the rest of their program.

Though the students are at vocational school, they are still considered students at their regular schools; so that their grades, attendance records, and other important data are transferred back to the home high school.

These regional vocational schools have made it possible for high school students to have a much better opportunity to explore vocational options and to get some training in vocations of their choices. Most of the students who complete the program are considered eligible for employment as soon as they graduate from high school. Since the courses offered are legitimate high school courses, students who attend can also be admitted into college programs should they choose.

What is an educational voucher and how does it work?

The idea of an educational voucher is based on the notion that parents should have some choice in where their children go to school and that any one school should not have a monopoly on education.

Thus, the proponents of the voucher would have the appropriate government agency give each parent an educational voucher which the parent could spend at the school of his choice by just presenting it to the school. In this way, the parent could make the choice and yet have some of his tax dollar back to help finance that choice should he not choose the local public school.

The notion of the voucher is not necessarily new, having been around for nearly twenty years. It has actually been tried a couple of times in experimental situations. The reports of the results are mixed. Some educational experts are strongly in favor while others are strongly opposed.

The proponents argue that the free enterprise aspect principle applied to schools would greatly improve the educational opportunity of all children. The opponents argue that such a system would actually create a segregated system of schools and eventually a segmented society.

What is a magnate school and how does it work?

The magnate school is one of the more interesting and promising experiments of recent years. Historically, one of the distinguishing characteristics of American education was what we called the comprehensive high school. In other words, every high school taught all subjects and conducted all programs for all students. Regardless of what a student wanted to study or what he wanted to do when he had finished high school, he walked over to the nearest high school and was educated. Though there wasn't a lot of room for specialization, he might take some extra courses in the field of his choice, such as business or vocational courses, or science or foreign language.

In recent years, some larger school districts have begun to think about specialized high schools. Why not have all these students who are interested in sciences in one school? They can take the required courses in English and history, but they can take extra courses in the field of their choice. Thus, the district can pick some of its better teachers for its specialized school, and since the students all choose this school, they will spend the day with people who have similar interests.

Districts have been rather creative in developing magnate programs throughout the United States. We have humanities high schools, science and math high schools, foreign language high schools, vocational and technical high schools, and (if we can believe the television program "Fame") performing arts high schools.

So far, the results have been positive.

When did the idea of Christian schools in America begin?

Actually, the idea of Christian schools began as early as the colonists first began settling here. In the northern colonies most children went to school in a district public school which was very religious in its tone and purpose. In the southern colonies, a good number of children were privately tutored by clergymen. But in the middle colonies such as Pennsylvania, many of the children of the original colonists went to schools maintained and operated by a specific religious denomination.

Shortly after the new Constitution had been ratified in the early years of the nineteenth century, there was some concern that this two-track system—a private or parochial system and a public system operating side by side—was not all that healthy for the new republic, so there were some major attempts to eliminate private education. One of the most significant attempts was the Dartmouth College case of 1819. The state government had decided to take over the operation and control of the privately controlled Dartmouth College. The case went all the way to the U.S. Supreme Court, where that court ruled that Dartmouth

College could indeed remain private.

Another test of the rights of private schools was in 1925 in a U.S. Supreme Court case called Pierce vs. Society of Sister. Again, simply stated, in that case, the state of Oregon was attempting to take control of the Catholic school system in that state. Again, the court ruled in favor of private schools.

In more recent years, the Protestants and, particularly, the evangelicals really got heavily involved in the Christian school movement during the turmoil years of the 1960s.

How are Christian schools financed?

First, we have to understand that there are various kinds of Christian schools, organized and structured in various ways; so let me answer that question by referring to those different kinds of schools.

1. The single church school—Many Christian schools are operated and controlled by individual congregations. For them, most of the funds for operating the school probably come from tuition charges to the parents with the difference between the actual tuition charge and the cost of educating the student to come from the church budget. They also may get some gifts from private donors.

2. The multiple church school—Some schools are a joint effort of several congregations. For example, several individual congregations may operate their own elementary schools but cooperate with each other to maintain a high school. Again, the bulk of the money usually comes from tuition charges while the remainder comes from the various church budgets. But they too may get some private gifts.

3. The corporation schools—Some Christian schools are formed and operated as private corporations. Parents and other interested people come together, pool their resources, form a corporation, appoint a board, and develop a school. Again, the primary source of financing for these schools is the tuition charges while other funds come from donations from interested people.

As you have probably noticed, there is a common theme running through all of these. The major part of the funds to finance Christian schools comes directly from the parents themselves. Actually these parents are paying for education twice. They pay their taxes to support the public schools; then they pay the tuition to support the Christian school.

The Christian school in our area is an A.C.E school. What is that?

A.C.E. or Accelerated Christian Education is a specific curriculum designed for Christian schools which is distinctive in two ways. First, the curriculum is Christian in content with frequent quotations and allusions to the Bible, suggestions for prayer and Christian growth, and references to many things religious. But, of course, there are more Christian curriculum companies than A.C.E. The other distinctive, however, is more unusual than the Christian content. A.C.E. is, for the most part, an individualized approach to both subject content and student learning.

In theory, the proposal is that any student should be able to take the prepared materials, follow the schedule, complete the work, and progress fairly much on his own with a minimum of supervision from a teacher or other supervisor. It is an approach to education which makes the student rather than the teacher responsible for his learning.

The subject matter and the class work is organized into little booklets called Paces. A student decides on Monday or maybe day by day, how much he is going to accomplish in each subject area during his time. He then gets his Pace, reads the material, and completes the assigned work. When he feels that he has mastered that concept or body of material, he takes a test and scores it himself. If the test proves that he is in command of that material, he goes on to another lesson or another Pace.

The faster students may complete two or three lessons a day while slower ones only work through one. Some students may even complete the work for their grade-level before the year is out and move on to the next. If a student is finished with all his Paces, he may graduate in less than four years.

While the student is working on his material, he sits at his own individual desk or carrel and works with a minimum of distractions.

The A.C.E. curriculum has been around since the early 1970s and has experienced a few minor changes. Yet, it continues to be popular as one of the means of educating children in a Christian setting.

We would like to send our children to our little church school all the way through the eighth grade. But our friend tells us that since seventh- and eighth-graders don't change classes every period like the regular junior highers do, we would be making it tough for

our children when they get to high school. What do you think?

I don't think it makes all that much difference. That adjustment from what we call a self-contained classroom to a departmentalized situation is an interesting time for any student, regardless of when he makes it. In some schools, students begin to make the adjustment in fourth or fifth grade. In other schools, students make the adjustment in seventh grade. In the case of your children, they will just need to make it in the ninth grade. It shouldn't be any more of a problem than it would have been earlier.

For some students, the adjustment doesn't seem to be all that great. In fact, I know some people who actually enjoy the departmentalized situation better and really begin to shine once they get out of the self-contained classroom. For others, the adjustment can be all devastating.

It is more than a simple matter of learning how to open a locker, of running through the halls to get to the next class before the tardy bell, and of carrying an armload of books all day. This changing classes means adapting to five, six, seven, or even more teachers. That is one of the rougher adjustments. It also means having 100 or maybe 150 different classmates when the student used to have only about 20. In other words, the student goes from a situation where he knows everyone and everyone knows him into a situation where he doesn't know anyone.

How well your children make that adjustment, whenever they have to make it, depends on how well they get acquainted with new situations, how they function with strangers, and where their friends are.

We have our daughter in a public school and that is fine. But our son is another story—unmotivated and a bit on the rebellious side. Would the Christian school be able to help him?

I would really like to answer this question in two ways. First, I would like to answer with a flat no and chastise you a bit for even asking. What do you think Christian schools are—some kind of reform school? Most Christian schools I know are solid educational institutions with professional teachers, an excellent curriculum, and at least their share of motivated students who are attempting to make the most of their gifts. Why would you want to send your unmotivated child to the Christian school when you aren't interested in sending the motivated one also? In fact, some Christian schools have a policy that requires that a family sends all of its children rather than selected ones, thus preventing the very thing you are proposing. The real purpose and real attraction of a Christian school is more than its ability to deal with the difficult student. The purpose of a Christian school is to provide a Christian environment and a biblical approach to all areas of learning.

But now that I have spoken harshly, let me hedge a bit. Perhaps this is the right decision for your son. Of course, you know him better than anyone else, but it sounds as if he has lost confidence in himself. (Remember that in an adolescent insecurity never looks like insecurity. Frequently it looks like rebellion and apathy.) Perhaps the best thing for him would be a change in scenery. Most Christian schools are smaller than the public schools, so that the insecure student has a little better chance of establishing some sense of identity and developing some friendships without getting lost in the crowd. Since the teachers usually have fewer total students during the school day, there is a better possibility that at least one teacher will have the time and the desire to show a special interest in your son, and will be willing to work with him through this difficult spot in his life. Since the content of Christian education is biblically oriented, perhaps your son, if he does have respect for the Bible, will find a new source of enthusiasm for the work he is asked to do.

As I said at the beginning, this is a tough question. If the Christian school is true to its purpose, it should attract students of all abilities who have a commitment to this kind of education. On the other hand, I have seen students like your son do a complete turn around by moving from the public school to the Christian school. In just a matter of months, they move from an insecure and apathetic student to one who enjoys school and does well.

Since I don't have an answer for you, I suggest that you go see the administrator at the Christian school. Perhaps he would like for you to bring your son for a visit, and you could even hear his opinion of the matter. If your son would rather be in the Christian school, that alone would probably make it a good choice.

CHAPTER TEN
Children and Preschools

One of the major changes in American education during the past twenty years has been the increased intensity on the education and formal schooling of young children.

In that time, we have seen kindergarten change from a simple luxury of the well-to-do to a necessity for all children. We have seen the purpose change from play-like socialization to heady stuff. We have seen kindergarten preschools spring up and prosper. The message is clear. The education of children is now serious business.

Of course, there have been some social changes which have hastened these changes in our thinking about schools. The increase in the number of working mothers, the deteriorating family structure, and even the immediate availability of television have had some influence on the way we think about children and what we do with them and their time.

Yet, this intensity on children's education is so new, it still remains something of a mystery. We do have some short-term evidence from research projects which show us some positive results of different methods and approaches. But we have yet to study the habits and attitudes of a generation of adults who began formal schooling one or two years earlier than our generation did.

For this reason, this chapter may be one of the most important in the book. If you are a parent or you anticipate becoming one, you need to educate yourself about this serious business of preschools.

How do I select the preschool which is a best for my child?

This is a significant question if for no other reason than you have the choice. As parents, we talk about exercising some choices in how our children are educated, but when we get the chance, we are sometimes awed by the responsibility. Another reason why the question is important is that you want your child to learn one very important lesson during her preschool career. You want her to learn that learning is fun and rewarding.

To find the school which can best teach this lesson, you should evaluate the technical aspects such as the quality of the facilities, the academic nature of the curriculum, the testimonies of other parents who have had their children in the preschool, and you could even consider the success of graduates of the various schools.

But since I take a simple approach to everything, I'll take a simple approach to this decision as well. To select the school which is best for your child, pick the one which has the best teacher. Now isn't that easy? Of course, you don't want to take this lightly. To make such an important decision, go to the various schools you have available and meet the teacher with whom your child will be spending most of her time. You will be able to get some kind of a feeling about that teacher in a simple conversation. You should be able to tell if the teacher is interested in students, if the teacher is patient, and if the teacher understands preschool-age people. Above all, you should be able to tell if that teacher is excited about learning and can make your child excited about it too.

That's the way to pick a school. Pick the best teacher.

In our area we have something called pre-first grade. What is that?

In this era of making kindergarten more academic and putting rather heavy demands on what kindergarten students learn, the first-grade work has also become more demanding and advanced.

If a student comes out of kindergarten and has not learned some rather advanced skills in study habits, language usage, and reading readiness, he will probably struggle for a while in the first grade. Unless he is particularly gifted and self-assured, this could be a discouraging and detrimental start which could affect his progress for several years. Thus, the proponents of the pre-first idea think that it is logical to put that child into a year of study which is somewhere between kindergarten and first grade. The child can then grow a year, mature a year, and develop the skills he is going to need in first grade.

Given the academic intensity of some kindergarten programs and some first-grade programs, it does probably require a rather mature six-year-old to handle some of the requirements. Though the pre-first program is still too young to fully assess, it may be one way of handling this recent trend to put more emphasis on learning during these early years.

Why do we need all-day kindergarten?

That is an interesting question. Though kindergarten has been a part of both public and private education for almost 100 years, it is only during the last 20 years that it has become viewed as an almost necessary part of a person's academic career.

Presently, there are two schools of thought about what ought to be taught in kindergarten. Some experts tell us that these ought to be highly structured academic programs which prepare and introduce the students to the academic rigors ahead.

The other school of thought maintains that kindergarten should principally be a time for the child to develop the social skills he will need during the rest of his school career.

Obviously, the people in the first school of thought would endorse an all-day kindergarten because we can get twice as much work done in a full day as we can in a half day. These spokesmen argue that the full-day kindergarten is necessary to update the quality of education in this country.

Another arguable reason for the all-day kindergarten is that with the working mothers trend, many children need the structure and organized environment which school provides. Thus, the kindergarten is the better choice for those children than having them a half day in school and a half day with a baby-sitter.

At this time, the all-day kindergarten is still an experiment. The problem is that with this kind of experiment, we won't know whether it is a good one or a bad one for about twenty years when these children become adults. In the meantime, there will probably continue to be two schools of thought.

We want our child to be a good student. How early should we put him into preschool?

How much preschool your child needs to prepare him for the long duration of thirteen years of intense, pressured education plus another four years of college plus another three years of graduate school depends on two factors. The first factor to consider is how much time you have to spend with your child yourself. If you are home all the time and if you spend time with your child talking with him, letting him use a pencil, teaching him colors, and helping him begin to learn the lessons of responsibility and necessary routine, he will probably accomplish academically as much at home as he would in the preschool.

The second factor to consider is how much opportunity your child has to interact with other people his age. Most preschool proponents tell us that the strength of a preschool experience is socialization. If children have many brothers and sisters or if they live in a neighborhood where they have friends their age or if they are active in church activities, they can begin to develop some of the social skills which school requires. But if your child has limited opportunities to interact with other children his age, you may want to put him into preschool, at least for a few hours each week.

To summarize, how much preschool your child needs and how early he needs to start depends on how much time you have with the child and how much opportunity he has to grow socially.

If we don't want our child to go to preschool, how can we prepare her for kindergarten?

At first glance, this could be a complex question because of the many varieties of kindergartens. Some kindergartens have more of a social thrust, giving children opportunities to play and interact and learn to cooperate with other children. On the other hand, some kindergartens have a serious academic thrust where the students are expected to develop readiness for reading, math, and the discipline of being a productive student. In other words, some kindergartens are about where kindergartens were twenty years ago while some kindergartens are about as intense and academic as first grade was twenty years ago.

To prepare your daughter for the experience, you really need to know what kind of kindergarten she will attend. You can probably determine that with one visit of no more than an hour or two. You should be able to see the thrust and direction quickly. Thus, you can begin to get some idea of how to begin to get your daughter ready.

On the other hand, there are some basics to help your daughter get ready for formal schooling, regardless of the kind of kindergarten she will attend. First, she will need to know how to take care of herself and be responsible for her own possessions. A few years ago I asked a first-grade teacher what she expected children to know when they came on the first day. She summed it up with one sentence, "I would like for them to know how to use the bathroom." Not a bad place to start.

You will also want to prepare your child by giving her opportunity to socialize with children her own age. If you have other children in the family of about that age, family relations themselves might be adequate, but probably not. You will want to give her opportunity in Sunday School classes and other church functions. You may even want to have a couple of get-togethers with mothers and children in the neighborhood so that your daughter will have some opportunity to develop an interest in give and take situations.

Academically, you will want to prepare your daughter by reading to her at least once a day. You will want to talk with her often, making sure that you listen as much as you talk. You will want to have her help you with chores, and you will want to give her some assignments during that time. As the two of you are setting the table, you will want to say, "Please run back in and get me four forks." These kinds of activities will help her get a sense of numbers. In the same way, you can teach her colors and anything else you think she seems to want to learn.

Finally, you can prepare her for formal schooling by making sure that she knows that you love her and believe in her. If she is clear on that fact and is confident in herself, both you and she should adjust to whatever kindergarten has to offer, even if it seems at first that she isn't ready.

The people brought their children to see Jesus. The disciples responded like too many of us respond. "Get those children out of here. Can't you see this Man is busy. We have adult things to do. After all, this is the Master Teacher and we need to hear the profound mysteries of life. This isn't fit fare for a child."

But Jesus rebuked them. "Let the little children come to Me." And then He said the real shocker, "Unless you become like one of them, you will never enter the kingdom of God."

I'm going to have to ponder that. I became a teacher because I wanted to be an influence on children. I wanted to be a model for them. I wanted to teach them how to live and especially how to live in such a way as to please Jesus. Now He tells me that I have it backward. I am a teacher because I should be learning from those children.

If I asked, "What did Jesus see in those children that He tells us to imitate?" you could probably give me a whole list of "childlike" qualities: honesty, loyalty, the ability to accept and believe, the ability to forgive, innocence. The list goes on.

But now I have a problem. In the past twenty years, I have watched closely all of our noble efforts to teach children, to put them into classes and educate them, to require them to discipline themselves, to have them sit and concentrate, in short to make them more nearly like us adults. I watch these noble efforts, and all the while I keep reminding myself of words from One far wiser than I. "You have to become like one of them if you are ever to enter the kingdom."

What should I do to prepare my daughter for first grade?

Thank you for asking this question. Thank you for being sensitive enough to realize that starting first grade (which for most children still means beginning all-day sessions) is a major milestone in the life of a human and requires a major adjustment. I am sure that your daughter will someday also thank you, if not consciously at least subconsciously. So now let me list the steps for you to follow, and I might add that I list them in what I think is an order of importance.

1. Make sure your daughter has a friend in first grade. I realize that I have harped on this twenty times already, but I say it again. Since learning is such a private and personal matter, it is criminal to send a child into a classroom unless the child knows someone there. This is especially true with first grade. Make sure your daughter knows someone who is to be in her class.

To manage this, go see the principal or school secretary and ask for a list of students who will be in your daughter's class. When you explain the reason, I am sure they will cooperate. Then call people on the list until you find some parent who feels as you do, and invite the parent and the child over. (If your daughter will have to ride the bus, make sure she knows someone else on the bus. Getting on a bus with total strangers is one of the most frightening experiences of a lifetime, except for people like Indiana Jones.)

2. Help your child get used to the routine of getting to and from

school. In fact, practice this routine. If your daughter is going to walk, walk the route with her two or three times. Point out safety procedures; get acquainted with the dogs along the way; and time yourself so that you will have some idea how long your daughter will be on the street.

If you are to drive your daughter, practice driving and stopping where you expect to stop. Also practice picking her up at that spot so she will have some idea of what to expect after school. Again, if she is going to ride a bus, as best as you can, help her determine where her bus will deposit her and pick her up. I know many adults who still have recurring nightmares about the time they got on the wrong bus during those early days of a first-grade experience. Your daughter doesn't need that psychological baggage, so do what you can to help her prevent it.

3. Help your daughter adjust her body clock to accommodate the school schedule. If your daughter is not already in a pattern similar to a school schedule, begin at least a month before school helping her to get up in time and stay awake for the length of the school day. Help her adjust her afternoon nap until after the school day so she can stay awake through class. School people—teachers and principals—are funny that way. They put a lot of importance on things like promptness and staying awake.

4. Get her the shots. In most states this is the law, but on top of that, it's wisdom. In classrooms children are huddled together and piled on top of each other in closer proximity than in almost any other situation. In that closeness they share everything: pens, pencils, toys, books, paper, ideas, and germs. They need all the help they can get. If you don't know what shots are required, call the school. They will be able to tell you.

5. Help your daughter build some positive anticipation for what is going to happen to her. Tell her stories of the good times you had in school. Convince her of the joys of learning to read and write. If your daughter is a little nervous about beginning the experience, you may want to plan some big event or reward for when the day comes. Get her the new crayons she had been wanting or plan a family outing to celebrate the event. Let her build some excitement for what is going to happen to her.

6. Prepare yourself for the event. It doesn't matter whether this is the first one or the fourteenth. That first day of sending a child away to school always produces some mixed emotions. In some ways we are

pleased and perhaps even a bit proud. This is our child and she is going to achieve so much and make us look good. Yet, a piece of you goes with her. Once they step into that school building to begin the first grade, we are reminded that they will never be little children at home again. I tend to want to cry right about then, but I never want the child to catch me at it. Maybe getting myself ready for the beginning of a new career or even a new year is as tough as getting the child ready.

We are not sure we want to send our child to preschool. Will we be cheating him academically if we don't?

That depends on two factors—you and the preschool to which you would send your son. Some preschools are quite academic in their efforts while others maintain that their purpose is primarily for social development. Some preschool teachers are quite good with providing academic experiences for the children and some aren't. Some preschools have a good supply of academic materials such as games and blocks and some don't. In other words, preschools are not all the same.

The other factor in this question is you. Will you have time to talk to your son a great deal? Will you read to him, take him to the library, and buy him books of his own? Will you take him on field trips? Will you read his interests in such grown-up activities as writing and coloring and provide him the materials should he develop an interest? Will you provide him an opportunity to talk with other adults?

From all these questions for your thought, let me make a neutral observation, but one that I think is accurate. Some children are better off in preschools, but some aren't. There is no need to feel guilty because you are not sending your son to preschool, so long as you make the most of the opportunity.

We think our three-year-old daughter may have unusual talent in gymnastics. How early should we start her in formal training so we won't limit her success?

Three things distinguish a successful athlete, or a successful anything else for that matter—basic, God-given talent, hard work, and enthusiasm. Talent alone is never enough. The decision you have to make is a complex one. You have to consider at what age you can start your daughter in the formal training so that you won't kill her enthusiasm while giving her an opportunity to develop her talent.

Though the decision is something of a risky one, I think you might get a little better clue by being subtle (the nice word for sneaky). Give your daughter an opportunity to watch gymnastics. Of course, you will want her to watch the great gymnasts on TV, but you will also want to take her to the local club and watch the younger people and the less skillful. She may watch the great ones with awe, but she will watch the others with identity, and both emotions are important. Too often we pick models for children who are so good that the children are actually turned off rather than turned on.

By doing this, you should be able to tell the level of your daughter's interest. There should be several signs. You may catch her trying to copy some of the moves during her play. You may be able to see the enthusiasm in her eyes. Or she may tell you, "I like that and would like to try it." That is the right time to start her in formal training.

When that time comes, pick your school carefully. Actually, choosing a good school is easy. Pick the one with the best teacher—the one who best understands children and can provide an environment of learning without being harsh. Whatever you do, don't start your child's Olympic training schedule when she is three. Wait until she is at least five. I jest, but you get the picture. Too much, too intense, too early will do as much to destroy your daughter's enthusiasm and chances at success as any other factor.

CHAPTER ELEVEN
The Primary Grades

In recent years, we have all heard some talk about the major transition points in our lives. We move from high school to college; we move from school to the working world; we get married; we become parents; our children leave home; we retire; we lose loved ones. As we have been told and as we have experienced, there is a certain amount of stress attached to each one of those transition points. In fact, if we rush out to our local bookstore, we can probably find some special book to help us through the stress of whatever particular transition point we happen to be dealing with at the time.

That is all good, but probably one of the major transition points in our lives we don't even remember. Every once in a while we even have the opportunity of watching others go through this great period of transition and stress, and we don't really know how to help because we don't remember going through it ourselves. That special time is when we first start to school.

We can talk about the importance of a good beginning, of how important the first-, second-, and third-grade years are, of the educational value of those years. And as adults, we know that those years are important, but too often we get so caught up in our own concerns that we forget about what is happening to the child during this crucial period of transition and stress.

When a child starts to school, we ask him to change his body clock, his work habits, the way he spends his day, his loyalties, his approach to the universe from a personal experience to a reading experience, his social habits, his friendship patterns. And all the time we expect him to remain the same sweet child he always was.

The theme of this chapter is that the primary years are important years, even crucial years, but they are also years filled with stress and often anxiety for the child. I hope that as you read through this chapter, you will spend at least a bit of your time and energy trying to think like the child.

What is meant by the primary grades?

This is just another classification educators are using to help identify different levels of school. The three major divisions of the school ladder are the elementary school or grammar school, or in some cases the common school; the middle school or junior high school; and the high school.

Another division which is a bit more specific is to talk of the primary grades, which usually include kindergarten through grade three; the intermediate grades; and the upper intermediate grades.

In other words, to answer your question briefly, the primary grades usually include kindergarten through grade three.

In my day we didn't have a kindergarten, much less preschool. Is all this necessary?

The times, they say, are a-changing, and the educators are always trying to keep up with those changes. Granted, the educators don't always make the right decisions, but at least they make an effort.

The emphasis on early childhood education such as preschool and kindergarten is one of the more recent trends of the past twenty years. There are several reasons for this trend and perhaps some dangers.

The biggest reason for this movement to provide formal schooling for younger children is the changing family structure. The number of mothers working outside the home has increased to the point that recent statistics indicate that only about 4 percent of the children in school have an original father at work and an original mother at home during the school day.

Based on this, you may protest that the preschool and kindergarten are just a glorified baby-sitting service, and that does have a ring of truth in it. Yet, something educationally positive is occurring during this time for these children.

Smaller families have also created an interesting new dimension in education. I was a child in a family of four children, so I had a lot of playmates without leaving home. Now, we have several families of one or two children, so these children will need to leave home at least to some degree to learn how to establish and develop social relationships and to learn to interact with other people.

As we gather more research in how people learn and grow, we have become increasingly aware of the impact of those early years on how people develop. We have learned, for example, that children who are read to during their early years have a much better chance of learning to read. Children who have language experiences—learning and speaking to other people—will have a much better chance to become good readers, good writers, and better students. Since we really can't control what is happening in the homes, the proponents of early childhood education argue that preschools and kindergartens will give more children a head start.

At the same time, the whole schooling process has become more pressure-packed. We are just demanding more of students at an earlier age. (I know some people don't agree with me, but at least I am convinced.) Some people would argue that we need to maintain highly academic early childhood education to prepare the children for the work ahead.

But herein may lie the danger as well. It is difficult to tell whether this emphasis on early childhood education is a cause or a result of that pressure to academic performance. Kindergarten teachers sense that they must start their students into reading because most people now entering first grade already know how to read. If one teacher attempts to fly in the face of the demands and not start her children, she will only be cheating them.

In the meantime we are starting children into the academic work earlier and earlier. Have we lost sight of what childhood is about?

Do you remember the 1976 Olympics and the little girl from Romania who won all of our hearts? Nadia Comaneci—brilliant, beautiful, so innocent, and yet so assured. I sat glued to the television and watched in awe of the sheer beauty of physical talent used to its maximum potential. Mary, my wife, sat with me, glued to the TV as well; and when it was all over, she said, "But she has such sad eyes."

Somehow I had missed it in all the splendor and near perfection. But I will always hear a mother talk. Now when I watch the great ones race or ski downhill with the wind in their face or jump or shoot or block or throw, I remember what Mary said; and I look at the eyes.

As a proud parent, I wouldn't mind having a laurel wreath or a medal or colorful picture to hang on my wall, but I would really rather have happy eyes.

Can we really put too much stress on learning when the children are in the early years?

Since you have used the word stress, I am going to say yes. Learning is the process of developing our minds and abilities to their fullest capacity. The whole process should be one that is not merely pleasant but exciting and inviting and encouraging. The implication that we have to force people "to learn" for their own good is dangerous.

There is no better clue than to watch little children at play. They will become so involved in their games of playing school or playing home or playing adult, and during this process they are learning—learning much. To strip this natural and spontaneous learning opportunity from them and force them to sit quietly and master the arts we want them to master is not really helping them to learn at all but is an aberration to learning.

Oh, I am for teaching children, teaching them from the minute they are born. I am for speaking to them in wholesome language; I am for playing games with them which will require them to develop hand and eye coordination; I am for reading to them from the minute they are born until they leave home to study at the local university and maybe after; I am for putting them into social situations where they must interact with other children, particularly those similar in age; I am for congratulating them when they have accomplished something significant for the first time, such as tying their shoe; I am for taking them with me to church or to shop or even to the job if possible just to let them watch me be an adult; I am for giving them space and time to play and be children.

But I also believe with all my conviction that if I do all of those things, if I do those things with joy, the child will learn to read and count and solve bilinear equations as early as he is capable of mastering such things. But then he will do it because he chooses to do it and not because I have stressed or forced or demanded. When that happens, he will then have learned to love learning; that is really the only lesson he will ever need to learn anyway.

Is the first grade the most important year in school?

I used to say that and so did nearly everyone else. In fact, that used to be a part of the school recital. You remember the speech, "If they have a good first-grade experience, the rest of them just fall in line." "Put your best teachers in the first grade. That is where the action is."

I think I still believe this, but in recent years a couple of developments have caused me to question it a bit. First, as my own children pass through childhood and adolescence and into adulthood, I am beginning to believe that every year is the most important year in school. Now, I rather would like to believe that maybe the most important year in school is that first year they are out of school. I am only partially jesting, because there is a danger in putting too much emphasis on any given year of development. If we convince ourselves that the first grade is overwhelmingly the most important, we may relax a bit when our child makes it through the first grade just to wind up with all sorts of heartaches as the child goes through seventh grade.

The other development in more recent years which affects the importance of the first-grade experience is the increasing educational demands of preschool and kindergarten. Some children are now coming into first grade already about two thirds educated.

Yet, in the light of all that, first grade is still a significant year filled with significant new challenges and adjustments. Most children still learn to spend all day in school during first grade; most still learn to read, at least at more than a rather simple level; most children begin to reason mathematically. These are major developments which are significant in helping the child make the adjustments into the educational demands of future grades. Obviously, the child who gets a good start during first grade is going to have an easier time of school in the second grade and probably through all the other subsequent grades. Yes, first grade is important.

There is another thing important for a first-grader to learn. Sometime during the year they need to learn to love learning. I thought about saying to like learning, but that isn't strong enough. If there is one lesson that a first-grader could master which would make all his other years not only more pleasant but easier it would be to learn to love learning. In this era of push and shove, it would be nice to think that first-grade teachers and parents of first-graders understood that.

Do first-grade teachers get special training?

No, they don't usually get any special formal training. Most first-grade teachers get about the same training as all other elementary teachers. Some may specialize a bit early and do some of their intern work in the first grade. Some may take a course or two in early childhood education. As elementary teachers, they are actually certified to teach any of the elementary grades, perhaps as high as ninth grade.

Most first-grade teachers get into their positions by interest and promotion. Some teachers are just naturally gifted to teach that age. Some aren't. Usually, the teachers themselves have a sense of that gift.

It is rather common for school districts not to put beginning teachers in the first-grade level unless such a situation can't be avoided. They actually fill their first-grade slots by moving the experienced teachers in from other grade levels.

Now that I have said all that, let me add that in my visits around schools throughout the nation, I have come to believe that as a group, first-grade teachers may comprise the most dedicated professional group in this country. If you were to line up any 100 people in any other profession and compare them with 100 first-grade teachers, I think you would find a far greater percentage of dedicated, capable, sensitive professionals among those first-grade teachers.

At least, that is what I have discovered.

Our son's birthday is in July. The cut off date for starting school is September 1, but we are thinking of delaying for a year. Would that be a mistake?

In my best judgment, I don't think it would be. Of course, the question is more complex than that simple answer. Several factors enter into the decision which you have to make. Different children mature at different rates. Some children with summer birthdays are mature enough to go to school on schedule while others aren't. Actually, that statement is more complex than it sounds, because there are so many variations of maturity. Some children are mentally mature enough to do the schoolwork. They can read, count, and write a bit. By all accounts, we would probably guess that they should be in school.

Yet those same children may be a bit slow emotionally or, even worse, socially. Now the question is whether the parent puts the child in school so he can keep his mind busy while he cries himself to sleep every night.

As far as I am concerned, knowing when to start a child in school is one of the most difficult decisions a parent ever makes. They all mature at such different speeds and in so many different areas.

On the other hand, I look at your question from another perspective. I visit middle schools where I watch classes of sixth-, seventh-, and eighth-graders. At that level, I see much correlation between physical maturity and academic success as well as social success. I know you have a tough decision to make, but I strongly feel that it is better to err in being too late rather than too early.

What changes occur when a child starts first grade?

Though the answer to this question will vary depending on how much formal school the child has had before he enters the first grade, it is still a very thoughtful question because any first-grader, regardless of how educated or sophisticated he may be, is going to encounter a ton of changes during that year. If parents realize this, they could be in a better position to help or at least to lend support. Let's list some of those changes so that we can take a look at them in some organized way.

1. Most first-graders learn to read. That in itself is one of the major transitions in human life—to move from a nonliterate to a literate world. Learning to read is a form of independence. If you can't read, you need to climb up into a parent's lap fairly regularly to get at those mysteries of the printed page. But when you learn to read, you don't need that lap as much as you once did. Learning to read is moving into a whole other world, a much bigger and more complex world, a world of printed words and meanings.

2. Television watching takes on a new dimension. I know that some people are going to protest what I say here, but for the most part, watching TV is a qualitatively different experience for readers than it is for nonreaders. Readers get more of the plot and more of the inferences. They get more involved in the whole process. I strongly urge parents to be aware of this. For the sake of family unity you might have to let your child play in the room with the TV blaring when he is

young, but as he becomes a more proficient reader, you may need to begin to monitor the time he is in front of the TV set. You will particularly want to help him with questions which come up while he is watching.

3. First-graders begin to lead a regimented life. Of course, this happens earlier in preschool and kindergarten, but the first-grader really must buckle down to the regimen of being in a specific place and working on a specific activity at a given time each day. Often for the first time in a child's life, someone is interested in his being prompt, diligent, attentive, and quiet. Some children have trouble adjusting to that regimen.

4. First-graders establish strong friendships. At least, that is the normal pattern. Prior to first grade, children have playmates and establish special friendships, but during first grade, some of those friendships grow into bonds. That probably comes from the fact that they live those regimented lives together. They have more in common and more to share. Of course, stronger friendships are another kind of growing independence. The child who has a good buddy at school doesn't need to talk to his mother as much as he used to.

5. First-graders encounter a much wider circle of people with authority over them. Before a child starts to school at all, most of the people who have the right to order him around gained that right through love. He may forget this sometimes but that love is still present. When the child moves into the order of a full school day during first grade, several different people now have some right to boss him around—the teacher, bus driver, principal, lunchroom aide, and school nurse. One of the biggest lessons a first-grader has to learn is how to respond to people in authority.

This list is offered not as a complete list, but only as a beginning to establish the point that first grade is a time of abrupt and often significant change in a growing person's life.

Last August, I heard a sad story. This lady I know, the mother of one, had just sent her child away to the first grade. For the past six years, these two people had been almost inseparable. They were constantly together, learning, walking, going to the library, and shopping. And now the son had gone away to the first grade.

Each morning, after the bus came, the mother cried for several minutes. For one thing, there was the mystery of it all. Her son had disappeared into the mysterious world called school and she really didn't have any idea of where he was or what he was doing. But she was also lonely. Instead of filling her days with all the exciting things she had often thought of doing, visiting friends, cleaning the house, planting flowers, she just sat around being lonely. But then, she reminded herself that this schooling experience was going to last at least thirteen more years, and she was really sad.

Yes, this was indeed a sad story. But I wasn't sad because of the mother. I was sad for the boy. If the mother thought she had to make adjustments, she should have been in her son's shoes; but at a time when her son needed her the most, this mother was so wrapped up in her own problem that she did not have any feelings left to help her son with. That is what makes this a sad story.

Our school principal just abolished show-and-tell for all first grades. How could she be so cruel?

Some principals practice cruelty and others take pills to get that way. Yet, others aren't really cruel but are sometimes forced into making decisions that appear cruel.

I suspect that is what has happened here. In its original intention, show-and-tell is a good learning activity for primary-age children. By showing something with which they are familiar, these children get a good opportunity of making a class presentation where they can practice not only using language, but also some of the aspects of formal speaking. On top of that, often the presentations help the students get acquainted with each other and form some social bonds based on common interests. For all these reasons and others, show and tell is a good activity.

However, even the best of activities can get out of hand. Under unusual circumstances, I have heard several reports about a rather interesting phenomenon attacking the old wholesome show-and-tell and turning that rather good learning activity into a nightmare for children, teachers, and especially parents. "What is this monster that could yield so much power in an average first-grade class?" you ask. Simple—competition. The old human emotion of competition.

It starts innocently enough. Some girl brings in her new stuffed bear that her father bought during his last business trip. Since it is about the biggest thing those students have ever seen, the little girl gets oohs and aahs from the crowd during the presentation, and she becomes the center of attention for the rest of the day. Well, the poor child who is on tap for tomorrow has got to get on her knees and do some heavy pleading to top what her colleague had. With that, the race has begun, and the only boundaries are the children's imaginations and the parents' indulgences. Within a matter of days, the whole thing can get out of hand and ugly. (I'm not making this up. This is actually happening in many schools throughout the country.)

The problem is bigger than what it might cost the parents just to help a child stay in the competition. The real problem is the idea of rank materialism, the idea that bigger and more expensive is more impressive. This is a sad lesson for anyone to learn at any age, but it is tragic for first-graders to learn it.

When this gets out of hand, the only alternative is for the teacher (or the principal) to cancel show-and-tell and come up with some other activity where the children can make an oral presentation without being materialistically competitive.

I suspect this is what happened in your school. I recommend that you call the principal and check. (A special note for parents who are still caught in a competitive show-and-tell activity: Call the teacher and tell her what is happening at your house. If your child is pestering you for something bigger and more expensive every time it is his time to present, you can be assured that this is happening in other homes too! The teacher will want to know that.)

Our first-grader tells us that she hates school; but when we ask why, she just says that she hates the bus. Could this really be the problem?

Yes, and a thousand times, yes. Your first-grader is no different from the rest of us. Regardless of how the rest of the day goes, one little event can ruin the whole day for us. You know how it is. You wake up in the morning dreading that unpleasant moment. The thought of the possibility tortures you all day long, and then after the nasty moment comes, you still can't get it out of your mind.

Well, obviously your daughter is having a bad time on the bus and that is overshadowing every other part of the day. Since you must get to the bottom of this quickly, you need to survey your options.

First, if there is any way possible, I would suggest that you take her and pick her up for a few days. I know that may be a rather difficult task, but that bus ride is apparently frightening her severely. If you could take her, she could then focus on the rest of the school day; and you could monitor her moods to see if she could learn to enjoy school. As long as she is still riding that bus with all of its bad memories, I'm afraid she isn't going to like school very much.

If it is just impossible to take your daughter to school, your only other option is to see if you can find the problem on the bus. I suggest that you start with your daughter's teacher. She may be able to help you some. If not, she will suggest the principal. Before it's finished, you will also need to solicit the support of the bus driver. Find out the problem. There could be several. Your daughter has no friends so she sits in isolation. The other children pick on her. She forgets to use the bathroom before she leaves so she sits on the bus not only uncomfortable, but frightened to death that she is going to embarrass herself. She gets motion sickness. She falls asleep and she is afraid she won't get off the bus. Since the bus is a strange vehicle, she is frightened about her safety. Those are all rather common problems for bus riders, but it would take a bright first-grader to put her finger on the exact cause of her fear. If you can, find the reason for her dislike. Then enlist the people it takes to help you work out a solution.

Our son has been going to first grade for six weeks, and he hates it. He cries every morning. What could be his problem?

I am going to assume that this is the first all-day school experience your son has had. If he hasn't gone to an all-day kindergarten or an all-day preschool, he is now in the process of making a tremendous personal adjustment to an almost entirely new experience.

At whatever age, moving from the home to the school is a major transition in a person's life. Let's look at some of these adjustments one by one.

1. Social adjustment—the child at home must share his work and playtime with only the other children in the family. But school is about friendships. It is almost impossible to function in school without some friendships. You need a friend to line up with you in the bathroom line. You need a friend to share your eating spot at lunch. You need a friend to help you study. You need a friend to lend you a pencil when yours wears out and you forget to bring a new one. Establishing all those friendships is a very exhausting enterprise, even for gregarious chil-

dren, because there is a risk involved. You send out your feelers, and if no one picks up on them, there you stand with your emotions all exposed, and nothing hurts more than exposed emotions left out in the cold. Let's see if we can make this into a general principal—ANY CHILD WHO DOESN'T HAVE A FRIEND IN THE CLASSROOM WILL HATE SCHOOL. Well, it may be a little harsh, but I still think I am willing to live with it.

2. Adjustment to the regimen—Learning to go to school is learning to live with having someone in control of your body, mind, and soul from 9 A.M. to 3 P.M. The teacher really expects you to sit still, read when she tells you to, walk straight to the bathroom rather than looking at all the neat stuff in the hall (Aren't schools a puzzle? They put all that neat stuff on the walls in the hall, then they yell at you if you stop to appreciate it.), get a drink when she tells you to, go to the bathroom when she tells you, and keep from looking out the window even when the man is there mowing the grass.

I think I would rather be at home.

3. Adjustment to authority—When a child is at home, the only people who boss him around are those who love him. When you go to school, everybody yells at you—the teacher, the bus driver, the person in the lunchroom, the person in the office, and you don't know where they get the right to make all those decisions for you.

4. The adjustment to leaving family matters—As a parent, if I have a sick child, I would rather be at home than at school. In fact, I may go to school but my heart and thoughts are all going to be back at home with that sick child. As a child, if I have a sick mother, I would rather be at home than at school. In fact, I may be at school, but my heart and thoughts are all going to be back at home with that sick mother.

I am actually serious here. I know some children who are so sensitive that they feel that they are actually deserting their families to go off to school. The therapy for that is to wait until they are teenagers when they would probably rather be anywhere than at home.

5. Adjustment to the ever-present threat of failure—Failure is as rampant in schools as success is; and some children, without even knowing it, get caught up in it and are almost destroyed by that threat. You can fail in so many different ways. You can misspell a word that everyone else spells. You can color outside the lines. You can read too slowly. You can drop your books when it is supposed to be quiet. You can go to the bathroom in your pants. In other words, if you aren't

careful, you could make a complete fool of yourself. You always have to be on your guard, and that not only wears you out, but it makes life miserable as well.

Since this is only a partial list of adjustments your son is making right now, I can only hope I got something close to what might be bothering him. I am really glad you ask what could be his problem rather than asking what to do about it. It is much easier to try to evaluate than to try to help.

But let me be bold and risk a few suggestions which you might try. First, help your son establish a friendship with someone in the class even if you have to invite someone over every night for a week. At this point, you need to be diligent and frequent in expressing your own love for your son. Pick him up and hold him. Hug him when he isn't expecting it. Since his world outside the home is insecure right now, reaffirm his security in his home world. You may also want to help him select and start a hobby—something that he can be good at. Now that school has started, you may be pushing the studies so much that he really hasn't had time to work at what he enjoys. But that is a mistake. Right now he needs to do something every day that he enjoys and feels some success with. This should help him live a little easier with the threat of failure.

Now that our child has started to school, how can we continue to help her learn?

Now that your daughter has started to school, she probably needs your help more than ever. There is an unfortunate but rather prominent attitude that schools are responsible for all the education activity in a child's life once they have begun the process. That simply isn't true. Not only are parents still commissioned by Scripture to assume the responsibility for educating the child, but the schools simply can't do the whole job. (Isn't that a strange thing for a teacher to say, but I believe it completely. We have given the schools a greater task than they can possibly achieve.) If your child is ever going to reach her fullest potential, she is going to need some help from you.

Before you protest that I am just trying to make you feel guilty in an attempt to persuade you to overcome the inadequacy of schools, let's look at the very nature of learning itself. For the most part, human learning is a very individual process. The individual receives the new information, processes it through the use of his own personal experiences and then individually practices the new information until that information is assimilated or appropriated into his mind and life.

When a teacher has twenty-five students in a classroom, she can present the information and start the practice process. But unless she is grossly hyperactive and owns some fast skates, she simply can't get to all the children often enough for them to get as much practice as they need. That is where you come in.

Help your child practice what she is learning in school. Since repetition is a biblical method of emphasis, I think I will repeat that. Help your child practice what she is learning in school. First, listen to her read. Some children read as if they have read a lot and some children don't. The difference is that the children who read as if they have read a lot almost always have. Help your daughter get off to a good start in her school career. Listen to her read. You don't have to be an expert in reading. Just listen to her read. If she stumbles over a few words, that's all right. You can gently correct her if you want, but the important thing is that she is reading. If she wants to read the same story for seven nights in a row, encourage her. The important thing is that she is reading.

Now that she is reading, you can also begin to work on arithmetic facts and other material that she is covering in school. Remember that your major intent is to help her practice what she is learning in school. There is no need to rush her into new concepts and ideas. She just needs practice times.

There is only one more rule. Whatever you do, make sure it's fun. Don't force and don't set too high demands. Make sure your daughter is enjoying the work. Make games. Build in reward systems. Do what you have to do, but make sure she is enjoying it. Learning to love learning is the biggest lesson to be learned at this age.

We think our first-grade daughter may be gifted. How can we know for sure?

I am absolutely the wrong person to ask because my thoughts run almost counter to all the popular thinking right now, but since you asked me, I will answer.

First, I agree with you. I really believe your daughter is gifted. I get my idea, not from watching your daughter, but from reading Romans

12 in the New Testament. From that text, I have come to believe that everyone is gifted, except in different areas. Some people are gifted with hand skills; some are gifted athletes; some are gifted in the art of discerning colors. Some are gifted with words. Since schools are primarily about words, those children who for whatever reason have a little more ability with words sometimes become the only students who get burdened with that terrible label "gifted."

Since you suspect that your daughter has some special aptitude for school and schoolwork, apparently as of right now she seems to be a bit ahead of her peers in handling language. There could be several causes. Perhaps she has parents who handle the language well. Perhaps she has had lots of language activities in her life during her early years. Perhaps she has a rather special innate ability for language.

Despite my tone here, I really don't blame you for wanting to know which it is. Unfortunately, I am not convinced that we have any foolproof methods of discovering. We do have tests—all sorts and kinds of tests to give us valuable data; but they don't provide all the answers. Tests may tell you whether your daughter is ahead or not, but they can't tell you how she got to be ahead or whether she will always stay ahead. If your school has any kind of gifted program at all, someone will administer these tests at the appropriate time, so I suggest that you just wait and enjoy your daughter until that time comes.

Some parents tell me that they can tell that their children are gifted because they are bored in the class. I don't buy that. In fact, I find the opposite true. Really good minds are rarely bored. These people may not be thinking about what other students are thinking about, but they aren't bored. No, I've found that too often boredom is the result of a misjudged overconfidence or comes from the inability to see the purpose of the activities of school.

I also think that parents need to realize that growth often comes in spurts. A child who is progressing quite rapidly at a certain stage may not be so rapid within a few months. I would be reluctant to label a child gifted from a few months of evidence.

We think we would like for our son to take first grade over. Will the school let us do that?

The answer depends on two factors: Why do you want your son to take the first grade again? and What is the school's policy?

First, I would recommend that you be very clear on the way you answer the first question. Some educators and experts on children are opposed to repeating a grade for any reason. I don't necessarily agree, but I do think that the people involved in the decision so significant to this child need to be very sure of what they are doing. I feel that there are some valid reasons for asking your son to take first grade again, but there are also some wrong reasons. You must know the difference.

If your son is on a different maturity rate than most children his age, he may be a good candidate for a second year in first grade. Usually this is obvious. The child doesn't walk on schedule, doesn't potty train on schedule, doesn't lose baby teeth on schedule, or doesn't grow physically on schedule. This different schedule in no way reflects the quality of his parents or the quality of his grandparents or the quality of person he is going to be when he grows up. It is just simply a different schedule of maturing. If it is obvious to you that your son is on a different maturity schedule during his childhood, there is a good possibility that he will be on a bit of a different schedule for the next several years. If that schedule is bothering him some—in other words, if he is having problems making friends or he is having problems in motor skills, or having problems sitting still and listening—you may be wise to think in terms of another year in the first grade.

On the other hand, if your son just had academic problems in the first grade, I would encourage you to consider the decision more fully. Explore the reasons for those difficulties. If a student is a bit behind the others academically when he enters first grade, the gap between them will increase some before the situation begins to get better. The children who already know some of the early concepts will make more progress. However, if your son is an intelligent fellow, he could close that gap in just a matter of weeks once he has learned the basic concepts. In this case, I would recommend extra help such as special tutoring or even summer school to see if your son can correct the problem and stay with the friends he has already established.

I also would never recommend repeating a grade as a form of punishment for the child who isn't interested or isn't motivated to do his work. If your child is on a rather normal growth schedule and if he has basically mastered the concepts required of first-graders, but he is having trouble applying himself to the work and finishing all his tasks, I just can't believe that having him repeat first grade will do anybody any good. If he is on course, someday, something will unlock his curiosity.

However, now that I have said all that, if you feel that you have valid reasons for having your son take first grade again, go see the teacher and present your case. If the teacher feels the way you do, you will have an even greater sense of peace about your decision.

If the teacher doesn't agree with you, don't be surprised to encounter some resistance. Usually teachers, administrators, and counselors will not support retention without what they feel are very valid reasons. If your son has made normal progress, they will probably disagree with your proposal.

Our second-grade daughter is in a new "Writing as Process" project. What does that mean?

In its best form, "Writing as Process" is just a new label for an old truth. We know that writing is a form of thinking and an integral part of thinking. As we think of the groceries we need, we write a list. As we think of the jobs we have to do today, we write a list. As we think of a new idea, we write it down so we can tell someone else.

By doing this, writing helps us remember, it helps us formulate, and it helps us clarify.

For a while, the people who taught writing seemed to be missing this function of writing. Instead, they were teaching students to write end products, to develop final papers. Rather than teaching writing as a process of thinking, we were teaching writing as a result of thinking.

The writing as process instruction is supposed to help the student learn to use his language ability and particularly his writing language ability to think through problems, make decisions, and even live a better life.

So far, this all sounds good, and for many students, the reinvented concept is really profitable. Unfortunately, in the hands of some teachers who are either too zealous or don't really understand the purpose of the concept, Writing as Process could become nothing more than an endless task of revising and rewriting.

Our second-grader is a happy, social little boy; but that is his problem. His teacher has already called us in twice about his constant visiting. What are we to do?

If I knew the answer to that question I would still be a second-grade teacher. This is one of the major dilemmas of being both a teacher and a parent. Here we have the classic case of a nice fellow who isn't vicious or mean or rebellious, but forgetful. We have to do something because he must learn the lesson of appropriateness, yet we don't want to discipline so hard that we kill his spirit in the process. You have yourself a rather nice tightrope to walk across. Let's review some steps you could take to come up with a course of action. Notice I didn't call it a solution. You may have to take several courses of action before you find a solution. That is just one of the things that makes working with this age person so much fun. We never know what is going to work.

1. Explore the possible reasons for the problem. You may want to do this with the teacher. As best as we can tell, there are three reasons why a good child disrupts with frequent and spontaneous talking. (a) He may not get enough attention at home. We all need a certain amount of attention to assure ourselves that we are real people and really matter in this universe. Sometimes students who don't get that kind of attention at home will use the classroom to their advantage. (b) He may get too much attention at home. Some children are put on stage. Even when they are quite young, they are always performing. When they say or do cute things, the parents call in the neighbors and relatives for a private showing, and here is this little actor going through his routine for public approval. As he gets older and moves into the classroom, he still needs that public approval. (c) He just may be the kind of person who thinks he has something to say.

2. Once you and the teacher have analyzed the problem, decide on a course of action. You have a wonderful opportunity to teach your son a valuable lesson. He needs to learn when it is appropriate to talk and when not. He needs to learn to respect the welfare of the group over his own feelings. These are really important lessons. Quiet for the sake of quiet is not the issue here. It is a much bigger lesson—something of a lesson of moral sensitivity. To teach your son such an important lesson, you and the teacher need to agree on a common course of action.

One thing that might work would be some form of positive reinforcement. Anything could work here. Make a big button for him. When he goes through a portion of the day remembering not to interrupt with his talking, he gets to wear his button. You may want to reinforce this when he gets home. Give him some special treat if he remembers the rules for an entire day.

You may also want to rethink your home rules for spontaneous talking. If your son is in the habit of interrupting home conversations, you may want to use the same techniques at home.

3. Be patient. This is a learned behavior that he is demonstrating. It will take him some time to unlearn that one and learn another one. Give him time and the encouragement he needs to master the lesson. Whatever you do, don't let this one thing affect the whole tone of your relationship with your son. Continue to have interaction with him in a lot of different areas and treat this as just something small which needs to be conquered. This young man has all the potential of becoming one of the great people of the next generation. Right now he needs your love, and a bit of correction.

Our third-grade daughter still has trouble with her math facts. How can we help her without making it seem like punishment?

Thank you for the sensitivity of the question. Of course you want this child to master those facts, and she needs to master them now before she convinces herself that the task is harder than it really is. If this happens, she will not only always hate math, but she will never have any confidence in herself, so she will never be as good as she can be. You are wise to realize that, but you are also wise to realize that you need to make the activity as much fun as possible. Obviously, what we are talking about is mostly memorization. Some people have fancier words for the process; but I can't remember them so we will just call it what it is. To be able to spout such eternal truths as $7 \times 6 = 42$ requires just a whole lot of memorizing—not too much higher-order problem-solving/critical-thinking skills here. It does help if she knows the concept, but she still has to memorize the fact. Memorization requires a whole lot of repetition.

Now your task is to make all that repetition and memorization fun. But that may not be as hard as it sounds. If you think of it, you can probably turn it into a game for all of you. Make flash cards with the facts in question. Carry those with you so your daughter can practice them in down times, such as waiting in the doctor's office. Given what's available to read in most doctor's offices, she ought to thank you for that. While she is watching her favorite TV program, run through a few flash cards during every commercial.

While she is helping you with the dishes, go through the facts orally.

221

You can ask her the problems for a while but switch off. Let her test you too. When you are in the restaurant waiting for the food to come, assign every family member the task of counting by a certain number (someone has to count to fifty by twos; someone has to count by threes, etc.). When you are in the car, play number games.

From this list, you should get the idea. Learning does not have to be regulated to the regimented, structured world of textbooks and school desks. Use the time the two of you have together to practice a very vital part of her growing. Turn the activity into a game, and in just a few days you should see progress. Your biggest problem may be trying to find some way to change the game to something else once your daughter gets comfortable with her math facts. Usually, they pester you to play all the time.

If I sound knowledgeable about this, it is because we went through the very same problem with a daughter in the very same third grade. When I first discovered how weak she was in her multiplication facts, I panicked. I blamed the teacher; I blamed my wife; and I blamed the whole American society for being so soft on children. But after I got all that out of my system, I designed some games and within two weeks that daughter was the best one in the family on those facts. Most children need a little individualized attention somewhere in their education; and unfortunately, teachers are often too busy to provide just the right attention at the right moment. That is what parents are for.

CHAPTER TWELVE
The Intermediate Grades

We call the fourth, fifth, and sixth grades the middle years for the student probably for the same reason we call the middle child the middle child. The symptoms are about the same.

When our children are young and just beginning their school experience, we worry about them; we worry about the schools; we help and encourage as much as we can. We see the children as potentially innocent victims in a world which might take advantage unless we are available to help.

When our children are in junior high and high school, we worry about them, and we worry about the schools, not so much because we look at our children as innocent victims, but we look at ourselves and possibly even the schools as innocent victims.

But when our children are in fourth, fifth, or sixth grade, we tend to want to relax a bit—let them find themselves, let them be independent. As parents, we meet the first-grade teachers; we are faithful about attending parent conferences; we attend school events. But as our children grow into those middle years, we sometimes forget the value of that school interaction.

I frequently speak at school P.T.A. meetings where classes are presented gifts for having the most parents at the P.T.A. meeting. I have never seen one of those gifts presented to a fourth or fifth grade. The first and second grades always have the most parents present at such meetings.

But for our children, the middle years are quite important. Somewhere in the process, the students have to surrender their hold on childhood and grow into adolescents, whether they want to or not. During the transition, they have to spend part of their time refining their learning skills such as reading and writing, but all the time, they have to be moving toward the future when the learning expectations change.

Since this is such an important time in the life of the student, this chapter is designed more to remind than to instruct. Don't ignore your child during his middle years. He needs your attention as much as ever.

We have never had any trouble with school until this year. Our son is in the fourth grade, and his teacher is terrible. The class is in constant chaos. How damaging could this year be for these children?

That depends on several factors. First, it depends on the individual student. Some students are so sensitive that a year like this could have repercussions for several years, not only in what they lost in subject matter but also in just being able to relate to a teacher. On the other hand, some people this age seem almost immune to this kind of situation. They just adapt, accept what is, and go on about their business.

Another factor to be considered is how you are responding to this. If you are panicking and fretting, you will surely pass part of this on to your child. On the other hand, if you are cool and accepting, your child will have a better chance of learning to adapt to an unfortunate situation regardless of his nature. In fact, if you are particularly skillful, you might even turn this situation into a learning experience in itself.

To work at this approach, the first thing you will want to do is check your own attitude toward teaching and teachers and make sure you don't let this isolated incident cloud all your thinking. Unfortunately, every student going through school will probably have an experience like this at least once in his career. I realize that shouldn't happen but it does. Regardless of how thorough our screening process is and how tough the standards we put on teachers, we still have classrooms which aren't positive experiences. We would hope that it doesn't happen too often, but it still happens; and when it happens to your own child, it is serious. When it does, we need to make sure that we don't lose our own confidence in teachers in general. I once had a bad experience with a medical doctor, but I still go to medical doctors and put my confidence in them because I know there are far more good ones than bad ones.

The next thing you will want to do is to try to decide why this teacher isn't getting the job done. Some teachers are just good with all the students. Some are effective with some students but lose others. This is a matter of chemistry, and since teaching and learning are human activities, it will always be a phenomenon in the classroom. On the other hand, some teachers are just a bad experience for all students. This sounds like the case you have.

Your next step is to try to decide why this teacher is bad. To decide that, you need to consider a few things that could go wrong with a teacher.

1. The teacher has trouble handling her own authority. When teachers have trouble handling their own authority, one of two things occurs. Either they are so inconsistent and disorganized in their attempts to maintain a proper learning climate that the classroom is in a state of chaos; or they come down so hard on students that they control through sheer fear; and the students don't get much work done.

2. The teacher is lazy, tired, burned-out. This is happening some these days. Some teachers simply spend so much energy that it finally catches up with them and they don't care anymore. They quit preparing lessons, or at least they don't prepare thoroughly enough. They don't read and grade the students' papers. They don't teach much. Students soon catch on to a teacher like this, and they not only quit working but they begin to play around in class in an attempt to justify why they are there.

3. The teacher doesn't know the subject matter. This is very rare and usually only happens to the beginner. Though most teachers have to go through a process of constantly learning and relearning, most of them do know what they are supposed to be teaching. This has been proved in recent years in those states where teachers are required to take tests over their own subject matter. We have found that most do know the material.

Now that you have spent some time thinking about why the teacher isn't getting the job done, you are in a better position to help your son. Let's explore some possible steps you can take.

1. Help your son understand what is happening to him. This is the first and most important project for you. You may be able to help the teacher improve some, or you may not be able to. But in the meantime you can help your son. As I said earlier, don't panic. Stay calm. Help your son with his lessons. Supplement if you have to. Read to him if you feel the need. And while you are doing all that, keep helping him understand that not all human beings he meets in his life will be

pleasant people. Help him develop some strategies for what he could do to establish some kind of working relationship with this teacher.

2. Go see the teacher. If at all possible, go under friendly terms. Invite her out for lunch. Meet her somewhere where she shouldn't be threatened about your roles. Try to find out what might be bothering her. You may find that she has some personal or family matter that is making her life miserable. You may find that she has lost her confidence. In other words you may find some perfectly reasonable reason for the kind of year she is having. If so, encourage her. Offer to help. And help your son understand. On the other hand, you may find that she is just a rotten person who acts that way in the classroom on purpose. If so, go to option three.

3. Go see the principal. Again, try to go in a nonthreatening but straightforward way. If the class is total chaos, the principal probably already agrees with you, but may not be able to admit it boldly. State your displeasure. Give specific examples where you can. Perhaps the principal already has some course of action planned to help this teacher improve. If so, give that new plan time to work. Offer your support but at the same time make sure the principal knows the problem.

As teachers, we need to be very clear with our teaching. I once heard of a teacher who planned a fine object lesson for her sixth-graders. She filled one beaker with water and another with alcohol. She dropped a worm into the beaker filled with water; and the worm frolicked around in obvious joy. She then fished the lively worm out and dropped him into the beaker filled with alcohol. Immediately, the worm sank to the bottom, dead.

"Now," the teacher asked in her finest teacher voice, "what have you just learned from this lesson?"

The silence which followed suggested that the students were working on an answer. Finally, one young man proposed a possibility. "I think I know," he said seriously. "People who drink don't have worms."

Joe and Jack were fifth-grade twins when I first met them. Joe was a bright young man. He was in the most accelerated fifth-grade section; he was active in the school chorus; and he was a disciplined and mature student. On the other hand, twin brother Jack was everything Joe wasn't—loud, chatty, prone to arguments, and, in general, an undisciplined student. Not only was he not in the most accelerated fifth-grade class, he wasn't doing too well in the regular fifth-grade class, so we called in Mother. She was a delightful woman—director of nurses at the largest hospital in the area—professional both as a nurse and as a mother.

She understood her sons and made no excuses for Jack. She could tell that he was a rowdy, undisciplined fifth-grade boy, and she was resolved to live with the consequences of his actions.

In the course of the conversation, I suggested, for no reason except that it sounded like something intelligent to say, that maybe she ought to have Jack's eyes examined—just to assure ourselves. She agreed, but only because she was a gracious professional. This not only was an attentive mother, but she was active in health care too. What could I tell her about eyesight?

Nonetheless, Jack had his eyes checked, and sure enough, he needed glasses. I will never forget the day he got them. He had left school on a Friday afternoon to get the fitting. That night, I was working the pass gate at the high school football game when Jack came running up with two unusual additions—the new glasses and a beaming smile unlike anything I had ever quite seen on his face before. When he was still more than twenty feet away he yelled out a brand new discovery, "Did you know that football players wear numbers on their backs?"

The last time I heard of Jack and Joe, they both were in medical school, but I don't know where they are now. Still, I wonder how many children are running around schools not hearing or not seeing and not even knowing that they aren't normal.

Our fourth-grade daughter wants to wear makeup and fingernail polish. How do we say no?

That sounds pretty good to me. Just say no. As a parent, you have a right to say no, and I would think that she can understand that, particularly if you say it loud enough. If you want to get more technical with your no, let's review the steps you may want to go through.

Step 1. Identify Miss Everybody. Let me guess what is going on. In your daughter's fourth-grade class, there is some young lady who is completely in charge, or at least in charge of a little clique of girls. This young lady has decided that all fourth-graders, or at least those who count, are going to wear makeup and paint their fingernails. Since your daughter wants to belong to the clique and needs to be approved by the lady in charge, she has committed herself to complete compliance. Your task, before matters get out of hand, is to identify the lady in charge. If you ask your daughter who she is, you will discover that her name is Everybody. "But, Mother," your daughter sobs, as she pleads, "everybody is doing it." Keep in mind that that is just one person. Now, find that person. Invite her over to your house for pizza. Check her credentials. See how much influence she has on your daughter. See if you and she might reach some kind of compromise. But make sure you meet Miss Everybody. This alone should help your daughter feel better about herself.

Step 2. Choose your war zone carefully. All growing people, children and adolescents alike, need some opportunity to express their individuality, which means that they need some opportunity to look like everyone else their age. Makeup and painted fingernails are such expressions. Is it worth the fight? I'm just asking, because it is your decision. For example, personally, I chose not to fight with my son over how he wore his hair. Rather, I saved my energy to fight over curfew. Now is a good time for you and your spouse to pause and think through where you are going to draw those battle lines. Is this one worth the fight? Again, it is your decision, though you know as well as I that if you ignore the problem, it will go away in a few months.

Step 3. Say no. If you have decided that this is an issue worth fighting over, just say no. You can sugarcoat it some by saying something like, "For whatever reason, God chose to put you in this family. Apparently He sees some advantage for your being here. Obviously, you sense some disadvantage just now. I do hope the pluses of living with us outweigh the negatives. But the answer is no. You can't wear makeup and paint your fingernails. Case closed." Now just assume that this takes care of it and go back into the relationship as if the issue never came up in the first place.

The school sent us a letter saying that the fourth grade would be departmentalized next year. What does this mean?

Departmentalized is a big word which says that the students will take science one period with one teacher in one room and the next period will go to another room with another teacher for language arts and then to another room the next period for math, etc.

The alternative is the self-contained classroom where the student is with one teacher in one classroom all day long.

Which is the better arrangement for fourth-grade students is debatable. The advantages of that departmentalized classroom is that teachers get to work in their strengths. Though elementary teachers have been trained to teach all subject areas, some have definite specialties. When they can work in the area of their specialty, not only do the children get better teaching but teachers are happier and more pleasant to be around. At the same time, a student who may have a personality clash with a teacher or has some barrier to learning with a certain kind of teacher at least won't have to be with that teacher all day every day. Some children really profit from variety. The school can also make better use of its facilities with departmentalization. Since one teacher is going to teach math, the school will need to buy only one set of compasses or one set of computer programs or one set of whatever teaching aid the teacher might need.

On the other hand, some students, particularly students that young, need the security of having one teacher and one classroom all day, so they might actually do better in a self-contained classroom.

If you have a child going into that departmentalized situation next year you will want to be alerted to the fact that it will require some adjustment. Your child will have to learn to be more dependable about keeping his possessions because he won't have one desk all day long as he does in the self-contained classroom. He will need to adapt and adjust to different teaching styles and personalities. He will need to work harder at remembering assignments and books.

Regardless of whatever age a student makes that move from self-contained to departmentalized, he will always face some adjustment. You will need to be especially understanding for a week or two.

CHAPTER THIRTEEN
The Middle School Years

Growth spurts; changing classes; lockers that won't open; falling over blades of grass; wearing jeans four inches too short; falling in love—twice a week; feeling awkward and conspicuous; knowing that everyone is watching; getting behind in the homework; and pimples. It's all part of life—part of that wonderful process called growing up, all completely necessary. But somehow it does seem a little cruel to have it all dumped on you at one time.

As parents, we worry about them, at least when we are not spending all our energy fighting with them. We love them, even though we may not always like them. We work very hard to try to understand them and their world.

This chapter comes equipped with two words of encouragement. Junior high is not terminal. Nearly everyone survives. And yes, even that is normal.

How can I prepare my daughter for middle school?

With love and tenderness. Moving from an elementary school to a middle school is one of the major transitions in a person's life. We rarely lose anybody, but we do confuse several. I am so pleased that you have asked how to help your daughter. Just knowing that you care should make it a bit easier for her. Let me suggest some of the changes that she is likely to encounter and propose some ways for you to deal with those changes.

1. Self-contained to departmentalized classes. Your daughter probably now spends most of her day in the same classroom with the same twenty-five students. When she gets to middle school, this will change. She will get a locker and a schedule, and she will have to learn how to

run at breakneck speed through crowded halls and treacherous stair-cases. That ordeal in itself could be worth a good six weeks of tear-stained pillowcases.

To save yourself a laundry problem, you might see if you could go with your daughter up to the school a couple of days before the whole deal is to begin. (Most schools have a day set aside just for this purpose. If your school doesn't, ask if the two of you can go.) Go with your daughter while she finds her locker and while she opens it a couple of times. Make sure she has the right combination and knows how to use it because to find out on the day school starts that she has been given the wrong combination could produce a long-lasting anxiety trip.

Then travel with her while she locates each classroom in succession. That way she will at least have one route in her mind. Take special note of such things as bathrooms and drinking fountains. She won't have time to search during that first week of classes.

2. Socialization. While in elementary school, your daughter probably knows everybody in her class. When she gets to middle school, thrown together with all those strangers, she will be fortunate if she can find those old friends. If your daughter is a special kind who has a strong need for friends, you may want to let her have a little party at your house sometime during the first or second week just to help her get reacquainted. If she brings the same old friends from elementary school, you will at least know she has some company.

Incidentally, this role will change for you too. If your daughter goes to elementary school in the neighborhood, you probably know all of her friends and their parents as well. In that middle school, the friendship pool changes; she may bring home some foreign names to you. You could get the idea that you are losing control at this point. That is another reason why you may want to host a little party.

3. Academic. Though this varies from school to school and teacher to teacher, elementary school is primarily about developing skills of learn-ing such as reading, writing, and working math. On the other hand, during middle school years, the students are expected to use those skills to learn such things as math and science and social studies. Most middle school teachers assume that the students have the skills and they go on from there. If your daughter is not at least at grade-level on reading and math, you may want to help her get some extra work during the summer. Any student who moves to middle school a bit behind is going to have some rough days ahead.

4. You. One of the biggest changes is what happens to parents as their children escape, trembling, from childhood into the wild years of adolescence. You may want to prepare yourself to offer constant reassurances to your daughter while you learn to live with a teenager.

What is the difference between a middle school and a junior high?

Sometimes the only difference is the name, but usually there is more. One criterion of distinction is what grades are housed in the building. Usually, if a building houses a combination of sixth and seventh grades, it is called a middle school. In fact, most middle schools seem to contain sixth, seventh, and eighth grades. On the other hand, if a building houses only seventh and eighth grades, or particularly if the building also houses a ninth grade class, the school is called a junior high school.

In the mid-1960s when the notion of middle school was just getting started in this country, the middle school was at that time a rather experimental project, and some schools called themselves middle schools because of various patterns of curriculum or instructional techniques. For example, some middle schools experimented with a core curriculum where a couple of subjects such as English and social studies were put into one block. Some experimented with combinations of large group and small group instruction where students would spend part of their day in a classroom with 100 students and part of their day in a classroom with 20 students. Some experimented with individualized instruction packets where students worked by themselves on preassigned projects for most of the school day.

Though there is much residue from many of these experimental projects still around in today's middle schools, usually the title of the school doesn't depend on a particular style of teaching or curriculum technique.

How are middle school teachers trained to teach that special age-group?

Frankly, I find your question embarrassing, not only for me but for educators everywhere. You are so correct in calling this age-group special. These are unique people. So many things are happening to them that they don't understand, so it is a small wonder that no one else understands them. Yet we aren't too sure who is supposed to teach them.

Let me illustrate that by using the certification patterns of our state. Though it is only one state, it does represent rather accurately most other states. In our state, teachers are trained and certified in two different categories, elementary and secondary. Elementary teachers spend a good deal of their college careers taking classes in instructional methods, materials, and techniques. Secondary teachers, on the other hand, spend that time during their college careers taking courses in a specific subject matter such as math or history. With their training, elementary teachers are certified to teach kindergarten through ninth grade. With their training, secondary teachers are certified to teach grades six through twelve.

Now look at what that says. We don't know who is supposed to teach those middle school people. I told you your question was embarrassing.

In all fairness, a few states do offer a special certification for middle school teachers, but that is rare. Across the nation, most middle school teachers were not prepared in any special way for that age-group. Now do you understand why they look so frustrated?

When our son was in the elementary school just around the corner, we knew all his friends. But now that he is in junior high across town, we don't know any of them. Are we normal in feeling that we have lost control?

Yes, not only normal but justified. That may be one of the first and worst confrontations with panic when you discover that you are suddenly the parents of a teenager. You not only lose control of his friendship patterns but you even lose contact with them.

That is frightening because you have to guess about who that awful monster called "Peer Pressure" is. When you conjure up those images in your mind, you almost always come up with something you don't like in your son's friends. Yet, you know enough to know that those friends are very important to him and his development at this point.

But you don't really have to despair—not yet, at least. It is true that your son does have a wider range of people in his friendship pool than those from your neighborhood; but if you work this right, you might be able to turn it into a positive educational experience, both for you and your son.

Though there is a much wider and more diverse pool available to your son, you will need to get to know those people. Of course, you may never know them as well as you knew the playmates from the neighborhood, but you can at least get an idea of what they look like and what they wear.

Encourage your son to invite his friends over. This means that you have to have the kind of home where young adolescents feel welcome. This may mean a few home improvements such as a basketball hoop out by the driveway or even a new stereo set in the living room, but these could be sound investments when you compare them with some other costs involved in rearing children through this age. If he still seems reticent, you may give him permission to have a party—with a minimum amount of adult supervision, of course. Thus, you will at least get a glimpse of the new friends when they come through the door.

If your attempts to get the new friends over to the house fail, try volunteering chauffeur service. Now, I know that is a big commitment, but the extra time is worth the effort. For some reason I don't fully understand, young people tend to loosen up a bit when they are riding in the backseat of an automobile, so you could get an even better idea of who those new friends are than when they come to the house.

If your son is involved in any kind of extracurricular activities, become a supporter. By doing this you will accomplish two goals. You will get to see his friends in action because in all probability his friends come not from his classes, but from his activities. But more importantly, you will be there to support your son and that action will make your relationship stronger.

I am actually serious about these suggestions. I do think that it is important that parents of adolescents make special efforts to know who their friends are. It will just help you so much in helping your child through some difficult periods and deciding what kind of direction you need to apply during those times. Besides, knowing his friends will help you sleep a little better and you will be easier to get along with in the morning.

Our seventh-grade daughter has so many different classes that we can't keep up with all she does have. Is this typical?

Yes. We're lucky we have kids in junior high because most adult minds wouldn't be active enough to remember all the different classes, much less the assigned seats and required materials.

Most educators see this junior high or middle school period as a time for academic experimentation. We need to expose these people to as many different kinds of studies and types of knowledge as possible. Consequently, the school day is divided into several different periods and typical students get a smattering of science, math, reading, literature, art, shop, homemaking, drama, foreign language, or whatever. For the most part, the teachers and administrators understand that this is only a sampling, but it should be enough for the student to find out what he is interested in and has ability in. This should enable him to do a better job of selecting courses and direction in high school and even college.

This is the theory behind the practice of having all those classes.

Our sixth-grade son tells us that he is to take typing. Isn't that a bit early?

In recent years, this has become a rather interesting problem among educators and curriculum planners. Now that many children are beginning to use computers at early ages, some as early as kindergarten, and now that many children are spending hours and hours at the computer, when is the appropriate time to teach people the correct fingering activities of a keyboard?

Some experts tell us that a child can properly finger a computer keyboard as soon as he is old enough to finger a piano. Others are telling us that people really can't be effective at the process until sometime in high school.

Some experts tell us that if a child is permitted to work at the computer with a one-or-two-finger hunt-and-peck system too long, it will probably be very difficult, if not impossible, for him ever to break bad habits and master a more expedient system. Other experts tell us that it doesn't make that much difference.

I am not sure I know with whom to agree, but I do have a couple of observations. (1) I have seen sixth-graders master the fingering process, so I am convinced they can do it. (2) Every student must take typing sometime. Let me restate that. Every student growing up in the United States in the latter quarter of the twentieth century must learn to master the keyboard. It would be criminal to let students out of high school without that basic skill, yet we are doing it. Already, I visit libraries where I can't check out a book without being able to type. I can't even imagine how important this is going to be in ten years.

Yet, we are graduating thousands of high school students every year who have never had an organized, structured time to learn appropriate keyboard maneuvers. The problem is simple—during the high school years, the good students don't have time to take typing. They fill their schedule with the more "academic" courses such as science and foreign language. They are so busy preparing themselves for a future that they don't have time to learn one of the basic skills of the future.

Our school district sent out a little survey asking us how we feel about organized sports for junior high students. How should we respond?

To begin, let me qualify my answer by saying that I am a sports enthusiast. I love sports, and I think that sports participation has a solid educational value for young people, and a definite place in our school programs. Obviously, my answer would begin there, but at the same time, I see some potential dangers to junior high sports programs which dictate that we move with caution.

First, I think that if sports participation is valuable for one student, it is good for all students, or at least all who have any interest whatsoever. Since junior high is a time for experimentation anyway, I think that a good junior high sports program would offer any student an opportunity. I could not endorse a program which would put so much emphasis on winning and success that students would be denied an opportunity to participate. A sports program for junior high schools should have as its primary goal to teach these people how to play the sport.

Now, the biggest problem with what I have just said is that too many people show up for the team. Basketball coaches may get as many as eighty candidates for fifteen spots. Obviously, not everyone can participate and the coaches have to make some cuts. But these cuts shouldn't be final at the junior high school. If eighty people want to learn to play basketball, then the school should provide some kind of alternative program for those who don't make the first team. Some alternatives could be intramurals or before-school practices.

One of the problems with making final cuts for this age is that some of these people will grow and change physically before they reach high school years, and the junior high rejects could well become the high school stars. There is just too much at stake to eliminate junior high students from sports programs.

237

There would be some who would argue with me on the grounds that in real life there are definite winners and losers—first-teamers and second-teamers; and we need to teach young people the lessons of real life. I am not sure I agree, but even if I did, there are far better places to learn the lessons of failure than in something which should be fun like sports at the junior high level.

On the other hand, I do understand why some schools really want a strong junior high sports program. It is a source of school pride and students who have felt some loyalty to their school are better students, better behaved, and even more studious. Besides, there are more people involved than just the athletes. Cheerleaders, pep band musicians, pom-pom squads, popcorn salesmen, and even the people who make booster banners for the halls all get into this school-pride thing and profit from a solid sports program.

Yes, I do favor such a program for its educational value, but still we must always approach it with caution.

Ever since my son entered junior high school, I feel that I have lost him. What went wrong in our relationship?

Probably just oncoming adolescence. Don't ask me to explain why people at this age get moody or grumpy; why they don't seem to be as friendly anymore; why they act as if they are ashamed of their parents; why they quit talking to people they have always talked to before. Don't ask me why they do it, but they do. Your relationship with your son is not all that different from what other parents go through. For whatever reason, communication breaks down somewhere in this process of a child becoming an adult. Your parents probably had the same concern about you when you were that age, but fortunately for selective memory, you have probably forgotten how rotten you were to them during your early adolescent years.

Though I can't offer you any advice for reclaiming what you have lost with your son, I can offer some advice about how to respond to this new relationship.

1. Whatever you do, don't ever give any indication on your part that you have closed the relationship. Regardless of what he does, regardless of how little he chooses to talk, make sure you keep the relationship open. Make sure your son knows it's open too.

2. Surprise your son with an unusual show of appreciation once in a

while. For no reason whatsoever, just grab him and hug him. Say something kind to him when he least expects it. Set up an appointment and take him out to lunch—just the two of you.

3. Meet his friends. At this age, his peers have probably become very important to him. They should also be important to you.

4. Work as hard as you can to continue to like your son. I know you love him and always will, but you may have to work at liking him when he goes through adolescence.

5. Try to remember yourself when you were this age. That is probably an almost impossible order. But work at it. If you can come up with a few memories about how you felt and what went through your mind, perhaps you can understand your son a bit more.

Our son never talks about school. How can we learn what is going on without seeming to be prying?

This is an excellent question, and I suspect a common one. We would all like to know what is happening in our children's lives, and since school is such a part of their lives, we really need some idea about what is happening to them during that time each day when we are more or less closed out of their existence. Yet, some young people choose never to want to talk about school, and some go through periods when they don't share a whole lot.

The first reaction from parents caught in that "Great Silence Chasm" is usually an unfortunate guilt trip. "Oh, there is obviously something wrong in our relationship. My sister's kids share everything. On the soap opera I watch, they talk all the time. What could have gone wrong? Where have I failed in this relationship? Communication is the key and I'm failing as a parent." If you think you have shortchanged him, do something about it; but if it isn't true, don't kick yourself. Again, some young people just choose not to talk. They may be the silent type.

They may be the kind of people who think that their experiences are not worth sharing with anyone else, that nobody would be interested. Or they may be the kind of students for whom school is a rather painful experience and they just don't want to talk about it all that much. Or they may be in a stage of their lives when they are striving to find out what it is like to feel independent. Since school is about the only thing they have outside your immediate jurisdiction, they (probably subconsciously) choose not to talk about school because that is their cloak of independence.

Since we don't know what your son's reason is for not talking about school, let's just list some possible things which you can do to help you catch a little peace of mind.

1. Make sure you have some kind of relationship with your son. Find some common ground where the two of you can talk to each other as human beings—a hobby, a favorite TV program, an upcoming vacation. Try to make these conversations for both of you. Avoid those issues where you may have to show your authority as a parent and come across sterner than you think you are.

2. Encourage your son to have friends around—in the car pool—over to the house. Again, you don't want to dominate the conversation. Just sit on the sidelines with your ears open. To paraphrase that great philosopher, "You can hear a lot just listening."

3. Get in contact with a teacher at school who knows your son. If your son is still in elementary school with one main teacher, that should be easy. If he is in junior high or high school, you may want to look for signs about which teacher your son seems to be close to. Go see the teacher during some relaxed time—over breakfast is often good—and tell the teacher your problem. The teacher may be able to provide you with insights into your son's life that you don't get to see right now.

4. Attend school functions. Go to open house. Make whatever sacrifice is necessary to get to teacher conferences. Go to ball games, concerts, plays, and activities. This probably won't help your son talk any more, but it should give you some feeling about what is happening in his life.

5. Don't close out your son while he is closing you out. Even though he chooses not to share his personal world, you can share yours with him. Someday he may need to come to you with his problems and then he will know that he is welcome.

The other day, I met a frustrated mother. Her twelve-year-old son had just been asked to leave high school (yes, you read correctly) and enroll at the university. In the year and a half that he had been at the high school, he had mastered all it had to offer and was now on his way to the university.

The mother was distraught.

One of her problems was that she didn't quite know how to relate to her own son. She had come to hear my lecture on the early adolescent, and she had read some books on the subject; but this was a special project. She was a mother of an early adolescent who acted mostly like an adolescent but carried a college schedule. That was tough for her.

She did tell me one thing that will always impress me. I asked her if her son was bored a lot. She answered as if she were almost impatient with the question. "Oh, no," she said, "with a mind like that he can entertain himself anywhere."

Our son used to be so cheerful and pleasant, but now that he is in seventh grade he is frequently moody and cries a lot. What is happening?

My guess is that he is a typical adolescent. That is a rather common pattern for the age, and I suspect you may as well learn to deal with it.

I realize that his attitudes and moods frighten you and tire you, but I think I understand his side a bit too. It isn't easy being that age. Have you ever stopped to ponder that everything about his world is in a state of change and sometimes rapid change? His body is changing every day. One day his pants fit and the next day they are three inches too short. One day he sings in the choir and the next day his voice sounds more like that of an owl with postnasal drip. One day he is agile and coordinated. The next day his feet are so big that he trips over a blade of grass and falls in front of people he was trying to impress. One day his skin is all right. The next day he has a huge pimple right on the end of his nose.

His friendship patterns are changing just as rapidly. One day he is popular and well liked. The next day his best friend has grown six inches and has hair on his arms, so now he is the most popular boy in class. One day your son has friends from the neighborhood elementary school. The next day he is thrown into a school packed with 600 strangers.

His daily routine has changed. Last year he had class with the same twenty-five people all day, every day. This year, every forty minutes, he picks up his earthly possessions and runs to a new and strange room filled with even stranger people.

His way of thinking is changing. Once he thought about and believed in what he could see and touch and smell. Now people are telling him that there is beyond all that a world of abstracts that he must learn to master.

Well, I don't blame him. With all that change, I would cry too. Actually, your son has only one way to deal with all those changes. He has to experiment. He has to experiment with different emotions and moods. He has to experiment with different ways to respond to situations. He has to cry and laugh, pout and throw temper tantrums. He may not realize why he has to do all that and parents rarely realize his need; but he has to experiment in some ways. At this point, I recommend two things for you. First, I recommend patience. Your son's behavior is not all that unusual. Be patient. If there is a bigger problem which requires more attention, it will reveal itself in due time; so now just accept what is happening as the expected.

Second, I recommend that as best as you can, provide your son some stability and consistency. Since there is so much change in his world outside the home, try hard to make homelife predictable and constant. Give him a specific set of goals and rules. As best as you can, remember to do everything that you said you were going to do. In other words, keep your promises. Don't give him any more adjustments than you have to.

I just saw a story in today's paper about a school principal who made students carry bricks to class all day when they forgot to bring their books or other paraphernalia. Of course, wiser heads prevailed and the practice was quickly stopped. Everyone seemed to agree that carrying a brick was cruel and unusual punishment.

But I would like to take this issue a bit further. Imagine for a moment that you are a seventh-grader just getting used to middle school. If you are in a typical school, you probably have about eight classes a day. For the first-hour class of math, you will need to bring a #2 lead pencil, a #3 lead pencil, graph paper, a compass and protractor, and a notebook. But on Mondays, Wednesdays, and Fridays, you are to bring your red textbook except every other Friday when you are to bring your Math Tricks book.

For second-hour English, you will need to bring a red pen and a blue pen, your journal spiral, your note spiral, and your test spiral. On Mondays and Tuesdays, you are to bring your grammar book; on Wednesdays, Thursdays, and Fridays, you are to bring your literature book, except every day you are to bring your approved and unapproved library books in case the teacher gives you free reading time.

Well, I have worn myself out just talking about the first two classes, but you do get the picture. Unless, of course, you were in that school in Texas where you would also have to remember to bring your brick.

Our eighth-grade daughter is studying the same thing in math that I studied in college algebra. Is this typical?

I think it is. There don't seem to be too many people who agree with my answer, but I'll stick with it. As I travel about schools and as I watch my children and other people's children do their schoolwork, I am convinced that today's students are about three to five years ahead of where I was when I was a student during the decade of the 1950s.

This push begins early. Five-year-olds are now expected to know what we used to expect six-year-olds to know. Second-graders are expected to master concepts that we used to present in fourth grade, and eighth-graders work on college algebra.

I hear the talk that we have dumbed down the curriculum and the textbooks, yet in the classroom I see the students interacting with concepts far beyond what was expected of us at that age.

Now, I'm confused. I don't know whether to celebrate or despair. Obviously, your daughter is a bright student who is probably mastering the work presented, so I suppose I am happy for her. On the other hand, I am not sure I know the purpose of the push. Where are we going so rapidly? Now that she has had college algebra, what will your daughter study when she gets to college?

Do high schools tell junior high schools what to teach to prepare students?

That situation that you describe has an important sounding name in educational circles. It is called articulation. In some situations, the junior high schools and the high schools are in the same school district, so the curriculum and the activities are planned and coordinated throughout the entire school program. (In other words, there is a great deal of articulation.) For example, eighth-grade students may all be required to read *To Kill a Mockingbird* as a part of eighth-grade literature class. Thus, the high school teachers would know that every student in high school once read *To Kill a Mockingbird,* so they could use that book as a reference point or even a starting point for other experiences with literature.

Though the high school teachers and administrators do not necessarily dictate what the junior high schools do, the school can coordinate learning experiences so that students are better prepared for the next step.

In other situations, the junior high and the high school may not be in the same school district so it is much harder for teachers to get together to make plans and coordinate. In other words, there isn't as much articulation. Whether this becomes an educational problem depends on the teachers and the students involved.

Joseph and Robert have been close friends even before they started to school. Almost the same age, they were the natural next-door neighbors. They played together, cried together, built the tree house together, fought together, and even had the paper route together.

Recently it has become hard to tell whether they will stay close friends. Joseph is almost six feet tall and Robert is all of four feet, six inches. What has happened is completely natural—natural at least for middle school people. Joseph has had his growth spurt and Robert hasn't had his yet. When they do get through growing, they will probably be about the same size again. In fact, Robert may be a bit larger. But for a while, there is going to be one giant difference. What's that difference going to do to their friendship?

Should junior high children be permitted to date?

Are we talking about your children or mine? Obviously, this isn't a simple question with a simple answer. So much is involved. What is meant by a date? Who is involved? What happens on such dates?

Since I can't anticipate all the answers to those questions, let me make some general observations which might help you form some kind of answer.

1. People do not always mature in all areas of their lives at the same speed. Usually, a person is going to have a real growth spurt somewhere between the ages of twelve and sixteen. After that rapid growth spurt, that person will probably begin to look rather mature physically. When you walk down the halls of a junior high school, it is easy to pick out those who have already had that spurt and those who haven't. The

common response is to treat those who look more mature as if they are more mature, but this is often a mistake. Just because a thirteen-year-old girl has begun to look like an eighteen-year-old girl does not mean that she has the emotional maturity of an eighteen-year-old. When we answer significant questions like the one you have asked, we must remember that a thirteen-year-old is thirteen years old.

2. I personally don't think it is a good practice for these young adolescents to date people much older than they. I may be an old stick-in-the-mud, but I could never approve of junior high students dating someone from high school unless there are highly unusual circumstances. Now, when I attach that opinion to the rather common observation that junior high girls are usually a little more mature than junior high boys, I do eliminate a favorable climate for much dating.

3. I highly recommend that parents make sure they agree on this one before the issue comes up and that both parents speak as one voice. If you have a child about to enter this interesting age, anticipate the question. It is surely going to come up. Get together and decide what your answer is going to be. When is dating permitted? What are the rules such as your meeting the other person and curfews? How many dates a week are allowed? What is off limits?

If you get some indication that your young adolescent is anticipating dating, you may even want to find the right opportunity for both parents to sit with the adolescent and cover all the ground rules so that everyone knows the parameters before this becomes a serious family issue.

Our eighth-grade son is the smallest person in his class, and I think it's upsetting him. How can we respond to that?

Growth is such an unfortunate circumstance of this age. Heredity and God decide how big we are going to be when we reach our fullest size, but when we get there is one of the great mysteries of God that no one understands.

Most people this age have an unusual spurt of growth sometime between the ages of twelve and sixteen. Though they spend some time feeling awkward about their new inches added to their height and to their feet and hands and arms and legs as well, for the most part they look forward to the time when the spurt comes. Many things ride on this new growth. The bigger people gain advantages in sports. The more mature looking people have an advantage in social relationships. If we were to admit it, most of us adults actually expect the bigger, more physically mature eighth-grader to act a bit more mature too.

Your son can't help but feel all these pressures. Of course, his size is bothering him. And I am not sure you can do all that much about it. You can try to reassure him. You can show him pictures of uncles who are six feet, four inches, and you can try to persuade him that he is going to get that size someday too. That may help some when he dreams at night, but it doesn't help much during P.E. class when he is the last one chosen for the basketball teams. You can commend him for his other characteristics of maturity such as his ability to solve personal problems or make decisions. I would also recommend that you help him find some activity where his size is not a detriment. If he is at all sports-minded, explore such things as swimming or diving or gymnastics or wrestling. It could be that his size might even be an advantage in some of the sports which place higher emphasis on coordination than size.

At the same time, always keep in mind that he is constantly comparing himself to his peers. Size is a major source of self-image for people this age, so he is going to need a ton of support and encouragement from you.

I have one more request. Share your concern with other parents, particularly those who have younger children. I meet those parents who are in such a hurry to get their children into school that they rush them even before the legal entry age at times. They argue that their children are mature enough emotionally and intellectually to succeed in kindergarten or first grade before they meet the age requirement. I don't disagree with the argument, but you have just reminded us all that age and size can be an issue all through the growing process. When we make a decision to start a child early, we are going to have to live with that decision for the next thirteen years.

Come walk with me through a typical middle school, filled with preadolescents. In this typical school, the sixth-grade students are divided into sections according to their academic abilities. Some of those sections are labeled advanced, some regular, and others are basic or even remedial. I have a notion that if we watch carefully as we walk through each section, just noting size and other indications of physical maturity, we can identify each section according to its given label. The sixth-grade students in the advanced classes will simply be more mature than the students in the regular sections. Of course, there will always be exceptions; but if we note the physical maturity of the class as a whole, we should be able to make an accurate decision.

I have done this often enough to know that as a parent, I would much prefer that my child be a half year older than a half year younger than the other students.

Our daughter wants to take her lunch because she says she doesn't have enough time to eat in the school lunchroom. Is that true?

Probably! Though the lunch period may sound fairly long to me or you—thirty minutes, forty-five minutes, or maybe even close to an hour—that time has a way of getting away from a student quickly. First, your daughter has to go to her locker and put up her books because it would be so awkward and embarrassing to carry those possessions into the lunchroom. That takes no less than five minutes. Next, she has to go down and stand in line to wait for her food. How long that takes depends on several factors—the efficiency of the lunch crew, the discipline in the line as to who gets cuts and who doesn't, and whether or not your daughter can get to the line in time to get up near the front. Nevertheless, she will stand in line at least five minutes and perhaps even longer. Most administrators try to deny this, but students near the back of the line sometimes have their food for no more than five minutes before they are to leave the lunchroom.

Now that your daughter has her tray, she still has one more time-consuming and embarrassing task ahead. She has to try to find a table where she would be welcome to sit. If your daughter is one of those popular students who has a nodding acquaintance with several of her fellow students or if she is socially aggressive, she might be able to find a spot rather quickly; but most junior high school students don't fit into either category, so they have to stand in the aisle, holding a tray of food, and search for a friendly face and a place to sit. This also takes time.

Now, try to understand your daughter's point of view here. Ever since you yelled her awake at 6 A.M. she has been constantly hurrying. She hurried through breakfast. She had to run to catch the bus. She worried about getting her locker open; she had to hurry to first-hour class to complete some homework; she has just been through four hours of induced silence and passive receptivity; she hasn't heard her own voice since 8 A.M.; she is tired; she is weary; she needs a break from all this madness to catch her breath because she is going to have to do it all over again in less than an hour. She just wants to sit back, relax, and spend a few minutes of earned peace and quiet with her friends.

In the name of all that is decent, let her take her lunch, even if it means your getting up a few minutes earlier to fix it. Doesn't she deserve it?

She loves you. You know she loves you. You have always had such a good relationship ever since she was born. She has been so dependent and so appreciative through all the years. She has always been the kind who told you everything. Until she was almost ten years old she insisted that you read to her every night before she went to sleep. You have never had any cause to doubt her love or sincerity. In fact, not two weeks ago she told you that she loves you.

So why did she say this morning, in that pouty way, "Well, Mother, if you HAVE to take me to school in THAT car, could you let me out two blocks away and I'll walk?"

Congratulations. You have a junior high daughter. Aren't they wonderful?

The seventh-grade teacher had the class absorbed in a lesson on economics. As the new concept became appropriate to the discussion, she wrote on the board, "obsolescence."

She backed away, looked at the new word for a moment and asked, "OK, class, what does this word mean?"

Since she was a veteran teacher, she wasn't afraid of the silence that followed, so she waited as the seventh-graders furrowed their brows, and narrowed their eyes to demonstrate that they were searching through their minds to come up with some memory of that word which they had heard somewhere but hadn't recorded as a permanent mental concept.

Finally, one fellow hesitantly held up his hand and ventured a guess. "I think I know," he said, sounding somewhat sure of himself. "Isn't that what you go into when you leave adolescence?"

Somehow the teacher managed to keep a straight face through it all. Sometimes teaching is a rough profession.

The school reports that our daughter has been tardy to her third-hour class three times. What should we do?

Buy her new Reeboks or maybe roller skates. No, wait a minute; before you do that, I have a better idea. Begin by talking to your daughter to get her side; and I recommend that you believe her. I have a suspicion that her reason for those tardies is valid. Let me guess. She had P.E. the hour before and she just can't get her clothes changed that fast—valid reason. That is the exact time of the morning when the breakfast orange juice takes effect, and she has to go to the bathroom— valid reason. (Keep in mind that going to the bathroom may not be the simple task you think it should be. Some of the bathrooms may be locked, and some of the bathrooms have been declared off limits to your daughter by the crowd that uses a specific bathroom at a specific time. She probably has to search.) Or maybe your daughter's third-hour class is over in another wing where she has to go way around and come up the up staircase—valid reason. Perhaps the second-hour teacher is so lost in his own ego that he goes overtime in class. After all the principal has ordered the teacher to teach all the way to the bell and not give those students time to pack up early—valid reason. Perhaps the third-hour teacher requires a ton of books every day and your daughter has to stop at her locker to pick up the extras—valid reason.

Frankly, I think you ought to hug your daughter for the five times a day that she gets to class on time. No student gets to class without effort. Your daughter has already demonstrated that she is a responsible, caring, fast, and tough person just to get there as often as she does.

Now even though you understand, you still have the problem. I suggest that you do talk to your daughter, find out the problem, then request a meeting of the third-hour teacher, the principal, your daughter, and you. Go with a smile on your face with the intent of finding a solution. Show the teacher that you respect his need to have all the students in class on time. He is not making an unfair demand. But together, the four of you can come up with some workable solution to this problem.

Of course, if your daughter had been tardy thirty-five times, this would be a different kind of situation.

We are so afraid of peer pressure. How can we as parents help to defend against its having so much influence on our son?

What an important question! Would you like to take the anxiety out of being a parent? Simple, just pick your child's friends for him. "Yes, you can be friends with him. No, stay away from that one." Doesn't that sound easy? I dare you to try it. That kind of input from parents almost always backfires. No, somehow you have to accept those peers your son chooses; then you have to work alongside your son to make peer pressure a positive part of his growing experience. Let me make some statements which, if they don't give any specific advice, will at least help you assess the task you have undertaken.

1. Peer pressure is easier to define than I once believed. I used to believe that all adolescents met somewhere every Saturday night and decided what the group would stand for next week. In recent years, I have come to realize that is not accurate. Peer pressure is just one person, and that person is the person your son admires. Of course, at your house, that person's name is "Everybody." "But, Mother, Everybody will be there." "But, Daddy, Everybody is getting a Mohawk this year." It's a lot easier to deal with when you suddenly realize that Everybody is just one guy. Now, your next chore is to find out who Everybody is and invite him over to the house. You need to get acquainted with this person who has so much power in your child's life.

2. Peer pressure is important in your son's growth. I speak to church youth groups about value formation. After we talk awhile about what a value is and what it means, I ask, "Think of a value you hold and think about where you got that value." The most common response to that activity is "friends." In fact, that response comes automatically and easily. After more thought, these students will mention parents and the media. They almost refuse to name teachers as a source of values. By their own admission, adolescents do learn from their peers.

3. Peer acceptance is tied to self-concept. OK, do you like to feel good about yourself? Well, of course you do. Do you sometimes go to rather lengthy measures to establish a positive self-concept? Well, of course you do. So my next question for you is, What one thing in your life is most significant in your forming a healthy self-concept? If you are a typical adult, we can assume that it is your work, your productivity.

Most teenagers don't have that going for them, so they substitute friendships. They must be accepted by someone to feel good about themselves. That is why some of their actions and decisions in the name of friendship are so compulsive and bizarre. "But I must go to the mall tonight."

"But, Dear, we can't go to the mall tonight. It just snowed forty-two inches."

"I don't care. I'm going to the mall even if I have to crawl on my hands and knees."

Would like to hear something real bizarre? I understand that logic.

4. Your son doesn't have as large a pool of friends to select from as you may think. Though he does go to a school with 1,500 people his own age, he doesn't know that many. If he is in some activity that throws people together such as sports or a music group, he will know those people; but other than that, his opportunity to meet people is more limited than adults think. Thus, his friendship patterns and selections may not make sense. But friendship isn't ever a very reasonable enterprise.

Now that you know more about peer relationships than you really asked for, let me answer your question. How can you defend against peer pressure being such a force in your son's development? Let me list some suggestions.

1. Do everything you can to help your son develop a good self-concept. Since self-concept is addressed in another section of this book, let me say here only that if you help your son develop a healthy self-concept on his own, he won't need peer acceptance as much as he would otherwise. In fact, he might even act sensibly some times.

2. Make an effort to get acquainted with your son's friends. Make them all comfortable at your house. Demonstrate to your son an attitude that reminds him that he doesn't have to be afraid of you and doesn't have to keep secrets from you.

3. Help your son learn how to make decisions for himself. Show him how you make decisions. Help him weigh his choices in certain matters in such a way that he will know how to weigh his choices in other matters when you are not around.

4. Share your values with your son. Don't apologize. Just tell him what you stand for. But remember, you had better stand for it if you tell him because your son will be the first to know when your words and your actions don't coincide.

We are eighth-grade class parents. At a party the guys went off and played basketball while the girls sat around and talked. Did we do something wrong?

You volunteer to be eighth-grade class parents and you ask me if you did something wrong? Did you ask for counseling or prayer before you started? Actually, I am only jesting. I really like eighth-graders myself. As a species, they are one of the most interesting groups on the face of the earth.

It is about this time of physical growth and hormonal reaction that someone turns on the giant TV camera in the sky. Every normal eighth-grader knows instinctively that someone and maybe everyone is watching, and watching constantly. You don't dare take out the garbage unless you are appropriately costumed in the costume in vogue at the time. Who knows who may see you in the street? You don't dare go shopping with Mom but if you get caught and have to go, stand on the other side of the store lest someone see you and you would be mortally embarrassed for the rest of your life. When you are at a party, you don't dare talk to a girl. Even if you wanted to, you don't because surely everyone there would laugh at you. On the other hand, if you are an eighth-grade girl, you don't dare talk to an eighth-grade boy because they are so "childish and immature." Now, if a junior boy talks to you, that's a different matter. It's cool to talk to a junior boy but not to an eighth-grade boy.

Now, let's see a show of hands. How many of you remember feeling this way when you were in the eighth grade? Well, of course you don't remember it. You were so embarrassed and self-conscious the whole year that you have somehow put all that out of your conscious memory. You probably don't even remember eighth grade at all.

No, you didn't do anything wrong at the party. Don't worry. If you keep being class parents, when they become sixteen and all get their driver's licenses, you will be asking about too much interaction.

Of course, if you have another party, you may want to try some mixer games. Try making a boy and girl hold hands and play basketball as one unit. That ought to put some variation in the game. While it is going on, everyone will complain, get embarrassed, and protest. But when it is all over and they are lying in their bed at night with the light out, they will remember it as fun, and secretly, oh, so secretly, they will thank you.

What is a science fair?

Thanks for asking. A science fair is one of my favorite school projects. Though science fairs are good educational techniques for students of any age, they seem to be the most popular at the junior high level. Though some states have now developed them into competitive state-wide events, any school could conduct one.

In theory, the students in a school, either working alone or in groups of two or three, conduct some piece of scientific research, write a paper, and build a poster describing that research; and then they bring the whole procedure to the gym or some other big room where interested persons can come by to take a look at what students are capable of doing and perhaps even learn things. With our bent to competition and trophies, most often the projects are judged.

For the students, the fair is just the motivator. The real learning goes on in the research and the preparation. During these times, some students, and frequently some less enthusiastic ones, do very good work. There are those who would criticize science fair projects because of parent intervention. I do know this is a danger—that overcompetitive or overzealous parents might do all the work for the students—but I think that the students who do most of their own work and learn the lessons are worth the risks.

For me, the real learning goes on while I am at the fair. I must confess. I wasn't a very good science student when I was in school, and I am trying to take up some slack. I go to every science fair I can find. In fact, I'll sometimes drive miles just to get to one. Some people think I do it because I am supporting the students. Not true. I do it because I am trying to learn science. And I do. For example, I learned about casting out nines at a science fair once. Just the other day I learned that fish are color-blind.

Now, I hear of some schools which are planning a history fair built on the same model. I even heard about a school which has an Elizabethan fair where history, art, drama, and music all come together. If participation is the apex of learning—as most experts would tell us—these students should never forget these activities, and I just kind of believe that someday they could live a little richer lives because of it.

CHAPTER FOURTEEN
The High School Experience

The high school is something of a watershed experience for the American educational career. Students enter this experience as they are just beginning adolescence, and they graduate more adult than child.

Though this is a four-year transition, that four years is often so packed with different activities and different emotions and different periods of growth that it seems much shorter than that.

Since the Kalamazoo Case in 1874 determined that high schools were an integral and necessary part of American education, and since the Committee for the Reorganization of the American High School in 1918 set the goals and expectations, a high school education has become something of a necessity in American life. For many of us, it is a common bond, a mutual experience, something from our growing days that we all can share in.

Though the high school experience is something of a common bond, the American high school experience is uniquely American in at least a couple of ways.

For one thing, the idea of a comprehensive high school is unique to this country. In most countries, by the time students reach high school, they begin to attend specialized schools. Some will go to college prep schools. Others will attend all sorts of different kinds of professional schools. In some countries, students will select a specific high school because of a major study interest. In some countries, high school students are assigned to specific schools depending on their academic abilities.

But in the American high school, we see the epitome of the American dream. We put everyone in one school, the comprehensive high school. What is good for one is good for all. If one students needs algebra and chemistry, all need algebra and chemistry. The high school shall be the common educational experience.

The other feature which distinguishes the American high school from those in other countries is the emphasis on the extracurricular. In our country, playing chess or football or blowing a horn or singing in the choir may not be as important as algebra and chemistry, but it is still a part of the school and school life. These experiences become a part of the high school experience and high school memories.

Since the American high school is a rather unusual experience, we as parents need to study it carefully. Not only is it significant in what our own children become, but it is also significant in what this nation becomes.

Our daughter is very bright, but she wants to go to school every summer to finish high school in three years. Is this a good idea?

Sometimes it is and sometimes it isn't. Frankly, I don't see why any of these young people are in such a hurry to grow up, but some are.

Some people do thrive on pressure. Your daughter seems to be one of those. If so, perhaps her plan will work for her. She needs the pressure to motivate herself and to keep from getting bored with the slower pace of some high school work. Perhaps she even needs the pressure of future plans such as what she is going to do once she has finished high school or even when she has finished college. But she does need to know that completing high school in three years is a proposal to accept some stress. I have seen students who set their standards high, rushed through, then had to take some time off just to recover from the intense pressure.

There are always a couple of other potential dangers in completing high school ahead of schedule. For one thing, high school is as much a time for maturation as it is a time to pass the courses. People enter high school at fourteen years of age and come out at eighteen, nearly 25 percent older than when they entered. In addition to learning a little bit about history and literature and science and math, they develop attitudes about themselves and life; they develop strategies for establishing and maintaining friendships; they develop skills in leadership and following instructions. All these are important lessons which the person who hurries through may miss.

The high school time is also a good time for a person to develop a well-rounded approach to living in general. Students who hold down a part-time job do volunteer work in hospitals or nursing homes, participate in extracurricular activities, or take some elective courses during the summer can really turn these experiences into profitable learning experiences as they begin to decide how they are going to spend the rest of their lives.

I would not suggest that you discourage your daughter in her plan to finish high school in three years, but I would recommend that you help her explore all her options.

The other day I ate in a '50s restaurant. The decor and memorabilia had been chosen to remind us of the good times and the good memories of that era—the old-fashioned soft drink glasses, pictures of Edsels, waitresses in bobby socks, and vinyl booths all took us back to memories of thirty years ago.

To complete the image and the memory, the menu cover consisted of parts from an original high school yearbook from 1953. It occurred to me as I sat there reliving that decade of how appropriate that final piece of decor really is. The decade of our memories twenty, thirty, or even fifty years later is the decade of our high school days.

As I sat there and remembered, I was reminded again of how significant high school is to what we become, not just as professional people or spouses or parents, but as human beings and what we remember when we remember the good old days.

My daughter has the option of taking a course called "The Bible as Literature." What is such a course?

Regardless of who protests and regardless of the basis for such protests, the Bible is still one of the most significant documents in the history of the Western world. It has a definite place in the curriculum of our schools. The most common and perhaps the most reasonable place to study the Bible in public schools is in literature class; so many schools have developed a Bible unit in a literature class, or many schools have even developed a specific English elective course called Literature of the Bible.

What the course is depends on the teacher. Of course, that is true of all courses, but it is especially true of this particular course. Teachers can make this one of the most beautiful and profitable courses students have ever had. Teachers can make this one of the driest courses allowed to exist on earth. Or some teachers could even turn this into a course of controversy filled with cynicism.

Every time I have seen the course taught, it was taught by a Christian, and those Christian teachers made the course beautiful and profitable. They were able to achieve a very beautiful balance of preserving the integrity of the literature and the role of the author yet conveying the thought that this material is different because it was written by inspired people. Because I knew the teacher, I recommended the course for my own children. As a parent, I thought the course was more profitable to my high school children than a whole year of Sunday School.

For content, the course usually covers the poetry of the Bible including the Psalms, Proverbs, and Job; some of the archetypal accounts such as the story of Creation and of the Exodus, and the parables as examples of metaphors and the role of storytelling in literature.

If you are interested in finding out more about the course, Dr. Leland Ryken of Wheaton College has written some excellent books on the subject, some of which are used as textbooks for the courses.

My high school son has three difficult courses the first three periods of the day. Is that typical?

Yes. The logic behind it is simple. Students are more alert in the mornings, so the teachers want those difficult courses early in the day and those snap courses later, after the students have experienced a Twinkie high and a lunch of carbohydrates and sugars.

It seems to me that there is some wisdom in this thinking. How well a student does in a course does depend, in some measure, on when he has that course. The problem is what is happening to your son. Some students have those tough courses back-to-back and their minds are fried after the third period. Of course, he does have the rest of the day to recuperate.

I spend most of my time working with beginning teachers—people who are just getting initiated into the process. Almost 70 percent of all the problems those beginning teachers encounter come from their last hour classes. Another 15 percent of the problems come from the classes right after lunch. These statistics include all problems—classroom management, motivation, inability to comprehend. Frequently, those beginners suspect a conspiracy. They call and preface their request for help with an announcement, "The administration put all the problems in the sophomore class in my last hour section." But I think what they are trying to tell me is that by the last hour, they are tired and the students are tired, and no one wants to learn much.

Our son is going to enter high school in the fall but is still shy. Will that hurt him in class?

I suspect that every high school student is shy in some ways. The experts on adolescence have given this self-consciousness a big name—they call it egocentrism. What it means is that the kid is shy. These same experts tell us that it is the common syndrome of the age—everybody has it. So in those respects, your son is not different from every other student there. He just shows it differently.

But you have another kind of problem. Your son is not aggressive, and that is a bit of a concern. Will he be able to shove his way through the halls to get to classes on time? Will he be able to find a table in the cafeteria where he can relax during lunch? Will he be able to share a locker with a peer in P.E.? Those are the concerns. But the actual classes may surprise you. Most students don't talk in class. Yes, that is true. In the typical suburban high school most students go through the school day without saying one word in class. Even in classes where there seems to be a lot of discussion and student talk, most of that is carried on by a small number of students. Others just sit and listen. Your son would fit right in.

I do, however, have a couple of suggestions—one for him, and one for you. For him, I would recommend that he create some special problem in every class—he didn't understand the assignment; he really enjoys the book; his desk is too far from the chalkboard—some problem which demands some attention. Then he should go see his teacher in a private meeting to address the problem. Do you see what I am recommending? A private meeting with every one of his teachers. This doesn't have to be elaborate—just a few seconds to make sure the teacher knows that your son is a real person. The next time the teacher calls the roll, or grades papers, or has a special duty, he will at least know your son's name.

Now, I have a suggestion for you. Make sure your son has at least one friend in the building, even if you have to engineer this. Invite some mother over with a son the same age or have a party or something. Even the shiest people need at least one friend. If your son has that, his shyness shouldn't really matter that much; and could even make him popular with those teachers who despise social talking in their classes.

We are helping our daughter plan her high school courses. How can we decide which are the most important?

Before I answer the question, let's just celebrate what you are doing. Aren't you happy that you have those choices? Aren't you thankful for the comprehensive high school which allows young people some choices in what they will study? This is a rare privilege, almost unique to the American student, and we should make sure we celebrate it and preserve it.

Now let's get to the question. There are three factors to consider in planning a high school career.

1. What are the graduation requirements? That's obvious. This is a given. All states have basic requirements which all high schools must meet. But individual schools often have requirements of their own over and above what the state requires. Since the student's first objective is to graduate, those courses are the most important.

2. What courses teach basic life skills? I could get into two different arguments here. Some students might argue that no course is really that basic to life, and you may argue with what I put on my list. But I am bold enough to make the list regardless of the argument. First, I think that it is almost a crime to let any student graduate from high school who does not know the proper way to finger a typewriter keyboard. Maybe a student doesn't need a full year of typing, but everybody needs to know where to put his fingers on a keyboard and which finger punches which key. Your daughter is going to live in the computer age whether she wants to or not, so she has to know how to work the thing. In a few years, we won't be able to check a book out of the library in this city without typing skills. What's next? Grocery shopping? Banking business?

The second thing I would put on that list is driver's education. If your daughter has an opportunity to take a course in driver's education, thank all the powers and make sure she gets it on her schedule. In all my experiences around high schools, I have never seen driver's education taught poorly. I highly recommend what I see.

3. What does your daughter like to study and do? If there is anything left, after she meets the first two groups, your daughter should take something she enjoys. Some people—high school counselors, college advisers, and parents—often recommend the toughest and hardest courses available or the ones with the best reputations for being tough and hard—physics, foreign language, or calculus. I understand the reasoning for this. We don't want to see these young people waste their time. But a course in art or shop or child care or cooking is not a waste of time, and there will always be time for the heavy stuff later. The one thing that every student should get out of high school besides a diploma is some happy memories. That should be the key when you help your daughter plan her schedule.

4. What does your daughter need to get into the college of her choice? You can learn that by writing to the admission officer at the college.

I am amazed to see what computers can do for us. The other day, I went to visit a high school English class working in the computer room. These students had written a rough draft of a paper. They typed the paper into the machine and punched a button. That machine gave them a full analysis of the paper they had just written—sentence length, paragraph length, use of slang and informal language—those students learned more about their writing styles than they probably wanted to know. With the computer feedback, the students were then able to go back and revise and improve their rough drafts, coming up with a second paper much better than the first effort had been.

It was a wonderful process, educational and productive. There was only one minor hitch. Since these students were in an advanced class, they were some of the better students in the school, and they had never had time to take a typing class. It took them three or four times longer to type that paper into the computer than it should have.

There was something sad about the process—those good minds sitting all that time at those computer terminals taking far too long to complete a simple task—having all that technology available to them and not able to make the best of it because they lacked a simple skill.

Our ninth-grade daughter has moved to high school this year, but she seems so young to be with seniors. Wouldn't it be better for ninth-graders to stay in junior high one more year?

This is the age-old question. What grades fit with which; or in other words, what ages are most compatible with each other?

From all the changing that is going on in the name of experimentation we can come to one conclusion, the school people don't know the answer either. Originally in this country, there were really only two school divisions. There was one building to house everyone through eighth grade and one building to house grades nine through twelve. After the junior high schools came into existence sometime about the turn of this century, many communities took the seventh and eighth grades out of the elementary school, and the ninth grade out of the high school to form the new junior high school. During this time parents and school officials raised serious questions about the age and maturity gap between seventh-graders and ninth-graders.

Sometime in the early '60s, some communities began to experiment with the middle school concept, and began to group sixth-, seventh-, and eighth-graders into one building and shipped the ninth-graders up to the high school. For the most part, high school administrators and teachers accepted this grouping with something between subdued and open anger and hostility. Nevertheless, this has become something of an accepted grouping, and high school personnel seemed to have accepted it.

Of course, this isn't a perfect model. Probably the ideal model would have every grade in its own special building because there is so much change and diversity between the age-groups of adolescents. But since this isn't practical, in the name of curriculum and administrative efficiency, the nine through twelve high school is a workable model.

I do agree with you. There is a wide age and maturity difference between freshmen and seniors (at eighteen a senior is 20 percent older than a fourteen-year-old freshman.) But most high schools have the personnel and programs to accommodate the differences. For the most part, students accept this arrangement and live with it.

On the other hand, I applaud those schools which are sensitive to the adjustment freshmen have to make and develop specific programs to help with the transition. For example, some schools are now having a special day sometime about a week before school starts for the freshmen to come into the building, find their lockers, make the journey from class to class so that they can find the most efficient route, buy lunch tickets, get acquainted with each other, and meet their teachers. This couple of hours before school starts can save the average freshman student weeks and weeks of anxiety, embarrassment, and needless activity.

If your school doesn't have such a day, suggest it to the principal. He may hug you for your ideas.

Our sophomore son has almost three hours of homework per night. Is that typical?

What would you like—research statistics or my own nonscientific personal observation? Research tells that the average high school student spends forty minutes a week doing homework. My own personal observation based on my experience as a parent, my experience of being a high school student in 1984, my conversations with students, my classroom observations, and my conversations with parents is that your son's workload is fairly common.

The next question is whether all this is necessary or is even educationally defensible. Some would argue that whatever else it might be, school needs to be hard. Students need to learn discipline, the value of hard work, and good study habits. In fact, some college counselors tell us that the most important thing for high school students to learn is good study habits. Obviously, your son is learning that lesson.

Others would argue for the homework on its own inherent educational value. Students need to learn the curriculum; they need to interact with the ideas; they need to practice the material; and there just isn't enough time in the classroom to get everything done. Thus, the homework is not only important but necessary.

Since I am not all that concerned about keeping up with the Japanese or any other country we are trying to compete with right at the moment, I could accept the second position much quicker than the first. Yes, there are some activities which have to be done outside of the class. Since most high school students are actually taking classes every period of the day and aren't in study halls, this constitutes homework. Unfortunately, it often disrupts the student's life, and even the family life, infringing on family activities and chores (and even television watching). But it may be necessary.

The test of the value of this is whether this piece of work is important. If the activity isn't worth doing in the first place and the students are only doing it in the name of homework, then I suggest that it is worthless and actually infringes on the rights of the students. Adolescents don't need busywork to keep them busy. They are busy enough without it.

A good rule of thumb for the test of importance is how important the teacher thinks it is. In other words, what does the teacher do with the work after your son has done it? If the teacher checks it, makes comments, and returns the work, then it has been of educational value and your son has learned from the homework assignment. Thank the teacher.

On the other hand, if the teacher never collects the work, collects it and throws it away, or collects it and keeps it in his desk drawer unread, then the homework is busywork with no educational value. If I were a student in that situation, I could lose my motivation in a hurry. Then you could call the teacher and tell him you protest.

When I was twenty-seven years old and one of the smartest teachers in America, I took a job teaching high school English at a university laboratory school. The students were pleasant people, very bright, and educationally sophisticated. They knew that they were in a fishbowl—that they were being used for lab purposes—punched and probed and observed and experimented on. But in spite of all this, they kept their sanity—just another indication of the brilliance of adolescents.

But those students knew something that I didn't know when I first started. They knew the difference between busywork and good work. They soon taught me the difference. Sometime during the first week, I gave them some earth-shattering, terribly important assignment— something like write down all the uses of commas that you can think of and illustrate each. One of my special friends in the classroom, a handsome fellow who was both student body president and captain of the football team, held up his hand and announced that the assignment was busywork. Twenty-five others nodded in unison, and the next day not one student had done the assignment. I don't mean that they hadn't completed it. They hadn't even started. I ranted; I raved; I went home and cried and begged my wife not to make me go back tomorrow. But I did go back, and that day I gave another assignment. "Now that we have read *Julius Caesar*, whom do you think would make the better President of the United States—Brutus or Mark Antony? Write your response."

All night long I stayed awake and practiced what I would say when that crowd came with empty hands and minds the next day. I practiced both anger and toughness, so I was ready.

As they walked into class the next day, each one of the twenty-six walked by my desk and carefully laid his response down. Most were typed. All were neat, the products of careful thought and work. And the average paper was seven pages long. All the ideas were valuable and some were even worth publishing.

I had learned the difference between busywork and real work. I wish all teachers could have such an education.

Our son is artistically talented, but he absolutely refuses to take art classes. Why?

There could be several reasons, all of them valid. One is just the nature of our society. In His infinite wisdom, God created some of us more gifted with words than with our hands. Your son seems to be the other kind—somebody gifted with his hands. Unfortunately, schools are about words—we speak words, write words, read words, think words. The students who work better with their hands than with words struggle throughout their educational careers.

In elementary and middle schools, art and hand activities are at least put on a par with the rest of the courses; but all too often, during the high school years, any hand activity, art included, takes on a stigma. Art classes are filled with students who haven't been too successful in the "more important" classes, such as chemistry and foreign language. Unfortunately, regardless of how serious the work is in the art classes, that stigma still exists in too many schools.

Most high school students tell me that art classes in their schools are filled with "burnouts." I offer that as their observation instead of mine because I think it carries more weight. It is this perception that causes most serious students to avoid the art classes.

Another reason your son avoids art classes may be one that we have already discussed. Perhaps your son has his life's goals in mind already. He wants to get into a good college and move into a career, and no one is talking about the importance of art or music or shop or typing. We just talk about chemistry and math and literature. Those are the important courses.

Since you didn't ask for advice, I will give some anyway. Whatever his reasons for not wanting to take art, I doubt that you are going to change his mind. At his age, perception is reality. (Maybe it is at my age too.) Thus, if you really want him to develop his talent with expert instruction, why don't you investigate the possibility of a night class at a local community college? Just the idea of going to the college erases the stigma problem, and many of those instructors are very good.

I enjoy going to daylong conferences for adults—teacher conferences, church conferences, study conferences, business meetings. I thoroughly enjoy watching adults who have just had the pleasure of listening to lectures for four or five hours. Their eyes are glassy; they have trouble sitting still or holding their heads up. They listen as if their ears have glazed over. Even with the funniest joke, the speaker has to pause and let the laughter catch up. Many of them are in some form of disrobing. Men have their ties loosened and the women have one or both shoes off.

If you have ever been there, you know what I am talking about. It is tough work to have to listen to lectures for four or five hours in a row.

But have you ever stopped to think about the difference between the adult after going through a day filled with lectures and the average student? The adult is probably going somewhere and relax when it is all over. The student still has to go home, complete his homework assignment, and memorize all those lectures for a quiz tomorrow.

Our high school just sent out a flyer saying that it was using the "effective schools research." What is that?

In recent years amid this talk of improving and reforming schools, some researchers have begun to study schools which are considered to be good schools, or in other words, effective schools. What qualifies as effective varies some but, generally, the researchers have considered such evidence as scores on national tests, community opinion, the number of students who continue education after they leave the school, the rate of dropouts, and the rate of attendance.

The researchers, using some or all of that evidence, identify the schools which seem to be effective; then they begin to dig deeper to see if they can find some common qualities which might, in fact, help those schools achieve those goals.

The researchers have been almost reluctant to make a list of characteristics of effective schools because they are afraid that other schools will use the list incorrectly in changing things about that school. In other words, the researchers maintain that having an effective school is more complex than just ticking off a list of characteristics.

Nevertheless, despite their reluctance to establish such a list of characteristics, such a list does exist. It includes such things as:

1. The school has a distinctive and recognizable educational mission which teachers, students, and administrators can state.

2. The school provides a safe and pleasant environment for students to learn.

3. Principals are seen as master teachers rather than as policemen.

4. Teachers have some voice in establishing school policy.

5. There is evidence that teachers have specific strategies for maintaining classroom control and presenting lessons.

Our daughter is in some classes called accelerated and some called regular. What is the difference?

This practice, called tracking, ability grouping, or homogeneous grouping is based on the assumption that teachers can do a better job of teaching classes where students are similar in their abilities and interests. In other words, classes with nothing but good students can move faster than classes where the instruction has to be slowed to accommodate slower learners. Usually, there are at least three tracks and sometimes as many as five. The labels for those groups may vary from school to school.

Since an individual student may be stronger in one area than another, that particular student may be in different tracks in different subjects. This is what has happened to your daughter.

For some reason—past performance, test scores, or a combination—the school people have decided that she is one of the top students in some areas, so she has been placed with other good students in something called an accelerated class.

But now that this has happened, the difference between the accelerated class and the regular class depends on the teacher involved. Normally, the accelerated classes would move a little faster and cover a little more material. Sometimes there may even be some variation in curriculum materials. For example, in literature classes the accelerated students may read a more sophisticated work than the regular students would. At times, there could even be some variation in teaching methods. Some proponents of tracking would recommend that the accelerated student should do more individual work on his own or small group work.

Of course, this is always the ideal, and doesn't always work this way. The deciding factor is the teacher involved.

We have been transferred, and our sophomore son will have to change schools. What will be his biggest adjustment?

Changing schools at any time always provokes a bit of trauma, fear, and frustration; but changing schools during the high school years can be a major upheaval if it isn't handled correctly.

The biggest adjustment, of course, is social. Your son is going to have to give up his friends and try to find some new ones, and that isn't easy. The friendships in the new school have already been established. It isn't so much that people are rude; but many of those friendship circles (social cliques) just don't need any more membership, and a new student is an intrusion. Usually, the only place where the new student is really welcome is with that group of students who haven't had much success themselves—the kids who are struggling in classes or with authority or with their own social positions.

If your son participates in some extracurricular activity such as athletics or music, he can facilitate the friendship problem a bit, but he will still have a struggle.

For one thing, your son could use some help just getting through the school day. In every building, there is an unwritten code—a sort of conspiracy of survival, a set of instructions for getting through the day. This code that the students know, but the adults in the building don't, includes such pieces of information as: What teachers police the halls for running and which don't? Where are the jams during passing period? What do we have for lunch on Tuesdays? Which teachers grade homework and which don't? Which bathrooms are OK to use and which aren't? That code is so large and involved that a new student just can't discover it all on his own. Your son will need a friend to teach him the ropes.

Another reason that friendship is important is just the very nature of learning and the classroom. Learning is a very private matter, just one isolated mind against the material, but the classroom is one of the most public places around—scores of strangers sitting so close while the person works his own mind. Knowing someone in the classroom just helps this process work better.

Because of that, we are back to my second rule of school survival. Never send a child to school without the child knowing someone there. I don't know how you are going to handle this. Get involved in church as soon as you get to the new town—invite some people over who have children your son's age. Whatever you do, help your son get acquainted with somebody. And while he is in that process of reestablishing close friendships, he will need more from you—more of your time, more of your interest in what he does, more of your participation in activities that he enjoys.

Of course, there will be other adjustments involved in changing schools. The curriculum may be a little different or on a different time sequence. For example, in some schools, students take American history as sophomores, while in other schools, they take American history as juniors. If something like this happens to your son, he will be a bit out of sequence; but these problems are solvable if he has solid enough friendships to feel good about himself while he makes his way through the rest of the maze.

The other day I was walking through the halls of a high school where students decorate the insides of their lockers. As I passed one girl's open locker, I was struck by the homey, attractive presence. She had some of the usual posters and signs, but she had arranged everything with taste and color-matching in such a way that the whole thing was pleasant, comfortable—a place where she could go even for a fleeting moment and recoup from the harsh reality of colorless halls and demanding classes.

The whole display was so appealing, I even paused for a moment just to enjoy. So I said to the girl, "My, your locker's nice."

"Well," she said in something of an "I tried but lost" tone, "the one next door has carpet and curtains."

With that she slammed the door closed as all students slam locker doors and scurried off to another class. Even in decorating a locker, they have to compete.

Our sophomore son wants to take some easier classes next year—art and wood shop, but we are afraid that he won't be able to get into college. Should we give in?

That question used to be easier to answer than it is now. In the good old days (a couple of years ago), most colleges in this country were just seeking high school graduates who had reasonable grades and decent test scores. But in recent years, this has begun to change.

Now the answer depends on two factors: (1) In which state do you live? (2) Where will your son want to go to college? Some states have changed graduation requirements so drastically that it now requires almost a college degree just to get out of high school; and in keeping with that trend, some colleges now expect incoming students to have about half of their college work completed by the time they start. Your task is to find the answer to two questions. (1) What does your son need to graduate from high school? (2) What does your son need to get into the college of his choice? For the first one, the high school counselor can help, but be careful. He may recommend the more "scholastic" course for your son; but while he is doing that, ask him outright what the requirements are for graduation. To answer the second question, you may need to write the college admission officer and ask for the requirements for incoming freshmen. Again, you may need to discern between recommendations and requirements.

But now that you have done all that, I think I am on your son's side. If he is going on to college, he still has a lot of time left to study foreign language and nuclear physics, but this may be his last shot at a wood shop class. Why not spend some time in high school learning such skills and hobbies which help make his life a little richer?

I have a friend who has a Ph.D. and teaches tough university classes where he encounters pressures and stress. On weekends, he buys, rebuilds, and sells clocks. I envy him for one course he took during high school. Guess what it was?

Our school principal told me that he is thinking about going to official school uniforms. Why would he want to do that?

Competition—it is as simple as that. In the teenage world of costuming, fads come and go, but the present fads are costly—stone-washed jeans and silk blouses and hose and high-heeled shoes. I don't know how a parent keeps up.

The other day, I visited a class of high school sophomores. One young lady came in and sat in front of me. She was wearing an expensive silk blouse and an expensive wool skirt, hose, high-heeled shoes, earrings, matching necklace, and a bracelet. I thought for a moment that I was lost—that I had slipped into some bank official's office by mistake. Yet, she took her seat, arranged her books, and blew a bubble with her gum. I knew then that I was in a high school.

Recently, I saw a survey of students in a rather typical suburban high school. One of the questions was, "What do you worry most about every day?" The possible choices included some biggies—friends, AIDS, grades, parents, life after high school—but the number-one most-popular worry among these high school students—the winner by a big margin was appearance. Eighty-five percent of these students reported that they worry most about appearance.

I don't know whether uniforms are the answer to that worry and to the competition and expense that follows, but some schools are trying it. We will just have to wait and see.

CHAPTER FIFTEEN
College Preparation

Sometimes when we compare the American educational system with other systems or even when we compare the system with that of the past, we fail to realize the role that college education has come to play in our society. Not only have we pushed the formal schooling age down to include younger children, we have also continued to push formal school up to include at least some college and sometimes as much as seven or eight years of college.

This trend began with the rise in the popularity of high school education following the events of the earlier part of this century, but it really took off following World War II and the availability of the G.I. Bill of Rights funds. That was the spurt, but the trend continues. Though college attendance fluctuates some from year to year, colleges are still growing and the opportunities are growing as well.

For this reason, some parents have begun to look at college possibilities as early as the birth of their children. We worry about whether our children will be able to get in, whether they will succeed, and what will become of them when it is all over.

This chapter is designed to address those worries, even for those parents whose children have just been born. It is never too early to start.

Our daughter is only eight years old, but we want more than anything for her to attend our alma mater. How do we influence her without putting pressure on her?

So you want me to participate in your conspiracy, eh? Actually, it shouldn't be too hard to accomplish your goal. If your family is typical, that is probably the only college your daughter will ever know anything about. You will take her to games and activities. You will encourage her to attend camps and summer programs the college conducts. You will buy her banners and knickknacks with the college motto.

If your daughter is typical, she will find all this connection with a college and college life highly exciting and romantic during her growing years, and before her time comes, she will probably be more eager than even you are.

At least, that is the way the process works in most cases. I have known of a few examples where the children have rebelled against all that emphasis on one college over another, but those are rare.

Of course, you might be able to avoid that last possibility by giving your daughter some options. If your old alma mater is really the right place for her, she might make that choice all on her own when she compares it with other colleges.

By the way, I don't see anything unusual about your hopes for your daughter. I think there is something valuable about the children attending the parents' alma mater if it is the right choice. It really contributes to communication during the college years. When the student writes home and drops names of buildings or even events, the parents will be able to relate to the references. When the student graduates, the family will always have something in common to discuss at reunions and other meetings. The college years are a critical time of growth because the students come as adolescents and leave as adults. There is something of a common denominator among people who spend those years at the same place, even if the careers are generations apart.

When should a person begin to apply for college admission?

The answer to this question is as varied as colleges themselves, but I would recommend that high school students begin to write letters of inquiry to college admissions people as soon as they begin to settle on three or four colleges they think they might like. These letters don't have to take the form of formal applications. They can be simple notes requesting catalogs and application materials, but at least these letters will begin valuable correspondence. Prospective students should never feel that these letters are an imposition on the college admission people. This is what they get paid to do, and the more letters they get the better they can do their job.

College admission personnel complain far more about the late requests than they do about the early ones, so don't be afraid of being too early.

By being early, a student can obtain valuable information which may help him make plans for finishing high school. For example, some colleges require SAT scores while others require ACT scores. Since students usually take those tests sometime during their junior or senior year, the earlier they know admission policies, the better decisions they can make. Thus, a student who is wanting to be selective in his college choice probably needs to make initial inquiry at least by his junior year.

On the other hand, if a student misses all these deadlines or makes his choice about college late in his senior year, I would still recommend that he apply to the college of his choice. The worst that could happen is that the college would reject him because of the late application.

With all the colleges available, how does one make a choice?

That is an excellent question, one which probably perplexes thousands of young people and parents alike. But in the long run, aren't you thrilled about the problem? Aren't you thrilled that there are so many excellent choices?

I don't want to minimize the importance of choosing a college. I think that is one of the most significant decisions in a person's life. I am convinced that it does make a difference, regardless of what one studies or what activities one participates in. Colleges are different. The classes are different; the campus life is different, and the overall college experience is different. Since most people start to college as adolescents and come out as adults, it does make a difference where they spend that transitional period.

Yet, there are so many good colleges to choose from that the choice may be a matter of choosing from the positives rather than from the negatives. In other words, which college one chooses does make a difference, but it is rather difficult to make a wrong choice.

Nevertheless, the choice is still tough, so let's look at some questions which a prospective student and his parents can consider when picking a school. You can put these into any order of priority you prefer.

1. What is the cost and what are the family finances? The most expensive educations may not necessarily be the best in every situation. One of the nice things about this country is that lack of finances should never be a reason for a person not to attend college.

2. What major does the student prefer? I realize that this is a tough question for the average eighteen-year-old, but if the student knows what he wants to study, this will help him pick the college. Some colleges are good in one area and not so hot in another.

3. What kind of campus life is the student looking for? If that student wants to move away from home and interact closely with his classmates, the local community college isn't the best idea.

4. What are the family traditions?

5. What school acts as if it wants this person for a student? Some schools really pursue certain students—ones with particular interests or skills. To me that is a good sign that the person would be happy there.

6. Where does the student want to go to college? This is still about the most important question to ask. College work is too difficult to have with it the added burden of not wanting to be there.

We want our son to go to a good college. What courses should he take?

Planning any student's high school program is an important activity, but it is particularly important for students who have already begun to plan their college careers and even their lives!

My first piece of advice sounds like what doctors say—get two opinions. Often high school students and their parents consult only with the school counselor while making these plans. I have a great deal of respect for school counselors and for all the fine work they do, but we must realize that some of them have particular biases. Some are going to push certain courses; some are going to push certain students in certain directions. Though they provide valuable information, it should never be the whole picture. Listen carefully to what the school counselor says, but consider other opinions as well.

If your son has even a remote idea of where he wants to go to college and even possibly what he wants to study, write to the admissions counselor at the college and ask the very same question you have asked me.

Don't be too surprised at what you learn from your sources of information. Your son may have more options at the high school level than you think. Colleges might recommend but do not necessarily require a rigid high school program of advanced math, high level science, and four years of foreign language.

If this is the case, then you and your son have another problem. You have to decide how much of his time he wants to spend preparing himself for college and how much of his time he wants to spend on courses and even activities which will give him a little variety in life.

Based on my experience as a college professor for the past fifteen years and based on my experience not only in teaching and supervising college students but also watching them graduate and go off into the next step of their lives, I recommend two high school courses for every student. As far as I am concerned, these are the first courses any person ought to work into his schedule. "Quick, what are those courses?" you ask. Typing and driver's education. Fooled you, didn't I? But I am serious.

How can high school students prepare themselves for the rigors of college academics?

Actually, the "rigors of college academics" may be a bit overblown, particularly in the minds of high school students who have had to listen to vacationing college students tell war stories about all-nighters, 1,500-page reading assignments, and 25-page research papers. Though the facts may be basically true, the stories do get embellished some in the telling.

College academics is not all that different from high school academics with only maybe a couple of exceptions. If a student has done relatively well in high school and has developed the basic skills of reading, writing, and organizing, about the only thing he now has left to master are a couple of lessons in time management. So that I will be perfectly clear, let me list those.

First, the beginning college students will need to learn to go to class. Now isn't that a ridiculous thing to say. Surely they know that already, don't they? Unfortunately not. In high school someone cares if you don't go to class. Threats hang in the air heavier than the odors of duplicator fluid. If you don't show up for class someone calls your mother. Then when they find you, you are hauled in front of a tribunal more severe and merciless than the Spanish Inquisition. You soon get the idea that going to class is important.

But college is different. If you skip class, no one says anything, so the student assumes that no one cares. Since skipping class is not only easy but also rather inviting, some students soon develop the habit, and that is the first step down the road to degradation. I am completely serious. During my fifteen years of being on a college campus, I have never known a student who flunked who did not begin his journey to failure by skipping classes. On the other hand, the converse of that is also true. I have never known a student with perfect attendance who made less than a C in any course. Let me restate this point as emphatically as I can. The best piece of advice I can give to anyone about preparing to meet the rigors of college academics is to make and keep a solemn pledge never to cut class.

The second adjustment the new college student will have to make in time management is to learn to deal with long-range assignments. Most high school assignments are short-range ones. The teacher wants to look at it the next day or at least by Friday. Thus, the student is always working on day-by-day goals.

On the other hand, most college assignments are more long-term. The paper is due in fourteen weeks. We will have a test over this reading assignment in eight weeks. Now, the student will need to learn to set his own daily goals so he won't be swamped in the end. In other words, the student will need to learn to study from the first day of class even though he can't see the immediate value of studying.

This is a tough lesson, even for the veterans. That is why we still hear stories of those all-nighters. What they don't tell is that often the assignment that forced them into a sleepless twenty-four hours had been hanging around for at least twelve weeks and didn't get crowded into the schedule of parties, intramural games, and other diversions.

That's my advice. Two simple suggestions. Go to class. Learn to study from the very first day of class. And relax. It isn't as hard as the older siblings make it sound.

Mike majored in English and secondary education during college. Since he enjoys reading and has something of a poet's sensitivity, he thoroughly enjoyed the major. When he went out to student teach, his love of literature and his sensitivity to young people made him an excellent teacher candidate.

But he decided not to teach. He wanted to go to medical school instead. He went back to college, took some science classes, got admitted to medical school, and is now a happy, well-rounded pediatrician who keeps Dickens and Shakespeare in the waiting room along with *National Geographic*.

From the time he was a little boy, Tom wanted to be an engineer. He went to college with that in mind and thoroughly enjoyed his preparation. After graduation, he spent three years working as an engineer with a major corporation. Then he decided he wanted to be a teacher. Using his savings, he went back to college, took the necessary courses and is now one of the happiest high school math teachers I know.

A straight line may be the shortest distance between two points, but it may not always be the most effective way to get there.

Our daughter doesn't want to go to college. How can we persuade her?

You probably won't like my answer, but I am not sure you want to persuade your daughter to go to college. Obviously, you have made your feelings known and you have at least provided her with the opportunity. Now the decision is hers. After all she is almost an adult, at least by legal standards. She is entitled to her own decisions at this point in her life, and for you to persuade her to go to college when she really doesn't want to could have more negative results than positive ones.

Though I don't know why your daughter doesn't want to go to college, I can think of several valid reasons why young people don't go to college at the time they finish high school.

Some people simply don't belong in college. At most colleges, the education is rather one-dimensional in that it is primarily about words—reading words, writing words, and talking words. Even if a person majors in something that sounds mechanical like engineering or drafting, still much of the work is done in words. If your daughter doesn't excel in words, she is going to find college strenuous, pressure-packed, and impractical. With that combination, the experience could destroy her self-concept.

Some people really need some time between high school and college. Not many people believe me, but I maintain that high school is a very rigorous endeavor for many students. I can't blame them for wanting to take a year or two break before jumping back into that mess of constant listening, note-taking, reading, and writing. I know several students who have taken a break between high school and college to work. With this break they achieved several advantages. They earned some money. They rested and prepared themselves; and they developed an even higher motivation when they eventually got to college.

This is why I am not as alarmed by your daughter's decision as you are. Based on what I have seen during the last fifteen years, I would say that if she does indeed belong in college, she will probably get there before too long. I would just back off, stay close to her, and make sure she knows the option is open. When she realizes she needs it, she will find the time and the motivation. On the other hand, if after three years, her life is everything she ever wanted it to be without college education, she might not make it as quickly.

Now that I have said all that, let me tell you that my advice is easier to give than to take. I can be philosophical because this is your daughter. If she were mine, I would be asking the same question.

College is so expensive we will never be able to afford it. How do we look for scholarships?

Let's begin with a promising reality. There should never be a student in this country denied a college education because of lack of funds. Somewhere there is someway for your children to get through school. They may not get to go to the college of their first choice. Both they and you may have to borrow the funds to serve as an investment for a college education, but someway you can make it.

There is an unfortunate misconception about scholarships. Usually when we hear the word, we think of football players or supertalented horn blowers. But those represent only one kind of the financial help available to a student. Those scholarships, called performance scholarships, are not only difficult to get, but they put high demands on students while they're in school. For example, an athletic scholarship in a major program would obligate the student for about as much time as a full-time job would. If your children are supertalented in something, the performance scholarship might be worth considering; but if they aren't that talented, there are still many sources of funds available.

The first place to look is at the college itself. As soon as your son or daughter decides on a college, don't even look at the price of admission or room and board published in the catalog or other materials. These figures will just give you ulcers, so just think that they don't pertain to you. Instead, consult the financial aid officer of that school. Request and fill out all the necessary forms as soon as possible. The most common one of these forms is something like a workbook for an advanced Greek course. Just filling the thing out is going to sap most of a good weekend, but take the time. It is worth your effort.

After you have filled out that form or an alternative, the financial aid people at the college will be able to tell you what your student is entitled to. Usually, the people construct something of a financial aid package which tells you what funds are available through programs and what funds you are expected to raise yourself.

Many states have excellent scholarship programs for their high school graduates. Many colleges have scholarship funds from within the institution itself. There are even some federal funds still available for some situations.

This is the best source for funds and the recommended way to proceed. Your second place to look for information is with the high school counselor. Since these people probably have a bit closer tie to you and your family, they may know about special interest scholarships such as funds for veterans or people of a certain ethnic group or even people who work for certain corporations or have membership in certain clubs.

DATELINE: MINNESOTA

Carl tried four different times to get into college, but he kept getting the same response. "Sorry, your high school grades were too low and your standardized entrance test scores are atrocious." Even his own parents tried to dissuade him. After high school, he stayed out a year and worked in construction.

More determined than ever after that experience, he sneaked into a summer program at a local university as a special student. That summer he compiled a solid B average and was allowed into the school full time, but on probation.

Obviously, he succeeded because he is now a senior partner in a prestigious law firm.

DATELINE: OKLAHOMA

John graduated near the bottom of his high school class. He did manage to get enrolled in a state college, but was asked to leave after one semester because of poor grades. For the next ten years, he worked in a variety of jobs, married, and started a family, but he was still hungry for more knowledge. Finally, he enrolled in a local community college and stayed in school until he finished his Ph.D.

DATELINE: ILLINOIS

All during her school career, Sally struggled with school. When she finally dropped out as a tenth-grader, even the counselor concurred that she had made the right decision. Ten years later, with three small children, she passed the GED (General Educational Development) exam which is the high school equivalency test and then enrolled in a local college. She is now an excellent teacher, particularly effective with those students who struggle academically.

Isn't this a great system, this system of second chances?

Our son has not been a really good student in high school, but now he wants to go to college. Isn't that just a waste of time and money?

Oh, no! Never! I am going to resist my urge here to lecture you about this wonderful educational system we have here in the United States which allows everyone a second chance and even a third. And I am going to resist my urge to tell you that this is one of the factors that makes the American educational system the most sensible in the world. Rather than unloading the lecture, I am simply going to answer your question.

The educational system in this country is designed to recognize periods of maturity. Sometimes students aren't too mature in elementary school, but they find themselves in middle schools. Sometimes students aren't too mature in middle school but they find themselves in high school. Sometimes students aren't too mature in high school but they find themselves in college. Now admit it. Isn't that wonderful?

You don't tell me what your son's difficulty has been, and that does make some difference. Some students don't do too well in high school because they have more important things to do such as work or sports or socializing. Some students don't do too well in high school just because they so choose. They are bored or turned off or can't really see the purpose of it all. Now, all these people usually have the ability to turn their academic fates around about anytime they decide to do it.

But there are some people who do struggle in high school. For them, the question is not so much whether to go to college, but where to go. If your son is one of those academic strugglers, help him to look for a college which offers some kind of effective study skills program for students like him. Some schools don't have any program at all; some have only casual ones which don't really offer much help; but some colleges have invested time and money in developing personnel and programs who understand people like this and some of their success stories are almost unbelievable.

No. I don't see your son's plan as a waste of time or money. But he will need your help. If you can, help him gain some understanding into why he has had difficulty in high school. He may know himself without any consultation, but if he doesn't, you may want to accompany him to visit counselors and teachers to gather as much information as you can. (Incidentally, if those people advise your son not to go to college, just smile and thank them. They don't always know either.)

Then, help your son make the right decision about the institution based on his personal choice and his special needs. If he is determined to get a college education, there is a place where he can succeed and achieve his ambition.

Our daughter is about ready to go off to college, but she still hasn't chosen a major. How can we help her make that choice?

My question is, "Why would you want to?" There is nothing unusual about a student going to college without a firm major. Some colleges will ask her to name some tentative major when she enrolls so they can assign her an adviser, but this is only a formality.

Most college programs are designed to recognize that beginning students haven't chosen a major. That is one of the purposes of the general education courses required during the first two years. Through these courses, students are able to sample a wide variety of different studies. They get acquainted with departments and professors. They meet the older students who are majoring in the various programs. Then the students who come to college undecided can make a far more intelligent choice, and there is still time to complete the program within four years.

Of course, I do have some advice for the student who is in the process of choosing a major. Pick something you enjoy studying. Surprised you, didn't I. You thought I was going to sound like a parent and say something profound like, "Consider the job market." "Pick up a marketable skill." I do realize those things are important, considering the cost of a college education; but I will still stick with my advice. There is no need for a student to be unhappy with his major during college, and there is definitely no need for a person to spend a lifetime of misery simply because he majored in something he didn't particularly enjoy. The first test then is, "Do you enjoy it?"

"We sent our daughter to one of the most highly respected Christian colleges in the land," the mother told me the other day, "and she lost her faith while she was there." Then we both stopped and cried for a while.

I suppose the first impulse is to want to fix blame. Parents and often back-home pastors know for a fact that something sinister is happening at that college, and that evil trapped and eventually engulfed that poor girl. On the other hand, the college people say, "Don't blame us. If she lost her faith here, she didn't have much faith in the first place. Surely the parents and the church have to stand guilty."

But I am not happy with all this finger-pointing simply because it isn't very helpful. Instead I would like for all of us who are involved with college students—college personnel, parents, students, and potential students—to stop and ponder those basic elements of college life which make it one of the most powerful experiences of our entire lives. Let's examine just a few of those.

1. Usually, students enter college as adolescents and come out adults. That is a major change in a short four-year span, and that transition from adolescent to adult can sometimes be painful. During the four years, many students pick up a mate, a career, an interpretation of success, and a lifestyle.

2. College is a place of ideas.

3. College life strips all incoming students of the high school image and requires them to start ego-building all over again. So your son was the captain of his high school football team. Within a week he will meet forty-five other captains and three who were captains of all-star teams. At that point, he will have to start building his self-image all over again, and some young people don't handle that too well.

4. College experience is more than classroom. During the high school years, the school and the home (and sometimes the church) dominate the student's life. In college, the student is not only adjusting to classes and assignments but he has to work out new friendships, new living arrangements, new time budgets, and often even new eating and sleeping habits.

I offer that list as a reminder to all of us about what is really going through a college student's life, and as a reminder about how much college students need warm and open relationships with adults they love and trust during the time that they make so many adjustments.

What special help can we give our son to prepare him for college?

I find this a very sensible question, but my answer may surprise you a bit. I am sure I should talk about academic preparation and financial plans and stuff like that. But instead, I would like to ask you to consider how well you have prepared your son in two very basic areas—a value system and social skills.

I am particularly concerned about a college student's value system. Regardless of where he chooses to go to school, your son is going to have to deal with ideas sometime during his college career. Ideas are found lurking almost everywhere around a college campus—in textbooks, in the libraries, in the minds of professors, in dorm bull sessions. Some ideas are great; some need to be weighed and considered. Some need to be rejected—completely and immediately. But your son has to make the decision about what to do with any particular idea. The yardstick he uses to measure and deal with any idea is his own personal value system.

I suppose there are some who would tell us that the purpose for going to college in the first place is to develop that personal value system, but I don't agree. I find that the students who are in touch with their very basic belief structure can handle the ideas more effectively and with far less mental turmoil and anxiety. To help your son work through his belief system will not only bring you some peace of mind, but it should help him cope with college academics as well.

Actually this exercise is not as tough as it may sound. Every thinker begins somewhere—with some absolute, nondebatable, self-evident point. Sit down in a casual conversation with your son sometime and help him verbalize his nondebatable self-evident point. You may want to couch that in a simple question, "What do you know for sure and will always know for sure, regardless of what happens?" The answer to this could be translated in a basic value system.

The other piece of equipment your son will need in college is some social skills. I find that far more students struggle with the social adjustment of college than struggle with the academic adjustment. (Of course, this statement assumes that the student moves away from home for the college experience.) To help prepare your son for this adjustment, make sure he has spent at least a week sometime in his life away from home before time to start college. Sit down with him and help him analyze himself—his likes and dislikes, his social frustrations and joys. All of this could be invaluable to him as he learns to live with that complete stranger called a roommate (and more often than not, roommates are pretty strange people).

If our son goes to college, he will have to go on an athletic scholarship. How do we let coaches know about him?

Tell them. Doesn't that sound crass? Wouldn't it be nice to think that college coaches will come beating at your door or will get your son's name from the newspaper, or will at least have his high school coach write. And this is the way it works for most. But if it isn't working that way for your son, take the initiative yourself. Tell them. Make a list of places where your son might like to go to school. Include big schools, small schools, junior colleges, and major universities. Make a little statistics sheet with such information as age, size, weight, speed, vertical leap, years played, and awards and honors. In other words, include any information which would attest to your son's raw athletic talent. Then send the information out to the coaches at the schools your son has put on his list. Don't be lazy. The least you can do is find the coach's name so you can make this a personal letter.

But also include on your information sheet your son's high school grades, his test scores, and anything else that might predict his ability to succeed in college. Despite what you might believe from all the news reports about college athletics, most coaches still want players who will be good students as well.

Now sit back and wait. The coach will put your son's name on his list of possibilities. He may write and ask for game films or other additional information. He may even come out for a personal visit. Then if he is interested, he will invite your son to campus to get acquainted with the school and the program. At that point, and not until then, should your son get his hopes up. If the coach invites him to campus, the school is probably interested.

Now that I have given you the information, permit me to give you a lecture. The free ride in college athletics is one of the biggest myths of this world—right up there with buying below cost and restaurant cooking like mother used to make. Keep this always in mind. There aren't any free rides. Some people, guys and girls alike, get paid for playing sports. That's fine when they enjoy spending their time playing sports. But keep in mind that the scholarship is nothing but pay for the time these people invest. It is not a luxury. I have had an opportunity to observe the scholarship athlete in both large and small colleges, and nearly every athlete I know is spending more than forty hours a week earning his scholarship.

Unless your son is an exceptionally gifted athlete, I would encourage you not to put all your hopes on that scholarship, particularly if he really wants to go to college. He may actually find that working in an ordinary job is less time-consuming.

Our daughter wants to stay at home and attend the local junior college for her first two years. Will that hurt her chances of getting into a really good school later?

No. Most four-year colleges and universities welcome transfers. In fact, some even go out and look for them. A few years ago as the junior college idea was first sweeping the nation, some state universities seemed to prefer most students to take their first couple of years at the junior college, leaving the university to focus on juniors and seniors and graduate programs.

I can think of a lot of reasons why your daughter's proposal sounds like a good one. The cost is only one. If you and your daughter can't afford four years at the college of her choice, then the wise decision is to take the first two years at the cheaper place and finish the degree at the other college. This way, she will be a graduate of her chosen institution.

Some students simply aren't ready to go off to school right after high school, so the junior college offers the opportunity to make some adjustment to college life with the security of the home.

The first two years of the college program is usually filled with general education requirements in a wide variety of fields so it would not be as if your daughter were delaying her program to attend the junior college. In fact, those general education courses are probably as well taught in the junior colleges as they are in the four-year schools. Junior college instructors are usually well-prepared and many have several years experience. On the other hand, some major universities use graduate students with limited teaching experience to teach those basic courses.

Nevertheless, if this is your daughter's decision, you and she need to remember a few pertinent details. Let me list those.

1. Some academic programs don't accept transfer work. For example, some engineering programs are five-year specified programs which allow little flexibility, so it is almost impossible to transfer in. If your daughter is anticipating some unusual college program, she may want to check on how much is specified during the first two years.

2. As soon as your daughter makes a decision about where she wants to finish her program, she needs to begin the application for admission process, and she needs to explain that she will be transferring from the junior college. The admission counselors may want to make some suggestions about which courses she should take at the junior college.

3. Both you and your daughter need to remember that each academic institution is different and each requires a certain adjustment program. The college she chooses won't be like the junior college, so she needs to allow some time for adjustment. She may have some frustration finding her way around, using the library, making friends, and learning how to function in the new classes. Don't be surprised if her grades go down during her first semester in the new school.

CHAPTER SIXTEEN
Extracurricular Activities

No study of American education is complete without some space given to the topic of extracurricular activities. For that reason, studies which compare American schools to the schools of other countries are never fully complete or accurate until we assess the education role and value of the extras in our schools.

To include such things as football, band, chess club, and school newspaper into our total school programs is at least unusual, if not unique, to our schools. There are those who protest that these programs are both expensive in time and money and have no worthwhile educational value.

On the other hand, I know several adults who now, thirty years later, have only memories of the extracurricular programs, so they would argue that such activities are actually the lifeblood of the educational system.

Regardless of where you stand between those two extremes, if you are going to be in a position to help your child through the whole educational experience, you need to understand as much as you can about the extracurricular programs, how they work, and how they can work for you and your child.

This chapter is not intended to be definitive about a position, but it is to encourage you to examine how such programs can be most helpful to your child and you.

Are sports overemphasized in schools?

I am not sure how schools in America got into the business of providing both entertainment and sports for the community, but they definitely have that function. In fact, too often a school is actually evaluated, not by the academic productivity but by the success of the sports teams.

There is no doubt about it. This is a costly role, both in terms of money and time. To construct and maintain playing fields and arenas, to hire coaches and staff, and to equip and transport teams demands a major part of the school budget. Teaching personnel spend hours on coaching duties; and students spend hours practicing, going to games, anticipating games, basking in glory, or suffering in defeat.

The question is whether there are any gains to outweigh all this expenditure of time and money. Let's look at some of the advantages that can come from sports in schools. Notice that I said "can." Let's not kid ourselves. Some sports programs offer more than others do, and some sports programs may even be detrimental to the school.

1. School spirit. This is something more than what the cheerleaders yell about at the pep assembly on Friday afternoons. I am a frequent visitor in about thirty different high schools every year, and some just feel better than others. You can tell a difference the moment you walk in. The students move through the halls with a certain air of confidence. They are more responsive in class. They seem to be happier and more at ease. Now, obviously, I don't know what causes all this, but having successful sports teams surely helps. As a high school English teacher, I would much prefer trying to teach Romantic poetry to students in a high school that just won the state football championship than to teach the same stuff to students from a school that hasn't won a game since the discovery of the forward pass.

2. Community spirit. The school is not an isolated monastery on a hill. It is an integral part of the community; and the more the school and the community interact, the more successful the education. Sports teams are always a source of community feeling and community support of the whole school program.

3. Student involvement. Sports keep students busy. Some people would complain about keeping them too busy so that they ignore their studies, but still, busyness, or at least legal and wholesome busyness, is always better than idleness.

4. Player development. Some high school athletes do learn the techniques and develop their talents and go on to win scholarships and maybe even professional contracts. For them, high school sports become another form of educational preparation. Though I hear this advantage coming out of coaches' offices frequently, I am not convinced

enough to make a solid argument. It is true that some athletes do go on, but the number is so small that I don't think this aspect justifies the time or the expense.

This at least begins the list. We could add other advantages such as discipline, self-esteem, and even memories until the list became even larger; but we still wouldn't answer the question. Are sports overemphasized? I think that the answer depends not only on a listing of disadvantages and advantages but on individual schools.

In my experience in schools, I have found that what gets overemphasized is that activity that the most excited teacher is excited about. If the drama director is the most excited (and exciting) teacher in school, then drama gets its share of emphasis. If the coach is the most excited teacher, then sports are likely to become the dominant activity.

Aren't all these extracurricular activities just frills which are really weakening the education of our young people?

No. I don't think so. Still, I do hear those cries for emphasis on the basics, and I agree. We must be diligent in teaching young people the skills of reading, writing, organizing, calculating, and using their minds. This is what school is about, and it would be a terrible shortcoming to fail.

Yet, at the same time, those extracurricular activities can, should, and do contribute to that mission—at least in a couple of ways. For one thing, the student who takes an active role in the extracurricular activities of his school is usually more excited about life, about school, and about learning. Because of that excitement, he is more highly motivated to apply himself to the sometimes-difficult task of learning the basics. One thing that we have learned from recent research is that the more students enjoy coming to school, the more they learn. Actually, when we think of it, that point is so obvious that we probably knew it long before the research proved it to us. So one of the tasks of educators is to provide an atmosphere which students would enjoy. One way to accomplish this is to provide some fun activities for every student at the school.

Besides, those extracurricular activities sometimes carry some significant lessons themselves. Notice how many military leaders were high school athletes. Notice how many corporate executives were active in a variety of extracurricular activities. These activities provide young people a very practical arena in which to develop such skills and attitudes as leadership, commitment to a group project, dedication, and personal discipline. I am prepared to argue that these lessons are just as important as the lessons of reading, writing, and calculating. After all, there isn't much value in learning to read if one doesn't have a real need to read.

For these reasons, I think the extracurricular activities are valuable. I would hope that we have enough variety—sports, music, speech, yearbook, etc.—that every student has an opportunity to participate. In fact, I think that providing that broad base of extracurricular programs within the school structure is one of the strengths of American education.

Of course, the problem is balance. When the extracurricular activities begin to dictate the school program or begin to command one individual student's life and study time, that is the time to teach students the very valuable lessons of making decisions and establishing priorities.

Our college junior varsity football team frequently matches a game with the state prison team in our area. Since those guys don't travel much to games, we always have to go down there. It is a good experience for our young players. To get to the playing field, we have to walk through the cell blocks and listen to the jeers of the inmates. It is probably a good, honest view of prison life, and a frightening one.

But every time I go down there, I am frightened even more by the looks of their football team. Those guys are big, strong, quick, and tough. I feel so sorry for our young kids against those Goliaths—until the game starts. Every year, we beat them. They may be big, strong, quick, and tough, but they aren't very good football players.

I once asked the coach of the team what the problem was. He explained to me that out of the 2,200 men in that prison, he knew of 2 who had played high school football.

What is the value and role of extracurricular activities in our schools? I am not sure I know anymore.

Our thirteen-year-old son spends much of his free time sitting around the house watching TV. How do we encourage him to join some extracurricular activity at school?

Let's suppose at the beginning that this is a healthy young man. If so, then this sounds like a rather typical problem of thirteen-year-old insecurity which is quite a common disease at this age. Remember first that thirteen-year-old insecurity never looks like insecurity; most often it looks either like arrogance or apathy.

Let me see if I can guess the conversation you two have had. You say something like, "Dear, have you ever thought about joining the band at school?"

And he answers, "Those people in band are nerds."

So two weeks later you say, "Dear, your cousin Mike is having such a good time in wrestling. Have you ever thought about going out for sports?"

And he answers, "Those people are crazy."

So two weeks later you say, "Dear, when I was in school I had such a good time working on the school newspaper. Maybe you would like that."

And he answers, "That's dumb—to write when you don't have to."

Now, let's translate all those responses. What he is probably saying through all this is, "I'm scared to death. Do you know the risk I would be taking? I could make a fool out of myself. Or even worse, I could fail. No thanks. Not now at least. I'll sit here in front of this TV with safe, false reality." The solution to this dilemma is simple. He needs some successes to reassure him. Look how easily I said that. Now your task is to implement it. Have fun!

You may want to begin by checking to see what his friends are doing. He is more likely to get into an activity where he already knows someone and feels comfortable enough to take a risk. You will also want to find out what is available in the way of extracurricular activities, and help your son assess some of the things he might be good at. If you can get just one hint of an interest in something, you may want to talk about some special instruction to help develop that interest. If he seems interested in music, let him get some private lessons before he tries it in band or orchestra. If he seems interested in sports, take him out in the backyard and help him work on skills. If he is a bit athletic but doesn't want to try the typical school sports, help him explore private clubs in other things such as karate or swimming or gymnastics.

As you know, there should be enough activities somewhere to meet his interest. But at this point, he just needs some success, even if it is nothing more than just mastering one small aspect of the activity.

Once he gets started, give him some room to grow in his activity before you crowd him. Remember that we are still dealing with a self-image problem here. If he wants to tell you about what he is doing, listen; but don't pry. Let him have this one thing all to himself for a while.

If he decides that he would like to try something, particularly if it is something that requires special instruction, just ask him to make a certain commitment of time to it. In other words, he should promise you that he will give it a good enough try. Sometimes these people don't enjoy an activity for a while but the more they work at it, the more they like it. I think most great piano players would have quit lessons during the second month if their mothers had let them.

Our daughter has the choice of playing soccer with the school team or with the park district team. How can we help her make that choice?

First, why don't you pause and celebrate the fact that you have the choice? This is excellent. I am so pleased to see that your daughter not only can play the sport of her choice but that she has some choice in the matter. Believe me—your question smacks of progress.

But now let's look at your decision by making a list of the factors your daughter and you need to consider.

1. Who is going to be in charge? Keep in mind that the coach/player relationship is one of the most vulnerable relationships your daughter will ever enter. If that relationship is healthy, your daughter will grow. If that relationship is filled with misunderstanding or insensitivity, your daughter could suffer. I am convinced that the significant difference between a good, positive experience in sports and a negative experience is how the coach or coaches relate to players. Now that I have frightened you, let me suggest that you investigate the methods of control available to you. I know enough about school sports to know that if you have some problem with a coach or an aspect of a program, you have avenues of complaint open to you—the coach, the principal, or even the school board, if necessary. What is open to you with the park district?

2. Which program best fits your daughter's level of participation?

One program will be more demanding and encourage a greater commitment and a higher level of competition. You know your daughter. Which one is best suited for why she is in soccer? If she is very good, you will want her to be in the most demanding program to challenge her to develop her skills. Yet, if she just wants to play for the fun of activity, you will want her in the less demanding program.

3. Where will her friends play? In the long run, this may be the most significant question because it will probably carry more weight than the other factors. But it should. If participating in soccer is not first a classroom for social interaction and acceptance, then it is a waste of your daughter's time.

Now that you know some of the things you want to look for, you can begin looking by going to see the coach. This is the place to start. Since I have been around athletics for the past thirty years and know how coaches work, I would never let my child participate in anything until I had a long conversation with the coach. Ask her about practice schedules and game emphasis.

After that, you can call other parents who have had children in the program, or you can even talk to the children. They will provide you with the best information.

When is the right age for a child to start organized sports?

I asked a neighbor when was the right time to pick my apples and he said, "When they are ripe." I will borrow his answer for you. A child should start sports when he is ready—not when his dad is ready or not when the cousin is ready or not when the neighbor is ready, but when he is ready.

But how do you know that? Let me propose a method of determining the age of readiness—when the child comes to you and asks your permission to participate in organized sports, then you will have some idea that he has an interest and that it is his decision. If you force him before then, you will have the nagging suspicion that he is "playing" just to please you, regardless of how good at the sport he becomes.

By using that simple test for readiness, obviously the starting age will vary from child to child. Some children are ready for organized baseball at six or seven. Some aren't. Some are ready for organized football by nine or ten. Some aren't. Some are ready for organized basketball at twelve. Some aren't. The difference is not just a variation of physical development but rather a combination of attitude, interests, and physical development.

As you have probably already guessed, there is one possible danger with my test. What if the child never asks? Well, you can prime a little if you wish. Take your child to games. Express your interest in some organized sports. Play catch with the child out in the backyard. If your child is interested, he should soon get the idea and ask you.

I do hear some parents say to me that there is a possibility that their child has exceptional talent in the sport and may need an early start to develop all the skills needed for the great Olympics. I don't agree. I coach sports at the college level; and at this level, we really prefer the athlete who started a little later, perhaps as late as high school. Too often those who started organized sports much earlier are simply burned-out with both the sport and the intense pressure required to play the sport well. I have a good friend who is a gymnastics instructor, and he reports the same impressions in that sport as well. Let me say that again in rather simple terms. If your child has exceptional talent in a sport, that talent will come out, regardless of when the child starts competition.

In other words, if you are going to err in the starting time, err by starting too late instead of too early.

Our daughter plays on the basketball team and sings in the chorus. Now the drama director has asked her to try out for the lead in the spring musical. We're afraid all this activity could influence her grades. What should we do?

Since your question is a rather common one for many parents of high school students, let me outline a procedure of response.

1. Draw a breath of awe and celebrate. God has given you what appears to be a wonderful and multitalented daughter. Aren't you excited about her range of ability and her participation in so many different activities? Aren't you excited that other significant adults—the coach and the chorus leader and the drama director have all put so much confidence and respect on your little baby girl? So while you shudder, praise God for the responsibility He has given you by permitting you to be parents of such a special person.

2. Don't get angry with the drama director. I know what he is doing. Anyone who has ever worked with teenagers knows. It's a variation of

the old adage, "If you want a task completed fast and well, give the job to a busy person." Your daughter obviously has established a record of dependability and cheerfulness along with her talent. Everybody in school is going to want her to do something before this endeavor is over. To have someone like that in your activity really cuts down on the Maalox consumption.

3. Turn this opportunity into a learning situation. You need to have a conference with your daughter—one of those times when you are both rational and logical—and assess the situation. Obviously, all this activity will affect study time. Are her grades suffering now? How much time does she need to do her school work effectively? How much time will all this participation take? Regardless of what happens, she will learn something from being in the play, but is that lesson worth what it is going to cost her somewhere else?

Frankly, making this kind of an assessment is a good activity during this time of your daughter's growth. I am happy to see that she has to do it now while you are available to help her. Nearly every human has to make some choices sometime in life about how to juggle fifteen responsibilities and obligations such as family and work and church. If your daughter can learn the process now, it will be a very valuable lesson for her later.

4. Support her decision. Even if she decides that she will have to forego the opportunity of the play, there will still be a few wet spots on the pillow for the next couple of nights. She will need your encouragement and support.

5. Play parent enough to know that she is getting enough food and rest. Insist on this. Most of us come equipped with an innate physical sense that often monitors our involvement. For active high school students like your daughter, that monitoring device is often called mononucleosis. Frankly, I am a little more worried about this than I am about her grades.

We have three children who are in everything. I am glad they are active, but I spend all my waking hours taking them someplace for practice or a game. What would you suggest?
1. Buy a bus.
2. Hire a chauffeur.
3. Keep donkeys so your children can have their own transportation.

4. Tell the family that you have to go to the store, and just never come back.

5. Shout a loud no the next time anyone suggests you take him someplace.

6. Teach your children how to make choices.

Life is a lot like going to a doughnut store. You can't have everything. You have to make choices. Sometime in your life, you have to learn how to do this. Now seems to be a good time for you to start with your own children.

There is an unfortunate false assumption in child-rearing that would have us believe that if children are constantly active, they will be happy That just isn't true. Believe it or not, there are some things which are more important and more conducive to happiness than your children's activity and participation in a thousand splintered organized programs. Such things as a solid family life, a little quiet time, and a stable, predictable environment are rather basic to a child's happiness. This may be the time to teach your children to make some choices from their many options of activities.

I hear your protests that you want your children to be well-rounded or you want your children to explore a variety of different activities lest they miss the one in which they have talent; or that you want to give to your children the opportunities you never had. I understand your concerns, and they are worth considering, but more important is the possibility that your children become so active that they get through childhood without some strong memories of family life. Besides, if your children have talent, they will surely find out before it is too late to develop it to its fullest.

Now let's talk about making choices. Sit down with each of your children. Help each child get a good concept of his strengths, both in talent and interests. Then help him or guide him, or even order him if necessary, into the activity or few activities which will give him an opportunity to express his talent. If he grows tired of these activities after a while, let him change into another, provided he gives up something to get there.

Learning to make decisions is a hard lesson, but one which is so valuable. Now is a good time for you to accomplish two objectives. You can simplify your schedule and teach your child at the same time.

My son really wants to play football, but I am afraid of the sport. What should I do?

Obviously, you have three choices. (1) You can say, "No, absolutely not, and don't ever ask again." (2) You can try the bait and switch trick (getting your son into another activity) which might or might not work. (3) You can cringe, bite your nails, hold your breath, and give in. But you knew that before you asked the question. What you really need is some method for dealing with your options, so let's look at this from two perspectives—your son's and yours.

Though he may not be able to give you a convincing answer, I think I can understand why your son wants to play football. First, probably most of his friends play football, and he doesn't want to be left outside the group. It is almost impossible for a non-football player to maintain a really close friendship with a football player. (We could add that this same principle holds with band or chorus or drama or other extracurricular activities. Friendships grow around shared experiences, and those extracurricular experiences are the most powerful experiences those people are having at that age.) In a rather fundamental way, your son probably understands this, so he has the desire to play football.

Second, your son may see football as a way for him to get glory and distinction. Face it. Some high school football players become community and school heroes. They have instant recognition and assured popularity. Maybe your son is good enough to distinguish himself. If not, at least he wants to nurture the dream for a while.

Third, your son may see playing football as a safe way to live life on the cutting edge. Adolescents seem to need a lot of thrill in their lives. That's why roller coaster rides stay in business. There is something macho or brave or daring or romantic about taking a risk, living through it, and bragging about it. Frankly, playing football is a fairly safe way of fulfilling the need for risk. It is much safer than driving the family sedan ninety miles an hour down city streets.

Fourth, he may enjoy the game. He may really enjoy hurling his body into other human bodies. He may like the competition and the contact.

Now, let's look at all the reasons you don't want your son to play football. First, you are afraid he is going to get hurt, and there probably isn't a second or third. I don't blame you. My son played football and I coach the sport, but I still lived in constant fear of injury. Some football players do get hurt. Fortunately, almost all of those injuries heal, but no parent ever wants to see his child suffer.

I do think you ought to consider the risks involved in many of the activities of growing up. Riding bicycles, roller skating, learning to drive, walking down the street, are all rather risky endeavors. Again some people get hurt and some don't. Also, do remember that if you deny your son football, he will probably fulfill his need for risk in some other way.

If you still have a debilitating fear of the sport, you may want to reason with your son about finding an alternative activity where he can fulfill his needs for friendship, thrill, competition, and glory, and you don't have to live in a constant state of fear.

Our son is getting ready to enter high school. We want him to be active in outside activities, but he isn't interested in sports. What else is available?

Your question has a sad ring of tragedy to it. Unfortunately, we have become such a sports-oriented society that when we say extracurricular activity, our only thought is sports. Yet high school can hold so much more for your son if he can find it.

Let's look at some of what is available: drama, including plays and musicals; about every kind of musical group for the talent including band, chorus, or orchestra; chess club; math club; creative writing club; science club; Junior Achievement, where students actually get involved in a business project; 4-H club or Future Farmers; vocational clubs for students in vocational programs; speech team; debate team; student council; technical assistants for the audiovisual department at the school; language club; school newspaper; yearbook; photography club; or even foreign exchange club. And this is only a partial list.

Most high schools believe in the value of a student's participation in some kind of activity, so they provide and sponsor a broad list of things for a student to do in hopes of having something to match the interest and ability of every student in school.

Your task is to help your son explore enough possibilities to find something that interests him. I would recommend that the two of you go to school together and talk to the counselor. He should be able to provide you the information you need.

It just seems as if schools are only concerned about athletes and sports. On the contrary, they are really trying to provide something for every student. Let me assure you that in high school there are a whole lot of guys who aren't interested in sports. Your son just needs to keep looking until he finds them.

What can we expect from our daughter's participation in school sports?

Well, that depends on three or four factors such as your daughter's interest in sports, the coach, and your support of your daughter's participation. But assuming that those are typical, let's look at both the advantages and disadvantages.

1. Socialization—For the most part, school is lonely. Students really don't have as much time to socialize and develop friendships as we think they do. When your daughter decides to join a sports team, she has just decided to spend hours and hours of informal time with a different group of students. She will probably have more friendships and deeper friendships with those people than with any other students.

For one thing, she will suffer with them—through practice, through pain, through losses. Together they will cry, and we are always a little closer to the people we cry with. She will also celebrate with them—when the play goes well or when the coach compliments or when the team wins.

Participation in any extracurricular activity can really boost a student's circle of friendships.

2. Discipline—To participate in a sport, you have to take charge of at least one aspect of your life, and that is at least a start at learning discipline. You have to get in shape. You have to practice when you don't want to. You have to push yourself physically beyond the limit you really want to. You have to learn to cooperate with other members of the team, considering others as well as yourself. These are all valuable lessons.

3. Self-identity—Since athletes spend a lot of time in sports, many put most of their emotions into the sport as well. Thus, success in a sport gives them emotional support, and they feel good about themselves. Though there are noted exceptions, most athletes in elementary, junior high, and high schools are also some of the better students. Frequently, athletes actually make better grades during the season when they are having some success in the sport than they do in the off season when they have more time.

4. Time constraints—A school sports team demands time—practice time, game time, travel time. Some students learn to manage that time constraint, but some don't. Your daughter's sports participation will interrupt your family schedule. You can count on that. She may never eat dinner with the family again.

5. A family activity—Again, this depends on you, but I know families which have rallied behind some member's sports participation and have grown into strong family units as a result.

6. Emotional highs and lows—Living with an athlete is not always an easy task. They can be rather moody. When things are going well and they are happy, they are pleasant; but when things go wrong, everyone around them suffers. And who is harder to get along with than a superstar the day of the big game? You may actually learn something about your daughter's deepest feelings from all this.

I will never forget Dr. Weber. I was a frightened third-year teacher and he was the school superintendent. But within a matter of minutes during our initial interview, I learned his style. He was a man of decisions. Over the next few years, I came to appreciate and respect that attribute. I would present my plan, often some harebrained scheme that was surely designed to bring at least chaos and maybe even worse to the educational endeavor. He would listen pleasantly and diligently, with just the hint of a grin at the corners of his mouth. When I finished presenting my proposal, I would then wait while the two of us stared at each other for what often seemed an eternity. Then Dr. Weber would respond. He was not a man of many words. The response was always brief. "Yes, you can." Or, "No, you can't." Nothing much more than that, but at least you got a decision. There wasn't any, "I'll take it under advisement." "I'll check with the board." "I'll ask my wife." No, when you went to Dr. Weber, you always got an answer, and somehow you knew that was final.

One day just before I began casting the parts for the fall play, all of us teachers received an official note from Dr. Weber. As usual, it was brief but reeked with the air of finality. Dr. Weber had made a decision. No one student was ever to be in more than two extracurricular activities. That was all the note said, but we all understood its meaning. Since we were a small school, many of our students were already in both sports and music; so those of us who directed other activities, such as plays, would have to use other students.

My immediate response to this note was to complain. I complained to the principal, to all the teachers in the lounge, and even to my wife. But I never thought about complaining to Dr. Weber. I didn't have that kind of courage.

So with his edict in my hand and malice in my heart, I started casting the annual fall play with the leftovers and rejects; but I was resigned to accept a dismal failure. The first night of practice, I caught my first glimpse of what was to be. Some of the people came to that first practice having already learned their lines—all of them. Now I wasn't used to that. I was used to the quarterback and lead actor learning his lines sometime between the last rehearsal and the first performance. Very soon, I realized what was about to happen. I had the smoothest, most pleasant time of play practice I had ever had. The students were eager and cooperative.

The performances themselves were among the best the school had ever seen; and the popular kids, those in sports and music, came to support their friends and applauded loud and long.

I still remember Dr. Weber for his ability to make a decision, but I also remember him for what he taught me about human nature particularly the adolescent.